Comments on Will Taegel's wo

"Dr. Taegel's words may well help readers recall their natural affinity with the Infinite. He attests that there is a realm beyond the usual that he and his Earthtribe folks have seen in their visions and concludes that we are all called to this realm from beyond ourselves. To respond to this call is the most important move human beings can make."

> — *Huston Smith*, author of *The World's Religions,* subject of Bill Moyer's PBS Special

"Dr. Will Taegel carries the gift of story-telling. His Native American roots provide a deep wisdom that comes through the gifts of deep reflection and connection to Nature, the Spirit World, and the power of the spoken word to teach through a story and in writing."

> — *Angeles Arrien*, Cultural Anthropologist

What people are saying about The Mother Tongue

"Everyone needs to read this book! At this critical time in our evolution, it's of the utmost importance that we reconnect with nature, and our own intuition about it. In *The Mother Tongue*, Will Taegel synthesizes science and spirituality through the lens of shamanism, and teaches us how to communicate with the Great Mother, Earth, by tuning into the primordial language of our planet's ecology. We are all indigenous to this luminous planet and there's so much to learn from her."

> — *Dr. Jennifer Howard*, author of *Your Ultimate Life Plan: How to Deeply Transform Your Everyday Experience and Create Changes That Last*

"Reading *The Mother Tongue* reminded me of Rumi's field beyond right and wrong. "I'll meet you there," the poet proclaims. Will invites us to meet him in the Eco-Field for an intimate experience of self, others and nature—the ground of everything. Weaving thorough scholarship, ancient wisdom, psychology of the selves and personal experiences together with a shaman's passion and sensibilities, the author takes us on a journey of the heart."

— *Lucia Capacchione*, Ph.D., author of
Recovery of Your Inner Child

"*The Mother Tongue* is a seminal book. In the past, people have been content to learn the languages of humankind—Greek, or Latin, or Chinese. We are now challenged to learn the language of the earth—to communicate with the trees, the stones, and the wind. All is alive, all is meaningful, all is in intelligible communication. Dr. Taegel's book points all of us to the language of the future. It is the language of nature, the language of the Mother."

— *Jim Garrison*, President and CEO
Ubiquity University

"When I finished *The Mother Tongue* this Sunday morning, I cried due to the feeling of a sense of ending with the connection I felt with you within the book. the standing waves flow over me in a wild untamed manner as I begin from the beginning to read this book all over again."

— *Susanne B.* of Boulder, Colorado

"Distilling ancient beliefs, cutting-edge science, and deep personal introspection, *The Mother Tongue* is a brilliant achievement. Will Taegel invites us to explore a visionary map of human consciousness that is imbued with disciplined mental clarity and the passion of an awakened heart. I intend to purchase several copies of *The Mother Tongue* as Christmas presents, so my friends will better understand where his revolutionary ideas are leading me."

— *Jai Cross*, New Mexcio

"Dr. Taegel's newest book, *The Mother Tongue*, blends deep heart and new science into a breathtaking, inspirational invitation to rediscover an old way of being that nourishes not only the self, but all of creation. Will's quest to discover how we humans became so out of balance with ourselves and with the language of nature takes us on a captivating journey from eco-fields to faith, from Aristotle to Einstein, from thinking to being. The personal stories of how those tuned to the Mother Tongue of nature do the "impossible," and detailed scientific research create a map to co-create a life of harmony, joy, and presence. A must read for anyone wanting to take the idea of deep connection into the experience of deep connection with all of life."

— *HeatherAsh Amara*, author of *The Toltec Path of Transformation*

"We yearn for intimacy but don't notice it's been in the 'field' around us since primordial times. Listen to Dr. Will Taegel's wise exploration to bring forward the language of the ancients, the Mother Tongue."

— *Reginah Water Spirit*

"In *The Mother Tongue: Intimacy in the Eco-Field,* Dr. William Taegel invites us on a spiritual and scientific adventure through the white water rapids of the river of our times. The currents are wild and a passionate journey unfolds through the co-mingling of ancient primordial and 21st-century physics ways of knowing. Dr.

Taegel has given us an understandable history of post-modern thinkers' two most favorite topics: science and spirituality. And to a much greater end, Dr. Taegel takes us beyond Rumi's field of 'wrongdoing and rightdoing,' and beyond Rupert Sheldrake's morphogenic fields, merging the ancient primordial with the most modern scientific information, calling us to our depths to dare to dream of the 'Eco-Field' of knowing that comes forth from his courageous hypothesis. This new relationship and communication between ourselves and the Natural World could be the most successful way for us to fortify our vessels for the forthcoming turbulence of the *Era of Natural Consequences* and successfully negotiating our way into the *Era of Natural Birth*."

— ***Karen Smith***, artist

"*The Mother Tongue* may be one of the most important books I will ever read.

"After going through for the third time and studying various parts to take your insights deep into my being and be able to speak about the content, I had a flash at 2:30am this morning of a communication I missed from the Mother years ago.

"I am always so touched at the way you weave your experiences over the many years with our beloved Bear Heart into your stories…

"I am indebted, in the best way, for all your diligent attention to things of importance for all of us."

—***Brown Dove***

"Tonight in my Shaman Journey Circle, we journeyed to the *eco-field* and our intention was to find out information: Why am I here? What message do you have for me? How can I be of service? I was inspired to do this journey after I listened to a talk about the eco-field when

I was on a train ride in India two weeks ago and I loved the description of Will Taegel's *Mother Tongue*. The eco-field journey was amazing and fun for everyone. I love how I can integrate the tools and knowledge into the work that I'm doing here in Istanbul. It's such a blessing!"

— ***Marla Kaya***, Istanbul, Turkey

"Today as I was walking to my car after lunch I saw an oak tree heavy with acorns; when I looked down they were all over the ground. Then I remembered a story told to me one time around a campfire by a Native American elder about how when the people would see the oak trees heavy with acorns they believed that was nature providing extra food to the animals to prepare them as a hard winter was approaching. I have been reading *The Mother Tongue* lately and I believe this is what Will is talking about early on in the book, about observing the world around us over a long period of time... generations... so we become in tune with our world to help us survive. I am anxious to continue reading *The Mother Tongue*... to learn to be more in tune with our natural world."

— ***Mark Weiler***, quality engineer

"In *The Mother Tongue*, Will Taegel challenges our assumptions, and invites us into a deep inquiry where we find ourselves questioning our core beliefs about our relationship with the Universe. He does this through the use of shamanic stories that resonated so deeply within me that tears sprung to my eyes, and through examples proven by the new sciences of quantum physics and the science of fields. Will carefully guides us into our deepest connection with Nature, and convinces us of our need to become fluent in the language underneath all modern language. I now have a conscious understanding of what Will calls the *Mother Tongue*, a language my body has known all along. I could string together the most memorable and powerful moments of my life and I now have a name for them - Mother Tongue Intimacy."

— *Shiila Safer*, author of *Born of the Earth: Your Journal, Poetry, and Meditations in Nature*

"Will Taegel writes from a place of deep wisdom that is often missing in contemporary literature. He creates his theories from many aspects of his vast experience in psychotherapy, shamanic traditions, religious and scientific research as well as a wealth of life experience. To hear the voice of our wise elders is profoundly important at this time of our fast-paced consumer-minded and somewhat mono-dimensional culture. *The Mother Tongue* is a continuation of the trajectory of synthesis of thought and experience that was presented with his previous book, *Wild Heart*. In *The Mother Tongue*, Will Taegel is going back to some of the thoughts from *The Many Colored Buffalo* and bringing them into renewed context, reaching at times both a philosophical and practical zenith. Will is obviously on a journey himself. It is good to follow along by reading his engaging and thought-provoking books."

— *Marie Trout*, CEO, Los Angeles, California

"The crises we face today on our planet are highly critical. Dr. Taegel offers scientific, philosophical, pertinent information on the navigation of the 'white waters' we face. His positive approach toward the future and resolution of these crises offers immense hope for our species and non-human beings. This is a book I hope will challenge our beliefs and actions into new awareness, insights and decisions. It offers us an opportunity toward significant change and optimism regarding our place in new eco-field understanding and relationship."

— *Lillie Rowden*, D.Min., psychotherapist and teacher

"I think that reading *The Mother Tongue* has given me a grasp on the concept of the *primordial mind/heart* and this in turn has allowed me to be open to new kinds of experiences."

— *John Rhead*, Ph.D., psychologist, Maryland

"*The Mother Tongue* is a map for the birthing of a new way of being. Be prepared for a sensual journey into the depths of the primordial self, through the eco-fields of Nature and the chaos of current times. Be prepared to be illuminated by the stars of the night and the starlight of the heart, all the while being held in the arms of community. Be prepared to be nourished as you stretch beyond the existence of who you think you are."

— *Two Trees Birthing*

"*The Mother Tongue* is such a wise work. Dr. Taegel's command of highly scientific research coupled with his depth of shamanic wisdom creates a logically inspirational call to become the best possible human while acknowledging, embracing and integrating the gifts and intelligence of our *more-than-human* compatriots. Through masterful storytelling Dr. Taegel leads us on a river adventure that fluidly moves through the challenges we face as individuals and as global participants connecting the latest scientific understandings and the centuries' old admonitions of *indigenous wisdom*. A feast for the intellect and comfort for the heart, *The Mother Tongue* instructs our *wild heart*."

— *Gayle Loyd*, educator, Seattle, Washington

THE MOTHER TONGUE

Intimacy in the Eco-field

Will Taegel

2nd Tier Publishing

Published by:
    2nd Tier Publishing
    501 Wimberley Oaks Dr
    Wimberley, TX 78676

ISBN 978-0-578-11079-0

Cover photograph and book design by Dan Gauthier
Stone art in section dividers by Sug′manitu Hota (Graywolf)

Table of Contents

A Reader's Guide

My intention in presenting this book is to express inner explorations as connected to various maps of the known universe and to create a dialogue with you, the reader, and the *more-than-humans* all around us.

When I presented material from this book to a potential publisher, she automatically thought my phrase, more-than-humans, referred to God-in-heaven or, at best, New Age jargon. That misunderstanding speaks to how far we have drifted from a deep connection with the other-than-human creatures in the ecology around us.

When I asked her about the New Age babble comment, she referenced my exploration of the electromagnetic field as being too far out for marketing. That misunderstanding underlines how little mainstream culture knows about 21st-century science. Hopefully, we can co-create a new found intimacy as we seek a portal to a lost language expressing in-depth awareness of ancients with sacred landscape and newer scientists with the interlocking fields that power the universe.

Along the way, I will question the foundations of industrial culture, including the method of knowing developed in Western Civilization, the Abrahamic religions, and the reductive science of the 20th century. That questioning will clear the space for a proposal that values the mode of communication and wisdom of the ancients in concert with the spectacular advances of 21st-century science. These two sources could provide us with a map describing a passageway of grace through turbulent forces all around us.

In creating this book I scour it with my editors and surprise myself with growing objectivity. At times I sound like I have the answers, and, in places, I experience myself as dogmatic, even as I state that I am opposed to dogma. You may notice this paradoxical tendency as well. That said, I hope to present awareness, passion, compassion, and thoughtfulness. I use the present tense in this paragraph because writing and editing with my publishers is an ongoing process, including feedback you supply. Every one hundred books printed, we review the book and integrate feedback. In that sense it is a co-creation with you.

In the first four chapters I will introduce a variety of terms. Some readers will want to explore the appendixes if they enjoy definitions and parameters. Others will plunge ahead, knowing I will unpack technical usages such as the Mother Tongue, eco-fields, vMEMES, newer sciences, epistemology, and a set of major hypotheses as we proceed. The Mother Tongue Hypothesis will unfold in the form of two offspring called Eco-field Hypotheses 1 and 2 (EFH1 & EFH2)

My approach alternates between subjective examination, shamanic stories, psychological models, philosophic observation, and scientific exploration. When I use the term, *Mother Tongue*, note that I refer not only to expressions of ancient wisdom but also to the science of fields. My aim is to be multi-lingual and thus able to explore multiple levels of the human epic, but always returning to the Great Mother's primordial wisdom and Her way of expressing Herself at the base of all things. Toward the end of the book I will open the door for an emerging expression of the Great Father, flowing from the stars, quite apart from the patriarchy.

In our conversation, it is important to delineate what I mean by research. In contrast to the field trial and double blind research of mainstream science, I utilize organic inquiry and phenomenological research. This research approach, developed by Clements, *et. al.*, (1998) for the social and transpersonal sciences, integrates subjective story, objective research, intuitions, dreams, and visions. Organic inquiry and research values the impact of the research on the researcher, as a reciprocal and transformative event and integrates phenomenological data as it arises.

At the heart of our journey, I will introduce Almo Farina's mainstream, scientific research on eco-fields (2010). Then, I will elaborate his startling hypothesis with my own data gathered in organic inquiry to open the possibility of a stirring intimacy whereby we humans return to our natural place in the environment. Fasten your seat belts. Away we go.

I

The Conversation Begins

CHAPTER ONE

A Primordial Story of The Mother Tongue

Rub your eyes to see if scales are falling.

Perk up your ears to a rumbling sound in the distance.

The systems of Western Civilization are failing us, sliding downhill before the incredulous eyes of all humanity. Alas, some see and hear while others do not. A crumbling of foundations sounds the alarm as the beautiful edifice of the industrialized culture implodes. The stark reality of the slide and, paradoxically, the inherent possibilities show up for us with a narrative that begins with a Christmas morning drink, 2004.

Join an imaginary scene in the narration with me.

In our story, we sit with our families on a pristine beach of Western Sri Lanka, gazing languidly at azure waters, tropical drinks in hand. A member of our family works for a multi-national corporation, and, as a reward for stellar profits, the whole lot of us receive the perk of this Christmas vacation. A rumor passes down the row of vacationers lounging on the beach. It seems, so the rumor goes, that

3

tribal people on this storied island, as well as other near-by islands, have abandoned the beach area and moved to higher ground.

"Why on earth would they do that?" someone asks with more anxiety than curiosity.

"They sense a natural disaster through their mumbo jumbo," another replies haughtily, lacking political correctness.

The rumor mill is sufficiently effective so that we hurriedly consult our latest smartphone apps to see if any data shows up to warn us of this unidentified danger. No information appears on the subject, not even Internet gossip. We are curious, of course, but since the rumor of catastrophe is not substantiated by our technological news sources, we have our doubts. After a brief and anxious conversation, we return to our texting and mystery novels, occasionally refreshing our drinks.

At breakfast the next morning someone surfaces a dream about frightened people fleeing from rising water. A sophisticated, psychological response comes, "If it were my dream, I would worry about inner disasters, perhaps an overbearing father. Water symbolizes rising consciousness. This dream is all about your issues. Maybe even about world problems." We continue to discuss the dream, using skills we have acquired from our various therapy sessions as we stroll down the stairs of our hotel, heads down, while busily texting friends between comments.

Then, we hear a blood-curdling cry from outside.

Over there!

Toward the beach where we are headed!

Looking up at last, we look aghast at a wall of water surging toward our hotel, tossing boats and autos in its wake, inundating houses, and swallowing people and other animals.

A tsunami!

We scramble back up the stairs to the roof of the hotel some eight stories high. Our hotel sits on a hill, so the massive wall of water sweeps down a valley near the front steps where we had just been discussing the dream. The roiling water spews dirty spray in our faces, but, thankfully, our lives are spared, though I might add, through no merit of our own.

During the next few days we give thanks for our safety but tremble with a vulnerability reaching our core, a fresh cut-to-the-bone. How could such a massive sweeping of the chaotic hand happen with no warning? How could we not have received any information, although we had been glued to our laptops and cell phones with excellent Internet connections?

Now, after the fact, the Internet is alive with reports. 230,000 people in a variety of countries have died. Billions of dollars of property washed away. Coastal infrastructure decimated.

Once back home, we continue to follow the news. Strange stories of tribal people in the island chains tell of some innate capacity they had for moving to high ground. We recall the rumors we discounted at the beach and get busy on Google to inform us of their origin. Here is what we learned: Off the coast of India, the remote Andaman Islands are home to the primordial Onge (pronounced OHN-gay) people, a hunter-gatherer tribe. It seems that they intuited the danger before it happened. Their inner radar downloaded troubling information in their dreams and their shamanic journeys. Unlike members of our vacationing party, they did not interpret their dreams through a reductive lens of modern psychotherapy. They knew the spirits were searching them out with important information, and they spoke well the primal language of the ancient Nature-spirit world.

Moving from their interior world to the exterior, one of their clan thought to scurry to a near-by creek. It was, he discovered, strangely running dry. Following the dry bed to the beach, he saw the seawater pulling away from the usual shore. He reported what he saw to the elders. They took stock.

Recognizing the clear and present danger, some tribal members wanted to move to higher ground immediately. But the tribal elders insisted on another course of action. A ceremony, passed down orally for generations, warned and told them precisely what to do in this environmental situation. Surprising to our modern minds, the elders knew exactly the course of action to take. But counter to usual rationality, they did not rush to high ground immediately.

First, the elder ceremonialists scattered pig and turtle skulls around their little village in a circle to communicate with the tsunami they knew was coming soon. Though strange to our ears, we can almost hear them talking intimately with the tsunami. Like the members of our vacationing group, they had received dreams the night before. Yet, they knew what to do with the dream time information given to them by what they called *The Great Mysterious*.

They perceived the mighty wave as a living being, not a sterile, geologic, or meteorological event. According to their primal map, the tsunami was a living being, and the map instructed them to engage in a ceremony focused on establishing a relationship with the waves. Later, the elders of the tribe explained to curious anthropologists that they accepted the formidable tribe of waves as honored, if dangerous, visitors to their land rather than a disaster sent from an angry god.

One by one, the Onge elders walked to the beach and threw stones into the sea as their oral traditions directed, and then they quickly gathered their possessions and scurried to higher ground. Only moments later, a 100′ high tsunami slammed into the Andaman Islands. Astonishingly, all 96 Onge survived the visitation of the wave, intimate friends as they were with their wave-relatives.

Courious happenings, yes, but the Onge were not the only people who tuned into the information available to those who had primal eyes to see and ears to hear. Other humans picked up the messages from the eco-fields as well, a point we will explore in Chapter Ten. A ten-year-old British girl, Tilly Short, heard the messages. She looked at the sea as it suddenly boiled, pulling away from the resort she visited.

Tilly Short's attunement to the primordial voices had not yet been covered over by post-modern rationalism, the so-called apex of human civilization. Tilly's body vibrated, and she suddenly recalled words from one of her teachers about the behavior of tsunamis. Quickly, with the intention to warn others, the young girl ran up and down the beach, and, later, authorities estimated she saved over 100 people.[1] It seems shamanic intuition is not limited to ancient hunter gatherers but can be awakened in post-modern people deeply attuned to Nature's cycles.

Interestingly, at Sri Lanka's national wildlife park at Yala—home to elephants, buffalo, monkeys, and wild cats—no animal corpses were found in the aftermath of the tsunami. Soon, the Internet was filled with photos people snapped of elephants moving to high ground and other animals following them—a Noah's ark with no Noah.[2]

What had happened? How were these animals receiving this information? The underwater rupture of the 9.3 earthquake likely generated sound waves known as infrasound or infrasonic sound. These low tones can be created by hugely energetic events, like meteor strikes, volcanic eruptions, and earthquakes. A current hypothesis is that the animals downloaded infrasound wave information, using primal and sensorial abilities.

Another channel of information available to the tuning devices of animals may have been ground vibration itself. In addition to spawning the tsunamis the Christmas quake generated massive vibrational waves that spread out from the epicenter on the floor of the Indian Ocean through the Bay of Bengal and traveled through the surface of Earth.

Known as Rayleigh waves, so named after scientist, Lord Rayleigh, who predicted their existence in 1885, these vibrations move through the ground much like the tsunami on the ocean surface. Yet, they move much faster; namely, at 10 times the speed of sound. These ground waves would have reached Sri Lanka hours

---

[1] www.montereyinstitute.org/noaa/   [View Lesson 9 - Ocean Waves]
[2] www.slate.com/id/2111608

before the water hit.[3] Mammals, birds, insects, and spiders can detect Rayleigh waves. Most can feel the movement in their bodies, although some, like snakes and salamanders, actually put their ears to the ground in order to perceive the waves. And, pressing their ears to Earth, they may well pick up electromagnetic signals, an ability humans had before dominant culture paved over such sensibilities.

On March 11, 2011, as we all now know, another powerful earthquake (9.1) near Japan sent energy across the face of the Earth. The force of the quake, including Rayleigh waves, took about fifteen minutes to travel from Japan to the Texas Hill Country where I live atop its famous Edwards Aquifer. When the wave of energy passed through the aquifer, it slightly compressed and dilated the giant water system so that the water splashed up and down; it was much like water in a bathtub if you rocked the tub. The water sloshed up and down by 15 to 17 inches within the aquifer.

How, you might ask, do scientists measure such an event? A float rests on the water surface hundreds of feet underground and is connected to a wire and a wheel that records the level on pen and paper. This technology, though interesting, is not nearly as sophisticated as that found in the innate capacity to listen and speak in a primal tongue, as demonstrated in the salamander, snake, elephant, the Onge, and Tilly Short.

Scientists, who analyzed the data about the animals in Sri Lanka, concluded that humans lacked attunement capabilities. Of course, the scientists did not, at that moment, know about the Onge or about Tilly Short. When they learned about the Onge's feat, they immediately assumed that the tribal people had just watched the animals and had followed them. Such an assumption postulates an in-depth resonance of humans with the animals, a skill which the vacationers did not possess. But we now know the Onge had tuning devices beyond this symbiotic relationship with the animals. Their

---

[3] www.slate.com/id/211160

primary information was transferred through dreams from an underlying source we shall see is a field of information.

The scientists could not yet fathom the shamanic dream world and the ceremonial capability of the Onge. The tribe received its information on the same infrasound network as did the animals, and the tribal people coupled this attunement with their oral stories to expand the information into a communal wisdom, an Earth Wisdom based on direct access to the Primal Presence. Were they speaking a language of the landscape long forgotten by modern humans?

When questioned about such an intimate relationship with the more-than-human community, a Potawatomi medicine person said simply, "They know me." And he knew them. Recovering such intimacy of the eco-fields is the aim of this exploration.

The first part of this chapter calls on us to use our imaginations as to what it might have been like in Sri Lanka for the 2004 earthquake, but the information about the Onge, about Tilly Short, and about the animals of Yala, though startling, is factual. Put together, the narratives raise profound questions:

* Are we moving into an auspicious moment in Earth's story, when primal forces are being unleashed and when humans become expendable?
* Where can we locate a wisdom sufficient to guide us in these wild times?
* How do we navigate this untamed white water, history's river, with its powerful currents?
* What kind of vessel is needed to carry us on this journey?
* What navigational and tuning devices are essential?
* Is it possible for humans to survive, much less thrive?
* Can we re-learn the Mother Tongue to experience an intimacy with all of Nature so necessary for our current journey?

With these questions spurring us on, let us move to a beginning statement of this book's hypothesis.

CHAPTER TWO

The Mother Tongue Hypothesis

The narrative in the previous chapter is, paradoxically, both disturbing and comforting. On the one hand it points out the failure of technology to assist us when the forces of Nature are fully unleashed, and, on the other hand, it links us to powers we have hidden in the depths of our cellular memories as a species among species, creatures embedded in the web of life.

The retelling of the tsunami event provides us with a backdrop to advance the *Mother Tongue Hypothesis.* By hypothesis I mean a map or proposal to guide us as we consider Earth's ecology, energetic fields, and specific landscape surroundings in a renewed and intimate partnership. First, though, we will consider briefly what meta-historian, Jim Garrison, calls the white water of our planet's conditions as a way to construct a context for the basic proposal of the book (Garrison & Taegel, 2010).

White Water: The Era of Natural Consequences

In a rich dialogue spread over several hours with David Abram, author of the ground-breaking book, *The Spell of the Sensuous* (1996), the two of us concluded that the direction of the conversation concerning the condition of the planet no longer centers on whether we are in difficulty or not. Look out the window, we commented to each other.

See the super cell storms.

Feel the earthquakes.

Breathe the polluted air.

Paddle through the Africa-sized gyre of plastic and trash in the Pacific.

Gawk at the bulging banks of the mighty Mississippi.

Cough as Texas wild fires clog your lungs.

The spray splashing from the standing waves in white water history already drenches us to the bone, washing away the sunscreen of our denial.

In our animated conversations, Abram suggested that we now are beyond crisis and catastrophe as isolated events. We are, he argued, in the *Age of Consequences*. Judith Yost, my spouse, injected the word *natural* to go with *consequences*. We both used that phrase through the years with troubled families in therapy as we drew on the work of Alfred Adler, a crucial shaper of modern psychology. Adler advocated discipline with children that assisted them in experiencing natural consequences of their destructive behavior as an improvement over corporeal punishment. Certainly, we humans, as Earth's children, have been profligate in our behavior and are now experiencing the initial results of our poor decisions. These outcomes are not so much the punishment of an angry Mother as the consequences of misbehaving children.

Take our relationship with the massive Mississippi River as one example among thousands that illustrates the natural consequences of living as if our environment could be manipulated as we please. As far back as the late 1800s, engineers sought ways to prevent the river from swallowing human communities during flood stages and debated whether to adopt a levee-only system, as opposed to one that would combine levees with outlets to allow the river to run free in spots and disperse sediment. This preliminary plan integrated our human growth with the natural inclinations of the river. It sought to protect human life while at the same time respecting the wisdom of Nature in allowing the river to seek its own course in many places.

But in 1927 a prodigious flood spawned fears that led to a levee-only approach in an attempt to squelch the wild in the river. Co-operation between humans and the river flew out the window and in came an even larger urge to control the so-called beast.

The levees, which seemed like a good idea at the time, have for decades deprived the world's seventh-largest delta of land-sustaining sediment by funneling the top-soil-laden river straight into the Gulf of Mexico. From 1932 to 2000, about 1,900 square-miles of land were lost near the mouth of the river and replaced by seawater.

Scientists estimate that realistically New Orleans will sadly be little more than an island within this century. John McPhee in his definitive book, *The Control of Nature* (1989), points out that the tail of the mighty river is like a snake, and it will move no matter what we humans do. The movement of the tail is especially powerful as the river builds up a head of steam with no outlets on its 2,320-mile journey. The land near New Orleans washes far out into the Gulf with Spring floods. Then, with hurricanes like Katrina, the water moves in where the land used to be, and the levees do not have the capacity to restrain the movement of the tail.

The loss of humans, as well as the more-than-human environmental life, is—it bears repeating—the consequence not of an angry Mother Nature but the result of human folly, hubris, and old-fashion ignorance. Our lack of intimacy with the mother river puts us in harm's way. The movement of the tail of the mighty snake is the disciplining mother speaking to us in primal words.

In the *Era of Natural Consequences,* we are experiencing the results of our human-dominant map of approaching nature. We see the results in the above example in climate warming, melting ice caps, super-cell storms, droughts, loss of top soil, and over-population. I cannot over-emphasize how vulnerable our excesses, our indulgent life styles, our arrogance, and, again, our cluelessness in such matters have made us.

If you transcend the conservative/liberal debate and behold the direct teaching of the primal forces moving in our midst, you can readily see that the unleashed forces are the consequential judgment by the organism Earth related to our human choices.

And that is not all.

These primal forces are likely a last judgment for humans.

It appears we are participating in the ending of the world as we know it.

The Hopi Prophecies—in contrast to 20th century evolutionary theories—tell us that we have had four cycles of worlds before this one. During each cycle, according to their oral tradition, humans have reached a technological apex, only to destroy their worlds. Now, we are at the choice point once again. Nature is revealing to us the folly of our life styles and giving us the option of changing. Believe me: the staggering national debts around the planet are the least of our challenges when compared with the supercharged and volatile environment.

Already I have engaged the metaphor of white water to describe our current planetary condition. Throughout the book I will use the images of a river journey rushing down a steep grade, throwing up eight massive, standing waves as the water crashes by boulders in the river channels. So, hang on, as we search for a map to guide us on such a journey.

The Mother Tongue Hypothesis

Here are the headlines of the Mother Tongue Hypothesis as a topological chart to assist us. Each of these points will be explored as we proceed with our trip and conversation.

- The information in the eight standing waves enters the individual and/or group through the tuning device of the inner council of selves. Although there are many tuning devices, all downloads finally have to come into human awareness through the inner council. Hopefully, an aware space opens (the aware-ego) through which the downloads can pass with discernment, thus creating a better context for choices and practices.

- The vessel for riding the ascending and descending currents lies in Nature-based communities strong enough to weather the turbulence of environmental and cultural pressure. Communities closely connected to Nature speak intimately with rising conditions in the field. Note the Onge.

- Both the descent down the river and the ensuing ascent upward move with the power of primordial energy retrieved from the shamanic domain. Sans high-grade shamanic and sustainable fuel, communities dissolve in the turbulence of external and internal pressure.

- In the crucial ascent after retrieving access to the primordial, the Earth-based community reads the code of each of the eight eco-field waves. It integrates the potential wisdom of each standing wave and transports the undigested wisdom to the apex of the spiral. Along the way a lyrical language of intimacy with humans and more-than-humans emerges. Sojourners are multi-lingual but always returning to Mother Earth's primal tongue.

- Finally, the Mother Tongue Hypothesis includes the Eco-field Hypotheses: one and two (EFH1 & EFH2), to be engaged in Chapters Seven and Eight.

Having advanced a basic hypothesis, I also encourage a holding of these proposals lightly, as only *possibly and incompletely true* as I write and you read. If you claim truth possessed, please continue with reading. I welcome you. Just keep in mind that my perspective is riddled with complexity and uncertainty as I raise larger and larger questions. I hope many of you will join me in the larger questions, including ones you have about my proposals. On the other side of the coin, you will notice that I often state my perspective passionately. In those moments I speak as if transfused with certitude, and, in that instance, I am. Soon, though, certainty dissolves into more questions.

With the Mother Tongue Hypothesis held lightly in our hands, we now proceed to a flesh and blood story aimed at giving sensuality and texture to what I propose.

CHAPTER THREE

Tongues of Fire

Spouting aims and hypotheses is one thing, direct experience quite another. Move out of the ivory tower and come with me into an experiment in the 2nd Tier of the human story. Later, I will explain in some detail what the 2nd Tier is, but for now it is enough to note that the 2nd Tier describes an ability of cultural creative humans to journey into and value the depths of human experience and into the Primal Presence. On this journey we gain, even for a brief time, an intimate exchange beyond our usual rationality.

As we enter this narrative grounded in sensual reality, we have the opportunity to experience the language of the landscape through our five senses. We will also need our sixth sense, our intuitive capacity, to grasp the import of the story. The narrative unfolds in an experiment by thirty-five thoroughly modern people, seeking the presence of the Primal, and an introductory, intimate exchange within Nature where Earth's base language is spoken. The story begins two years in the past when Lisa Dvorak, then Assistant Chief of a mid-level police department, felt drawn to a particular spot on a 500-acre outbreak of the Southern Pine Forest, Deer Dancer Ranch, near Columbus, Texas.

Lisa and a number of persons associated with a spiritual community called the Earthtribe and an educational partner, Wisdom University, are planning an event called *vision questing*. You may be familiar with this term, vision questing, but I use it in a very specific way. The vision quest experience is key to understanding how to gain attunement to the Primordial and a wisdom that lies hidden beneath the varieties of human-based wisdom.

As I use the term, the intent of the vision quest is to immerse in the vernacular of Nature, something like an immersion learning in a language school. In a similar way that you might live with a family in a foreign country to learn their language, so we live with a specific landscape to learn its inherent and intimate means of communication. As in any intimate relationship, we open ourselves to what is both pleasant and unpleasant.

Lisa's proposed vision site is remote from the main camp and requires quite a hike to explore, yet it calls to her as an intimate partner. The spot pulling Lisa into its bosom is not alluring to the other seven people who will be vision questing, nor is it particularly appealing to the twenty-seven supporters of the larger vision encampment. When Lisa tells her friends that she is considering the site, their response is tepid. Their nonverbals tell her selecting this site would be inconvenient for them when it comes time to hike out and check on her to make sure she is safe.

"Why not move toward the lake near the buffalo where you can hear sacred songs of the tribe as you meditate?" They speak to her. Unspoken: "Why make it so difficult for us?"

A prime focus of the proposed site is a pond, an attractor for thirsty wildlife that sends forth a gentle voice reaching out to Lisa. Tall loblolly pines enclose the area so that a sense of being held by a dense thicket prevails. A subtle beauty seeps through as wildlife are abundant, but the meditation site offers no vistas as some vision questing traditions suggest are necessary. Near the site, ranch hands travel a dusty road doing their daily chores, so Lisa will not have the absolute privacy often craved by persons fasting for one to four days in a circle as they seek access to the ancient heart of Nature.

Lisa raises questions as she considers finding another place: "Is this place too tame for a journey into the wild?"

"Can I learn new aspects of Earth through this sparse spot?"

"Will the Mystery speak to me?"

For a moment that seems to last forever, Lisa hesitates, considering the above liabilities to a space that will be her home for several days once the time of questing arrives. She reflects on what it will be like to expose herself to the powerful movements of weather patterns, storms, and wildlife. She imagines what it will be like to leave behind access to food with only a little water, not to mention technology and the comfort of her bed and house. She reasons with herself concerning the short-comings of such a vision site.

As she considers, a draft of primal wind tugs at her soul. At some level she knows this local habitat, a tiny eco-field in itself, has the potential to challenge the control system of her usual ego. Suddenly, she announces in a firm voice to her vision guide that she has found her spot. The selection makes little rational sense, but the discourse of the environs sent her mysterious information just beyond her usual waking reality. The communication enters at a limbic level that resonates beyond the reasoning of common sense. At the point of choice, the subtle idiom of the field is more important than Lisa's human resistance. Throughout the ensuing two years, Lisa will see this spot in her dreams and visions until it becomes a regular staple in her awareness diet.

Fast forward through time two years to April, 2011, and now Lisa is on the vision quest, sitting in her circle, the very place that she questioned and yet chose. Seven of her fellow vision questers are scattered throughout the ranch, but nobody is near her. When she selected the vision site two years in the past—or more accurately when the locale chose her—the ranch had been through a typical cycle of more than 40″ of annual rainfall.

But, as the time of sitting in her circle approached, Texas was suffering through its worst drought in history. In the seven months previous to the quest, scarcely three inches of rain had fallen. The 90′ tall loblolly pines and 60′ tall red cedars were tinged with brown, brittle needles as the trees' roots reached for water not there. The ground threw up plumes of dust behind the four wheelers driven by ranch hands. A thick carpet of needles, dried and thick, covered the area around her circle and, indeed, throughout the forest floor.

Back in the main encampment, the vision supporters participated in sweat lodges without fires to heat the rocks. Such a precaution was a first in the thirty-five year history of the Earthtribe. Vision questers were instructed not even to burn ceremonial sage because of the flagrant danger of fire. Coleman stoves to heat coffee in the support encampment were allowed, but still dangerous.

A large portion of Texas is perpetually arid, but Deer Dancer Ranch is less than a 100 miles from the Gulf of Mexico and thus semi-tropical in its weather patterns. The ranch consists of an outbreak of the Southern Pine Forest, which for reasons unknown to modern science, suddenly appears on the Gulf prairie in all its glory to cover a 100 square-miles and then disappear into rolling Gulf plains. This portion of the forest where the tribe quests is as thick as you will find in the heart of Virginia, or Georgia, or lumber centers throughout the South. Since it is still significantly old growth, the forest is a dense and comely reminder of North America before the European invasion.

To make another comparison, bring to mind the Northwest forest in Oregon where Judith and I spend many summers. The two forests are different in their ecological characteristics, but similar in the amount of annual rainfall and dense undergrowth. So imagine what Portland would be like if it received three inches of rain in seven months. Usually, Deer Dancer's 500 acres are dotted with brackish ponds teeming with systems of life, but, as we arrive for the quest itself, only the larger lakes are still viable as the yearning web of life cries out for water.

Lisa defines her vision circle by unwinding her prayer ties—tied on cotton string and wound around a power stick—in a circle about ten feet in diameter. She squints her eyes as the wind rises to between twenty-five and thirty mph. Usually, the humidity is just this side of oppressive, but the drought has sent the humidity numbers plunging. The conditions are ideal for wild fires, and, in fact, 1.5 million acres of prime Texas land burned in the weeks preceding the quest encampment, including the area immediately surrounding the famous McDonald Observatory. Learning the vernacular of drought is not easy for us or romantic.

Studies strongly suggest that the psychological trauma of drought is more devastating than other more dramatic effects of climate change such as hurricanes and tornadoes. Storms come and go quickly, but droughts persist, often over decades, thus stimulating prolonged anxiety and vulnerability.[1] As with any long term relationship, intimacy with a landscape means being with an eco-field in its pleasant and unpleasant energetic cycles. Nature's lesson for this week does not include conversing with spring flowers and languid sunrises. Rather, our intimates are hot winds, dust, and parched animals. Plus, an ominous danger lurks in the gusting winds. If the aspiration of the quest is intentionally to upset culturally-oriented systems of protection and control within the human personality, these severe conditions are ideal.

---

[1] http://dialnet.unirioja.es/servlet/articul?codigo=3030554

On the third day of the quest, a Friday, Judith and I sit in lawn chairs in our campsite drinking coffee and herbal, chai tea respectively. Off in the distance about a half a mile, I spot a figure running in a dead sprint toward us. It takes a moment for me to realize it is one of our questers. Immediately, I scurry to meet her, and I now can see it is Lisa. As soon as I am in ear shot, I hear Lisa shouting,

"Fire! Fire! Fire!"

We meet, and between gulps of Lisa's gasping for air, I discern from her wheezing report that the winds, still blowing fiercely after three days, have toppled a large pine tree on an electrical wire near Lisa's vision circle, sparking a fire. Leaving Lisa I race to the ranch house to fetch Jack Jensen, steward of the ranch. I find him shaving in the bathroom and shout the news through the door. Immediately, we crank up a four wheeler and speed toward the fire.

Arriving, I can see the flames already surging up the trunks of trees along an estimated quarter-of-a-mile line. Without delay Jack dives into fighting the fire by kicking and throwing dirt to smother the flames while I speed back to the campsite to gather tools and to enlist firefighters, or fire dancers as we would later call ourselves.

All the while I talk to the fire, "I know you have your job to do and I don't know what is best for this ranch, but I love each and every tree, bird, snake, and insect. If you can see fit, please hang on and allow us to dance with you."

I do not know if I am heard.

Judith and other camp elders mobilize those who are not working to manage the fire to enter into an animated interchange with the Sacred Web, asking for collaboration in saving the forest and all its inhabitants.

What specifically do I mean by the Mother Tongue in a setting like this? How would urban cultural creatives, gentrified folk, know something specific related to information from the eco-field? As the vision encampment gathers in circles to make plans for possible evacuation, tribal members pay close attention to a large red deer named Light Heart. He likes to wander in our midst.

At first he stands at attention with his nose in the air, every muscle flexed as if prepared to bolt. His knowledge of the fire is far beyond our human sensitivities. Then, over the next hour, he slowly relaxes. Finally, he grazes near the circle. Judith calls tribal attention to the deer, knowing that the danger must be passing. Tribal members then scale down their plans for evacuation even though they have no firm news about the progress of the fire from human sources. An unspoken intimacy between Judith and the red deer carries important information. Often humans speak to animals in a parentified voice, as if the animal was a small human. I do not refer to such anthropomorphic utterances here but to the base broadcasts beneath words, a hidden lingo living in our depths.

Soon, those engaged with the fire, race with two pickup loads of campers and shovels to the fire, while others call the county firemen. A ranch hand drives a tractor with a front loader while the buffalo, unconcerned thus far, stand at a distance watching the spectacle. When we arrive at the fire, several of us grab shovels and throw dirt on the trunks of the trees. The fire is now about head-high moving up toward the canopy, and if it reaches the upper system of branches, we know it will be unstoppable. Complete destruction of the ranch, thousands of acres of forest, and danger to our entire encampment is now on the table.

The tractor digs a trench on the wind side of the fire while the volunteers remove the undergrowth feeding the fire. Twelve of us work as one, and the fires moving up the trunks of the trees are now showing signs of waning. Just when I feel the first wave of hope, the local volunteer firemen arrive with two small fire trucks. They have less than 250 gallons of water. Not much to stop the fire as it barrels toward a large grove.

A man next to me utters between shovelfuls of dirt, "I am asking the fire to help us."

Another, "Mother Wind, help us."

At just that moment, the wind shifts from a prevailing Southeast to a light breeze from the West, Northwest, and the fire suddenly turns and heads back toward a dirt road, averting the grove of trees.

The man next to me looks up and grins through a charcoal streaked face, "We've been spared!"

We pause and rub our blistered hands. A fireman tells of a blaze his unit extinguished near-by that burned thousands of acres, and he estimates we were within ten minutes of a similar fire, or perhaps worse. "This ranch would have been toast in a couple of hours," he muses, as we now begin to laugh as our vulnerability passes into gratitude. In a similar situation a few months in the future, the infamous Bastrop County fire will erupt in exactly the same manner—a wind storm toppling a tree onto an electric line—and will burn 38,000 acres of this same forest, along with 2,000 homes.

From such a catastrophe we are spared.

Later that afternoon we gather as a tribe in a circle to give thanks. Judith tells the community that Lisa has returned to her vision circle to complete her quest. We are all acutely aware that Lisa's being in her vision circle saved a large portion of the forest. The fit was hand-to-glove. Of all the questers, she was most qualified to handle the situation because of her first-responder trauma training in the police department. She also was in good shape physically to sprint the mile trek to our campsite to act as a Paul Revere and deliver the warning. And she had felt a profound message sent to her two years prior to her stay in that particular place.

Did the landscape somehow know that it needed Lisa?

Jeff, the only quester who had already returned to camp, was also a police chief and trained in such emergencies; he was crucial in mobilizing the camp to attend to the fire. A tribal member reminded us that we had been working with Jack and Allison Jensen for twenty years in the restoration of the ranch since the previous owners had abused it. It had taken us ten years to convince the forest that we were there to renew the cycle of life. Eventually, we gained the trust of this local landscape.

In the circle of thanksgiving that day, we remembered a gathering in a tipi ceremony where the forest wrapped us in its arms and whispered: "We the forest have mended enough to send you humans visions." We recalled in gratitude how the forest had yielded visions for our personal and collective lives. On this day of the fire, we had a hand in saving the forest. Intimates assist each other.

When Lisa returned from her vision circle the next day, she told of the trees speaking to her, "We needed you today. Thanks."

Almost everywhere we turned in our conversations, transfers of information and meaning occurred as we entered a temporary grasp of the prose of the countryside. Later that night, one in our midst told of receiving a message in a dream that there was a hotspot still remaining where we had thrown dirt over the fire. Confident the forest had spoken to him, he went out to the charred area early the next morning to find the hot spot and put out the still smoldering embers. We were unaccustomed to such precise directions from more-than-humans. We questioned, yet obeyed the informational transfers.

The next day we convened once again to reflect on these dramatic events. Jack Jensen spoke with a tremor in his voice, "If our tribe had not been here, then the ranch would have burned." He did not use the word tribe lightly because his roots reach deep into the soil of his Potawatomi heritage.

He spoke truth. Jack and Allison do not have their permanent residence on the ranch, and the ranch hands live some distance from the fire. If the planners of the encampment had picked another date, if Lisa had listened to her rational self and not her visionary self in selecting a vision site, then likely the ranch and surrounding area would today be as barren as Mt. St. Helens, after the volcanic eruption.

Certainly, we were not as conversant in the native speech of environment as the Onge people in their relationship with the tsunami, but we joined Tilly Short, the young English woman who saved the 100 people in Sri Lanka, in conversing with the local landscape in enough fluency to avert a tragedy. We were not perfect humans or even as adept as the indigenous, but we were enough for that day. We continued to sense through the following months an undercurrent of gratitude not only arising in ourselves but within the entire eco-system.

Our momentary competency in the syntax of the eco-field was something like my visits to Mexico. Here is the analogy: I have studied enough Spanish whereby a two-week visit to Mexico allows me to converse adequately with those for whom Spanish is a first language. When I return to my home, I lose my facility quickly because I soon fall out of practice. My lack of practice means I cannot claim to be fluent in Spanish.

It will be the task of this book to explore the meaning transfers in such stories as this one and in the narrative in Chapter 1 and to probe the possibilities of gaining greater fluency in the primal. To follow the foreign language analogy a bit further, vocalizations of the eco-field are not only foreign to the modern ear but also are not spoken with consistent intimacy anywhere in the world, except in small pockets of people embedded in Nature. Watching the Nature channels on television or YouTube assists but is a long way from the requirements of intimacy. Such a situation presents us with a severe learning challenge.

We will look into how we can descend the rollicking white waters of the Era of Natural Consequences; down through the waves of the post-modern mentality; down through the rationality of modern science and the positives and negatives of current capitalism; down through the many traditions of laws, books, religions; down through armies and bands of warriors; down through the magic of the shaman; finally, down to the early voices of the first day.

We will utilize this story and other narratives to retrieve proficiency in the parlance of the primal, if only for brief, shining moments. It may sound strange to you at first, this notion of meaning transfers between humans, fire, trees, elk, grasses, insects, weather systems, soils, and even rocks.

Strange, indeed!

To soften the strangeness, I will encourage us to become multilingual in our river trip, sometimes speaking with the scientist, sometimes the psychotherapist, sometimes the poet, sometimes the philosopher, and sometimes the mystic shaman. All of these languages are needed for us to converse intimately with our landscapes. We will have to enlist many aspects of our inner councils, so these sub-personalities will give us permission to converse with mountains, plains, forests, hurricanes, and tsunamis as if they were actually intelligent beings.

And they are.

We shift now to consider a downward journey on the raucous river of the human story. Our aim on this river safari will be to reach the lower levels where we have heard distant rumors that ancient utterances are still spoken. We will need river mentors or field guides who have made the journey themselves and devised specific—though unfortunately incomplete—maps to assist us before we can navigate such a raucous river. The trip is far too perilous to travel without the information other sojourners have garnered.

CHAPTER FOUR

The Vertical Journey

Imagine yourself standing on an upstream bank of a swift flowing river. The flow of the river moves away from you and downward at a 45-degree slope and maybe even steeper. Your visual tells you there is a down and also an up. You perceive a difference in elevation, a verticality. If you journey down the river and then make a return trip, you will need to navigate using these terms: up and down. That seems simple enough.

Up and down. No controversy?

Maybe in terms of geography but not in regard to expressing the human condition utilizing the metaphor of a swift flowing river and standing waves. Let's see why the discussion and the journey veer into the controversial and complex when I use this metaphor of up and down the river.

There exists in our culture a strong argument to keep all aspects of life on a level playing field, a form of radical democracy. Horizontal is in, and vertical is out in progressive circles. In the latter half of the 20th century, it became politically incorrect and revealing of bias to state that one perspective was better than another. Nothing, in this view, was better than another, just different.

In cultural creative circles using terms like higher and lower provoked critical corrections and cries of *hierarchy*, or worse, *patriarchy*. These objections have a strong point. For example, the dominant cultural view is that we have advanced beyond ancient people, even most liberals espouse this view—moderns are more advanced than cave dwellers. This questionable assumption opens the door for one of the darkest moments in all of the human saga.

The Dangers of Vertical Maps for the River

Columbus—representative of European power brokers—automatically assumed that the indigenous peoples of the New World were inferior, so the Europeans as envoys of their supposedly advanced civilization were justified in a massive extermination. I will contend that the Western Civilization of Europe was and still is built on foundations that are basically flawed, and nowhere is this flaw more apparent than in the bellicose colonization of the New World.

Fueled by Roman Catholic theology, some conquistadors thought the primal people were not human. And even if they were human, they needed to be converted to civilization's lifestyle, savages that they were deemed to be.

Some scientists now project that the population of the Americas was approximately 80–100 million in 1492, and by the turn of the the 20th century the indigenous population had been reduced to less than a million in North America.[1] The figures of the population of the Americas have a great range in scientific circles, likely because American/European academia consciously and unconsciously direct their research to defend the atrocity of advancing Western Civilization at the expense of the native peoples and the environment.

If, however, the population estimates are even remotely correct, then 79–99 million people were exterminated in 500 years, tens of millions of them either directly ordered by the United States government or by its tacit agreement. Just as in Europe, so-called Western Civilization mowed down the forests as a giant machine rolled across the Western Hemisphere. No wonder some historians are calling this extermination, *The American Holocaust* (Standard, 1992). You can see the dangers of a vertical perspective, where one

[1] www.shmoop.com/columbian-exchange/statistics.html

civilization is given permission to exterminate another, because it is deemed to be more advanced.

Hence: my plan in this book to move up and down the river of development has certain vulnerabilities, made clear by the example of *The American Holocaust*. In utilizing developmental theories and approaches to the human condition, I risk putting myself in the camp with the exploiters of the Americas and of thinking our group is better than another group, so our group can exterminate or dominate your group. Who wants to be in the same camp with Columbus and Hitler?

Limitations of the Horizontal View

Yet, there are also difficulties with only using a horizontal map where every perspective is given equal billing. For one thing, not all ground is level. Rapids and whitewater do exist. Ups and downs abound. Therefore, some views of the horizon are better than others, and that is not just an opinion. You can see more from a mountain top on a clear day than from a polluted city street.

To continue for a moment in this vein, let us say that we want all life to be equal, the most radical democracy. With this view we should never make a judgment that one form of life has more value than another. In one sense such a view has validity. At base, all life, no matter what form, is precious. Plus, we could not live without simpler life forms such as bacteria. They are our earlier and absolutely essential relatives.

A wonderful community of these creatures lives in our intestines. Anyone who has contracted a intestinal parasite—or even a three-day virus—knows how important it is to keep the bacterial community happy. My intestinal community once ran my life for eighteen months when I came home from a shamanic dialogue in Mexico with a parasite. For what seemed like eons, these pesky invaders out-voted me at every turn on almost any decision that presented itself. Much more of this radical democracy, and I would have died.

With the strict horizontal view, the bacteria, numbering in the trillions in our intestinal tracts alone, will *always* prevail in any discussion. Antibiotics would be out because we could not judge a human life (or a dog's or a whale's or a dolphin's) as having more importance than a wayward bacteria from the jungle. In a strict democracy that gives equal votes to all life, bacterial communities always win. See what I mean. I can get on either side of this argument. I do not want to be in the camp with exploiters such as the Colonialists or Hitler, but I also want to kill bacterial infections and eat shrimp.

When I suggest we go on a journey down the swirling river of evolution, I am engaging in a risky suggestion that some perspectives are higher than others. The other possibility is to throw out discernment and live in the illusion of absolute equality. Another funny and complicating moment occurs on our journey down the spiral when you, the reader, will note my contention that primal people are in many ways superior to moderns.

And you will be right.

I do hold that position, often.

The Onge had superior abilities to perceive the telluric messages of Earth in the tsunami crisis when compared to the vacationers on the beach, Tilly Short excepted. So, for the moment in our discussion, down the river is better than up. In traditional religions you have been encouraged to climb Jacob's ladder, and here I am encouraging you to descend the ladder. Yes, indeed: the real action for today's world is at the bottom of the Biblical ladder. I will make that proposal time and again, so be prepared to note my possible imbalance.

The solution to this tension between vertical and horizontal perspectives is not solved, I contend, by balance. I am not going to look at the horizontal as much as I do the vertical. I have already stated that we are first canoeing down river. I also have stated that for the moment in the Era of Natural Consequences the descending current is more important than the ascending. In theological terms

I hold that immanence is more crucial than transcendence at this moment in Earth's story.

I have selected five researchers or river guides precisely because they are sensitive to the horizontal while at the same time seeing themselves as developmental or vertical researchers. As they explore the standing waves of the river, each researcher sees only what their lens allows. The particular *thing* they focus on also focuses on them. Truth be known what they are researching is a *power, intelligence,* or *force* that in many ways selects them. A bit confusing?

What I mean by this statement will be explored as we proceed. It is an axis on which this book turns. Now, we are prepared to look at the white water river using the lenses of five river or field guides. We need to grock the river and its various maps before we jump in head first.

Clare W. Graves: Field Guide #1

I begin with Clare W. Graves as our first field guide on this river trip because of his comprehensive research utilizing a statistically significant sample of college students over a seven-year period (1952—1959). His subsequent analysis of the data resulted in an early global theory of human evolution that includes both individual and communal or cultural dimensions (Graves, 1971). Moreover, he shattered the mold of reductive evolutionary theory by looking toward an open system and applying punctuated equilibrium to the human story.

Graves was a lesser-known colleague of Abraham Maslow, yet Maslow eventually revised his own paradigm under the influence of Grave's comprehensive approach (Wilber, 2000). Graves noticed, perhaps for the first time in research form, the emergence within human life of a new *bio-psycho-social system* responding to pressures from the larger ecology, a pressure I will argue later in the book comes from the eco-field through specific informational input.

We shall see that a specific landscape, or eco-field, actually *tells* the individual how to unfold as Lisa's vision quest site gave her very specific information that saved the ranch. Graves called this dynamic the interplay of external conditions (1971), while his student, Don Beck, labeled the pressure simply *life conditions* (Beck & Cowan, 1996). Although Graves did notice the influence of life conditions, his research was exclusively focused on humans, a flaw we shall see may be fatal to humans and other species.

But I get ahead of myself.

As Graves dove into the eight different standing waves, he called them *levels of human existence* (1974). Interestingly, he latched onto only one element in each wave, human values. Picture him with snorkeling goggles strapped on his face, looking around in the waves as he moves downstream. He excludes everything but *values*. He does not pay attention to any other of the trace elements in the waves. As he swims, he makes a map of the white water for our benefit. He uses the alphabet to map the trip on the river while his student, Don Beck, uses colors in his topographical depiction of the waves or stages (Beck & Cowan, 1996, 2002; Graves, 1974).

I prefer the colored map, so throughout the book I will refer to the different waves we splash through by the ensuing color code. Even though I use Beck's color code, I am not limiting myself to his perspective (Beck, 2006). We shall see I have a major difference with Graves and Beck: I engage many elements in all the waves while they address exclusively human values. Also, I will present the map of the river in this chapter, starting at the bottom of the rapids for convenience sake. Later, I will show how we can only start the journey from the higher elevation where we live; thus, we will in subsequent chapters make a descending journey in the safety of our canoe of community. For now, though, here is the Graves/Beck cartography of the river (Beck, 2002).

The First Tier consists of six waves.
- **Beige** Starting 200,000 years ago; habitual learning; automatic thinking, survival motivation; present day examples are African bushmen, tsunami survivors; mothers giving birth; Texas health care system. *Central value: survival and basic nourishment.*

- **Purple** Starting 50,000 years ago; world is magical and mystical intertwined with Nature; tribe is safe; ethnocentric; shamanic; cross-species communication and community; ethics limited to specific tribe or clan; free access to Primordial Wisdom; fluent in Mother tongue of the eco-field; present day examples are Indigenous tribes and Nature-based communities; *Avatar* movie; *Central Value: mystical connection to and communication with all the Sacred Web.*

- **Red** Starting 10,000 years ago; strong and cunning survive; avoid shame and get respect; take and do what I want; warrior identity; Comanches; Genghis Khan; present day examples are USA pre-emptive strikes; Mid-East terrorists; revenge television; street gangs; drug lords; akido; assertive skills; *Central value: assertive power for self.*

- **Blue** Starting 5,000 years ago; ordered existence under the control of ultimate and transcendent truth; life has meaning, direction, and purpose; literal myths; monasteries; cathedrals; King Arthur; Chartres; Puritan American; Evangelical Christianity; Tea Party; moral majority; rules to control impulses; codes of honor; academic lectures; *Central value: command, control, discipline.*

- **Orange** Starting with Plato and gaining momentum in 1859; questions authority; reason prevails; marketplace full of opportunities; self-reliance; entrepreneur; play to win; consumer mentality; Industrial Revolution; outlaw slavery; The Enlightenment; Silicon Valley; corporate states; dominate the Earth; *Central values: objective questioning and garnering wealth.*

- **Green** Starting 150 years ago and surging in 1960s; supposedly free from dogma but strangely self-righteous; sensitive to all perspectives; rebirth of community; sustainability; human rights; Woodstock; New Age; politically correct; horizontal views of leadership; inner exploration; Esalen; cultural creatives; Greenpeace; human rights; early Wisdom University; *Central value: sensitivity to and justice for all.*

As we peruse Graves' elevation drawing of the standing waves in the river, pause here. As he paddled around in the waves, he discovered to his amazement a human being of a different order. He called them "a different breed of cat" (Graves, 1971, p. 120). Remember, his research was in the 1950s when folks were listening to the Kingston Trio and passing separate-but-equal legislation with regard to the so-called race problem, not a likely context for a new human to sprout. Yet, this different breed of cat showed up in the waves, and it forced Graves to describe the river in a different manner. We might say, following my analogy of the river, that Graves encountered in his research a steep grade or waterfall. Such a waterfall required a quantum leap to the second tier or new level of the river to see what kind of human was living upstream (1971). Here we go in a jump upstream.

The second leg of the journey requires a quantum leap to the 2nd Tier to a whole other class of rapids.

- **Yellow**   Starting 50 years ago; comfortable with chaos and complexity; newer sciences; integral thinking; 3rd Way politics—Paul Ray's political north (2009); individual seekers; differences and change embraced; individual creativity; spontaneity; Fritz Perls; Einstein; Jean Houston; Carolyn Myss; Stan Grof; beginning use of the Mother Tongue; *Central value: holding opposites and paradox and a thirst for the wisdom of all the previous stages, especially Purple, or Earth Wisdom.*

- **Turquoise**   Starting 30 years ago; elegantly balanced systems; embrace opposites; participatory community based on all the standing waves; value of all living things; participatory learning; ongoing communities based on Nature's cycles; spaciousness of dialogue; moves easily up and down the river and embraces the highest values in each wave; Ilya Prigogine; Elizabeth Sahtouris; Mary Oliver; Gandhi; Dalai Lama; Gregory Bateson; Angeles Arrien; emerging Wisdom University; early fluency in the Mother Tongue; *Central value: everything flows with everything else in living systems within nature-based communities.*

We will return to this colored depiction of the standing waves shortly. Now, I want us to look at some of the other researchers who have been willing to dive into the waves. We shall note that each one of them researched only one element in the wave. Their goggles see exclusively their research target as they focus on various human-centered debris in the waves.

Carol Gilligan: Field Guide #2 for the River

Allow me to state up front that Carol Gilligan is a hero of mine. Let us see why. She was a junior associate of Lawrence Kohlberg, research giant at Harvard in the 1970s and 1980s (Kohlberg, 1981). Although it is difficult for us to imagine in this day and time, Kohlberg had researched the moral development of men and concluded that males are capable of a higher level of moral development than females even though he had not included women in his research design.

Come again!

Such a preposterous conclusion and deeply troubling distortion of the data pushed Gilligan to launch her own research map of the standing waves. She would eventually challenge Kohlberg, the most prestigious researcher of ethics of that era, and his male-dominated results. Kohlberg's manipulation of the research data, perhaps unconsciously, is a dramatic demonstration of how mainstream, industrial culture tends to view the world in a manner that defends its position in the name of objective reason and research.

As Gilligan swam in the standing waves looking through her own goggles, she tracked the moral development of women over an extended period of time. Her initial research sample included 4,000 women. When the results came in, she published the findings in a ground-breaking book, *In A Different Voice* (1982). The book knocked a hole in Kohlberg's map which stated that women develop morally in a horizontal (relational) but not vertical direction. Gilligan also took issue with the feminist models at the time which also largely ignored vertical development, and, in one fell swoop, Gilligan excited the ire of both academic patriarchy and early feminism—a nice day's work.

Here is her map of the standing waves in the river:

* **Selfish (Beige, Purple, Red)**   Women start their development, like men, with making moral decisions based on selfish or egocentric guidelines. "What is good for me guides me."
* **Care (Blue/Orange)**   Women next enlarge their perspective and make moral decisions based on what is good for the larger group, tribe, or even nation.
* **Universal Care (Orange/green)**   Women expand their circle to consider what is good for all people and, indeed, Earth.
* **Integrative (Yellow/Turquoise)**   Gilligan discovered a group of women who were able to integrate the previous levels of development, drawing on the wisdom of all of the standing waves for their choices.

Her later work points to the *different* voice inside for not only women but also men, data that will be critical to the direction of this book as we proceed (Gilligan, 2002). Over the years Gilligan refined her research interpretation and concluded that the lost voice is both female and male—a template human voice.

As she swam through the standing waves, she discovered a primordial voice, a base language that spoke with the intuitive, the feeling, the unguarded, the natural, the receptive, and, finally, the collaborative and higher moral voice. She pointed me in the direction of a natural dialect completely tuned into the landscape, though she herself did not explore such a direction. She inspired and anticipated my description of *The Wild Heart* self, a sub-self that lives close to the essence of the individual (Schnall, 2007; Taegel, 2010).

Gilligan provides the insight that boys have this lost voice covered over by the dominant culture by age four or five because of the manner in which boys are socialized to individuate; whereas girls, who are socialized to attach, do not lose contact with the primal voice until age nine. This research insight found in the standing waves is crucial for us when we begin our journey down the evolutionary spiral to the shamanic (Purple) where we are able to retrieve our untamed souls from the prisons of current civilization.

Now, I will consider three additional researchers or swimmers in the standing waves; however, I will touch on them only briefly. My intent here is to underline that there are many trace elements in the standing waves, that some researchers see one thing, and others another, and that often researchers surf waves and perceive only what is important to humans, forgetting other creatures important to the journey.

Jean Houston: Field Guide #3 for the River

Known for her wide range of interests and teaching, Jean Houston dives into the standing waves, adjusts her goggles, and hones in on the consciousness of the individual self (Houston & Rubin, 2009). Her goggles are greatly tinted by the research of Gerald Heard (Heard, 1963; Houston, 1987). When Houston comes to the part of the river where a quantum leap is required, she and Heard invent a term to describe the consciousness of the self at that point: Leptoid Man, from the Greek word, lepsis, to leap (Heard, 1963, pp. 128—135). Here their research reaches confluence with Graves in uncovering the need for a quantum jump in the river journey.

How to make this leap to the 2nd Tier?

Houston infuses into the discussion an important component she calls the *Life Force* (Houston, 1987). She postulates a moving Force that both pushes and pulls the process of the unfolding consciousness of the self. Under the influence of Teilhard de Chardin, her childhood teacher, she inserts a sense of Sacred movement within the process (Houston, 1988). Houston also recognizes the importance of community in fostering the consciousness of "the possible human" (Houston, 1987, p. 15).

Hence, the crucial leap up the stream is made through the push and pull of the Life Force, a Force I will state emerges out of the Primordial Mind/Heart through the means of the eco-field. Connecting with this Life Force, the élan vital, constitutes an important gift from this river guide.

Robert Kegan: Field Guide #4 for the River

If Jean Houston discovers the trace element of the consciousness of the self in the standing waves, then Robert Kegan puts on his goggles and sees the unfolding ability to observe that same self, or what he calls *the observing self* (Kegan, 1982). The central track of Kegan's research follows the observing self as it moves from first one standing wave to another on the evolutionary river.

Why is this important?

As we develop, we move to different levels of maturity. That maturity is measured by an increasing ability to view aspects of ourselves with an ever-enlarging perspective. Age presents a verticality. Six-year-olds are not equal in their grasp of reality to sixty-year-olds. Let us delve further into the matter.

As we age:

We learn to be more objective about ourselves.

We learn not to take ourselves so seriously.

We learn the importance of an ever enlarging lens.

We learn to put all stories on the table, no matter how strange they may sound to our ears.

Wisdom traditions such as Buddhism and Hinduism call this process the development of the *Witnessing Presence*. In shamanic communities this ability to make the story bigger is achieved first and foremost through vision questing, a time of fasting and seeing visions while close to the Untamed, the Primordial. Usually, a call to quest arises as the river sojourner moves from one wave to another. For example, Crazy Horse (Spirited Horse) had thirteen vision quests as he moved through his life. Some persons in the Earthtribe have been on at least eight quests, with each quest allowing a larger vision, an ability to see one's self and reality from a larger perspective.

Kegan uses the technical terms of the subject of one wave (the self who is looking through the goggles), becoming the object or target of the looking on the next wave (1982). For example, when you are four-years-old, you see the world through eyes not yet influenced by the logic of telling time. Then, as you reach puberty, say eleven or twelve, you achieve another identity informed by the alphabet and hormones, and make the four-year-old self an object of your observing self or witnessing presence.

"I remember when I was a little kid and couldn't tell time."

This ability to observe or witness yourself without judgment provides us with an important guidance system for moving through the standing waves looming before us on the journey up and down the river.

So, what have we seen thus far through the goggles of the various researchers? Values, morals, consciousness of self, and the ability to witness or observe the self as it moves through different standing waves. Now, we consider another researcher, one who tracks human spirituality in the different waves.

James Fowler: Field Guide #5 for the River

Fowler, Director of the Center for Faith Development at Emory University, defines spirituality or *faith*, as he puts it, as "the human quest for transcendence" (Fowler, 1981 p. 14). There is good news and bad news about his research. First the good news: Fowler's own spiritual practice is Methodist (Christian); yet, as he moved through the standing waves, he found amazingly uniform development through most of the world's religious and wisdom traditions as spirituality or faith evolved.

A person has a different spirituality that depends on the particular wave she is in at the time. For example, if you are in the orange or green wave, your spirituality will have a heavy dose of logic and reason, like the Unitarian Church. If you are in the purple standing wave, your spirituality will usually have a close connection with all the elements of Earth, like the Native American Church.

To choose another metaphor for a moment: What all of these waves have in common in terms of spirituality is the plucking of the string of the guitar. The pluck of the string is Spirit touching our heart strings in a mystical moment. But what Fowler discovers is that the sound that comes out of the guitar is determined by the type of box that the guitar has. To put the two metaphors together: the box of the guitar amplifies the sound. When you are in the orange wave, one sound emits from your soul. When you are in the purple wave, another sound rings out from your essence. The field of energy where you dwell physically and culturally determines the map you use to interpret Spirit's strumming your strings.

In a lifetime a person will, according to Fowler, move through different forms of spirituality in the quest for transcendence. You usually begin with an intuitive spirituality, move to a literal faith, surf to logic and questioning, begin to put things together, and end up with a universal spirituality. All this maturity unfolds if you continue the quest. Most people, according to Fowler's research, find a center of gravity along the way and remain there the rest of their lives. They settle for the smaller view.

I mentioned there is good news and bad news in Fowler. Like much of Western Civilization, Fowler is over-balanced in transcendence. His very definition of faith (or spirituality) is "the quest for transcendence" (p. 14). But what of immanence? What of the Ground of Being? What of the spirits of the meadows and tsunamis? What of the perceptions through our five senses? What of the trees reaching out to Lisa and warning of the fire at Deer Dancer Ranch? What of the wisdom of the eco-field? What of the most important language of spirituality, primal and felt utterances?

I know. I know. If James Fowler could respond (and he probably will), he would say, "Of course. Both perspectives are important." My point here is that the zeitgeist of civilizations' various forms of spirituality automatically frames the search as being toward transcendence, the sky god, up Jacob's ladder, up the Tower of Babel, Jesus in Heaven, toward Buddha's enlightenment, away from the flesh, away from the sensual. All the while, using field guides provided by the dominant culture, we ignore the beauty and Wisdom of Earth and consider Her our outlet mall to use pretty much as we want with a tipping of the hat toward stewardship.

We shall explore how, in my view, this prejudice toward Transcendence, the Absolute, Pure Reason, Enlightenment, and God-in-Heaven has plunged us head-over-heels into the Era of Natural Consequences. We shall see how Industrial Civilization, including the fruits of the Renaissance and the marvels of modern technology, are basically bankrupt to face our current era, literally. We shall see that, for all the beauty of the literature of Western Civilization and its moving classical music, we need a more basic but lost intimacy with Nature.

Now, we have considered five field or river guides, barely touching the scope of their research. However, the main point I make in the brief inspection of their maps is to note that they uncover through their research the two currents: descending and ascending. Though they record different elements in the waves, they all, coming from very different angles, note these two currents.

In the service of transition to the next chapter, allow me to shift metaphors for a moment. Let's assume that the five researchers noted in this chapter had tuning devices built into their snorkeling gear. Their tuning apparatus allowed only certain information to be fed into their maps. The limitations of their peering into the waves points us to important questions.

What about others of us as we splash in the standing waves? What are our tuning devices?

What do our channel selectors pull out of the domain of waves? What is even meant by tuning into informational waves?

These questions send us to the larger human experiences of *tuning into the signals of the fields.*

II

Fields as Utterances of The Mother Tongue

CHAPTER FIVE

Tunings from the Field

At Wisdom University and the Earthtribe, we launch our journeys from the matrix of direct access of our own deepest experiences. Our orientation point is the subjective, and then we move to the objective. We explore the interior of the I, move to the intersubjective of the we of community, and then to the objective reference point of incoming data and exterior maps. In that spirit this chapter concerns itself with a number of different tunings into the fields of energy that envelop our planet. In the next chapter, I will enter a more comprehensive dialogue about the scientific understanding of fields and eco-fields. For now I delve into our interior experiences of the fields.

Already I have mentioned the Onge of the Andaman Islands, ten-year-old Tilly Short in Sri Lanka, and Lisa Dvorak at Deer Dancer Ranch. Other tantalizing cases of tuning into fields follow, but first a few of my own direct tuning experiences, included because they are quite ordinary.

Will's Tuning into Fields
The year was 1992, and I entered a shamanic journey one night and saw a hurricane that hit Homestead, Florida, with considerable devastation. The next morning I talked of the dream/vision with Judith Yost, my spouse, and we immediately checked The Weather

Channel to see if there were any hurricanes developing either in the Atlantic, the Caribbean basin, or the Gulf of Mexico. There were not. We both dismissed my tuning in as pertaining to some aspect of my personal unconscious. We were beginners in the tuning domain of specifically predictive dreams.

Within a few days a large hurricane, Andrew, developed off the Eastern Coast of Florida and slammed into Homestead with catastrophic results, including twenty-five deaths and $30 billion in property damage. Questions pummeled me as the winds roared across Florida:

What was the origin of the information?

What was I to do with the information once I obtained it?

How had I been able to access the information?

Are there actual conduits to these fields that make sense to our modern minds?

These questions point us in the direction of the hunger of our inner world to connect in an energetic manner with the larger fields, or a dimension beyond ourselves.

Here is another example of an informational transmission from an underlying field. In 1987 Judith and I led a vision quest in the Adirondack Mountains of Northern New York. As was our custom, we conducted a pipe song meditation each night from 2:00 to 4:00 a.m. aimed at supporting the vision questers and educating the twenty or so supporters constituting the encampment.

At the end of the meditation period, Judith and I returned to our tents, seeking a few hours of sleep. As I lay there with my eyes closed in a shamanic state, I suddenly saw a string of advanced calculus formulae. I asked Judith if she were having a similar experience, and she answered in the negative. Tuning into this mysterious field lasted for about ten minutes, and then I drifted to sleep.

Two days later, we brought the vision questers in from their sites. It was our custom as elders to interview the questers, listen carefully, and offer beginning guidance. At the end of this processing of his quest, Dave, one of the questers, mentioned that he had an unusual experience during his time in his circle. He saw a series of calculus-type formulae in a vision that lasted for about ten minutes. The mathematical information, he explained, had little meaning to him and did not figure greatly into the thrust of his personal quest. He had a puzzled look on his face at this odd download.

Startled, Judith and I looked at each other but said nothing.

A day later we broke camp and drove back to civilization. We stopped at a restaurant in a nearby town and parked our trucks. I walked casually with Dave along shaded streets toward the café, discussing my experience of seeing the formulae. He was shocked when I told him the details of the equations because they were similar to what he saw. He used his math skills on a daily basis as a computer consultant, but still he had no clue as to their meaning.

It was apparent that we did not know what to do with the technical information, so the downlink receded to the background. We did not have the bandwidth to upgrade the information to the level of knowledge, much less wisdom. We speculated that an underlying field sought outlets that night, perhaps around the planet. Maybe there was a young person in Russia trained in probability calculus who received the transfer and knew how to amplify the data.

My personal experiences with the field recorded here are not remarkable, but rather suggestive of larger possibilities and of our yearning for points of contact with the beyond. Deeper entry into boundless fields of information present themselves once we notice a tuning possibility between our interior and the exterior. Let us continue in exploring more startling log-ins.

Friedrich A. Kekule's Pivotal Tuning

In 1865 German chemist, Friedrich Kekule, published a paper that opened the door to modern chemistry and the development of the benzene ring. His discovery made possible our understanding of all aromatic compounds and essentially led to modern drugs, plastics, synthetic rubber, and dyes.

How was such a pivotal scientific discovery made? For twenty-five years Kekule kept the account of his breakthrough a secret, thinking the scientific community would not understand. And he was right: they did not understand, as we shall see.

In 1890, the German Chemical Society organized an elaborate professional conference in Kekule's honor to celebrate the twenty-fifth anniversary of his first benzene paper. To their shock and, in some cases, dismay, Kekule offered a narrative describing his original discovery.

Here is the story he offered at the conference in his honor. For seven years he had pondered a bottleneck in the chemical understanding of benzene and the nature of carbon-carbon bonds. No matter where he turned in his research, he found dead ends. One day, he spontaneously went into a trance state of consciousness in which he had an elaborate vision. He was careful to explain that his vision was not from his internal imagination but elegant information that seemed to come to him out of—shall we say for the moment—the blue.

The essence of Kekule's vision included a snake seizing its own tail. Such a vision is to this day common in shamanic circles. The archetype is known as the Ouroboros or Endless Knot, so it is not unusual that in a shamanic type trance a person would see such an image. What was unusual in Kekule's case consisted in the specificity of the information given and its facilitating a quantum leap forward in chemistry.

Hear Kekule's own words:

"I turned my chair to the fire and dozed for a few minutes. Again the atoms were gamboling before my eyes…my mental eye… could not distinguish larger structures of manifold conformation; long rows, sometimes more closely fitted together, all twining and twisting in a snakelike motion.

"But look! What was that?

"One of the snakes had seized hold of its own tail, and the form whirled mockingly before my eyes. As if by a flash of lighting I awoke…"
(Weisberg, 1992, p. 43).

When he awoke, it was clear to him: the carbon-carbon bonding appeared in the form of a ring later known as the benzene ring, the details of which can now be seen in any chemistry textbook.

Four notes on the above vision:

- First, a few scientists continue to reflect the typical pessimism of our dominant culture and believe that Kekule concocted the vision in an effort not to share his discovery. Such comments reflect the limits of our current epistemology, or methods of knowing. Since many modern investigators are ignorant of shamanic trances, they assume such states of mind reveal frauds, much the way the vacationers on the beach at Sri Lanka assumed the Onge were imagining things when they went to higher ground as the tsunami approached.

- Second, Kekule became a field guide for all of modern chemistry because, unlike the vision I saw in the tent of the mathematical formulae, he knew what to do with his tuning into the field.

- Third, the cyclic nature of benzene was finally confirmed in 1929, sixty-seven years after the original vision by the further experiments of scientist Kathleen Lonsdale. Visions need communal and, sometimes, academic confirmation.

- Fourth, and perhaps most important, the role of the snakes and the fire arise, in my hypothesis, from a field of energy whereby the field itself seeks out Kekule as an outlet for its intelligence.[1] I will flesh out this statement in future chapters

We are beginning to warm-up to the access points of the Mother Tongue, information flows from the fields speaking to those who know how to decipher the language. As an aside, it is worth noting that Carl G. Jung was fascinated with Kekule's dream/vision and devoted considerable attention to Kekule in the

---

[1] dreamtalk.hypermart.net/teachers/famedrm.htm

symbolism of creative thought (Jung, 1983). Jung saw visions and dreams emerging from a domain he called the collective unconscious, his psychological version of the underlying field.

Abraham Lincoln's Tuning

Lincoln reported the following dream to his friend Ward Hill Lamon.

> "About ten days ago, I retired very late. I soon began to dream. There seemed to be a death-like stillness about me. Then I heard subdued sobs, as if a number of people were weeping. I thought I left my bed and wandered downstairs. There the silence was broken by the same pitiful sobbing, but the mourners were invisible. I went from room to room.
>
> No living person was in sight, but the same mournful sounds met me as I passed alone. I was puzzled and alarmed. Determined to find the cause of a state of things so mysterious and shocking, I kept on until I arrived at the East Room. Before me was a…corpse wrapped in funeral vestments. Around it were stationed soldiers who were acting as guards; and there was a throng of people, some gazing mournfully upon the corpse, whose face was covered, others weeping pitifully.
>
> "Who is dead in the White House?" I demanded of one of the soldiers.
>
> "The President," was his answer. "he was killed by an assassin."[2]

Comment: In shamanic domains, traditions tell us that the sacred web (field?) will give us a glimpse of our own deaths, even a song to propel us through death. Was this dream a message from the underlying field to Lincoln to assist his journey? Does this account suggest that we can recover the lost pathway through

---

[2] rogerjnorton.com/Lincoln46.html

death itself to the larger domain? Is there a resource intelligence just waiting for our tuning?

Is death itself the principle verb of the lost language?

Though some scholars question the historicity of Lincoln's dream, the questions remain, and, for me, the dream rings true.

Guiseppe Tartini Tunes with the Devil

The Italian violinist and composer, Tartini, composed his greatest work, The Devil's Trill, after he had a dream in 1713. In the dream Tartini handed his violin to the devil himself, who began

> "to play with consummate skill a sonata of such exquisite beauty as surpassed the bold flights of my imagination. I felt enraptured, transported, enchanted; my breath was taken away, and I awoke. Seizing my violin I tried to retain the sounds I had heard. But it was in vain. The piece I then composed...was the best I ever wrote, but how far below the one I heard in my dreams."[3]

Comment: Trained in the philosophy of our transcendent-oriented culture, Tartini associated the sublime from the field as the devil where often the beauties of nature are seen as evil. Still, the music of the spheres seeks outlets through those who dive deeply into the waves.

Are actual sounds available through the primordial fields for the ordinary seeker like you and me? Are profound songs seeking entrance through fields?

9/11 Tunings: Precognitive Dreams

An avalanche of premonitions and precognitive dreams have come to the surface since 9/11, and following are a few that have surfaced in my research.

> On September 10 I dreamt of my classmate of school days, now President of United Airlines.
> In my dream he and I met on the streets of New

---

[3] www.geraldelias.com/music_DT_tartini.html

York under the background of the twin towers. He rushed toward me and we embraced as two old friends should, but he was crying. I mistook the tears for joy. He then told me that something dreadful had happened and both of us turned to see the twin towers in flames.

Anjan N.[4]

Here is another:

I saw the bombing of the towers in a dream a week before. The problem with my gift is the interpretation. In the dream I did not know where it took place or the date. In the dream I was watching TV and saw the disaster unfold with no sound or voice to say what it was. I told my daughter that I saw an explosion in my dreams. I have this gift, but it is hard to understand or interpret.

Cheryl G.[5]

Comment: Notice the precision of the first dream down to the name of the airlines involved. Also, be aware of the recurring theme of the person tuning into the field and yet not knowing how it was done or, as my story in the vision quest with the calculus equations, not knowing how to interpret the information.

The various hypotheses of this book will explore how we must recover the ability both to tune into the field and to translate through the medium of nature-based communities. 9/11 itself has brought thousands of dreams like the above to the surface, pointing to the link between historical events and primal intelligence in the field and to a Wisdom seeking to assist in Earth's well being through messages from the field.

Let's continue our dance with field guides and their tuning abilities.

[4] paranormal.about.com/library/weekly/aa100101.htm

[5] paranormal.about.com/library/weekly/aa100101a.htm

Tunings from Ordinary Life

> My father was at a local swimming pool. He was looking toward the road, and he saw a car come around the corner and smash into another vehicle. He smelled fumes and heard sounds of the crash. He shouted for help, but his friends just looked at him strangely as if he was going mad. Nothing was there; nothing had happened.
>
> The next moment, the exact scene took place exactly as he had seen it moments previously.

Here's another:

> We were out camping by a river that runs from the Rocky Mountains just west of Nordegg. My dad had a dream about a small pond lined with skulls. The next day we went out fishing and my brother got really sick with Beaver Fever because he had drunk some contaminated water.

And another:

> My grandfather once mentioned in a passing conversation that he was glad that my Aunt's leg was healing well even though nothing was wrong with my Aunt's leg. He explained she had slipped on a dock. Two days later she slipped on a dock and broke her leg in two places.[6]

Comment: A major emphasis of my research centers on how we ordinary humans have the ability to tune into the fields if only we can recover an intuitive tongue described in these tunings. This possibility lies mostly dormant in our cells. Covered with the overlays of dominant civilization, we have lost the value of these

---

[6] religousforums.com/forum/mysticism-dir/84560-predictive-dreams-vision.html (accessed on August 4, 2011)

moments and, to emphasize again, our ability to interpret and translate them into usefulness for the larger planet.

Tunings with Ancient Structures

A journey to the pyramids of Teotihuacán, located about an hour north of Mexico City, is stunning in its impact. When there, I am aware of a profound kinship with distant planets and star systems. My body vibrates or resonates as I stand atop the Pyramid of the Sun, especially when I am in the midst of a resonant community.

To explore intuitive transfers at the site of the pyramids, I delved into the research of Peter Tompkins and Hugh Harleston, Jr. (Tompkins, 1976). With a grant given by the Smithsonian Institute, Harleston spent twenty years working through the mathematical relationship of the pyramids in the Teotihuacán complex and made a startling discovery. The layout of the city is an accurate representation of our solar system, including the celestial entity, Pluto, which is sometimes classified as a planet and sometimes not.

When I realized that the Teotihuacán complex is an accurate representation of the solar system, I was shocked. Let us see why as I put the modern discovery of Pluto in context of field attunement. The head of an astronomical research team, V. M. Slipher, at The Lowell Observatory in Flagstaff, AZ, had followed the mathematics of Percival Lowell that suggested the existence of a small planet at the edge of the solar system. Yet, the research team had reached an impasse. Slipher had read an obscure reference by a self-taught astronomer, Clyde Tombaugh, who combined his intuitive education on a Kansas farm with his homemade telescopes to make amazing, if scientifically unsubstantiated, observations.

Slipher invited Tombaugh to join his team and was savvy enough to utilize Tombaugh's intuitive skills combined with the best astronomy of the day to search the skies for the elusive and small planet located in our local solar system and predicted by Lowell's mathematics.[7]

---

[7] planetary.org/explore/topics/pluto/plutodiscovery4.html (accessed August 4, 2011)

Each night, when the weather was clear and the Moon was not shining, Tombaugh placed a photographic plate, 14″ by 17″ in size at the focal point of a 13-inch telescope. In a process called *blinking* with an instrument called a comparator, Tombaugh worked nine-hour days in an unheated observatory where temperatures were sometimes below zero. In the process he scanned a million and a half stars. Then, on February 18, 1930, he located Planet X, predicted by Percival Lowell's mathematics and called it *Pluto*.

The Tombaugh story is astonishing in and of itself, but it pales beside the reality that the Toltecs at Teotihuacán not only knew about Pluto but also had worked out the mathematics some 4,600 years before Lowell. Catch your breath for a moment. The Mexican pyramids were completed while Europe was still in the midst of the Dark Ages, thinking the Earth was flat and the center of the Universe.

Comments: The pyramids themselves point to a journey down the river of evolution to ancient people who spoke the language of the stars, a trip that we will take shortly. As we journey, we will need to put aside our tendency to think the ancients knew less than we. We will need to put aside our prejudice that European knowledge predates the wisdom of the New World. We will need—gasp—even to consider that the planetary migration theories of human beings may not be large enough to hold unfolding reality when we become fluent in template language of the eco-fields.

We will continually be reminded that a new epistemology is developing that tells us the ancients are completely necessary for a wisdom that takes us through the current era. Evidently, the builders of the pyramids had tapped into an underlying pattern expressed in mathematics before the formidable power of antiquity, Rome, had even thought about invading the backward tribes of Europe. The Toltecs apparently had advanced into the universal structures of numbers long before Pythagoras formulated his famous theorems.

And where did such a basic dialect—one reflecting an underlying architecture—originate? The builders of Teotihuacán's pyramids tell a story of receiving the information from the stars. If such a statement sounds preposterous to your rational sensibilities, then remember, I assert, we need the largest possible grasp of language if we are to navigate this mighty river, no matter how preposterous the suggestions may seem.

Such openness is the essence of authentic science.

Nevertheless, my tale here verges on completely offending our scientific and skeptical selves as they sit in our inner council. So, before I continue with such science, shall we say for the moment, "science fiction," let us proceed to an exploration of the newer science of fields to see if these tales of booting up to an underlying consciousness are fiction, or not.

CHAPTER SIX

Field Theory as The Mother Tongue

In the previous chapter we tasted the fine wine of direct access of a larger domain I called the underlying field. So far so good. I hope your curiosity is whetted. Mystical literature is full of such accounts, stretching back into pre-history.

But what of us moderns and post-moderns and our rousing skepticism? If I mention that the base language of the planet came to us—like the oceans and all the cells of our bodies—from the stars, we likely will wrinkle our brows and roll our eyes.

We all have in our inner council of selves an inner scientist and an inner skeptic (Taegel, 2010). Even if you don't consider yourself a scientist or a skeptic, it is impossible to live in our dominant culture without having these powerful influences speaking, or at least whispering, through an inner microphone on a daily basis. These two inner aspects form a coalition within our council that is useful at times but often paralyzing.

This chapter respectfully addresses these inner scientists and skeptics. These subunits within want to know what we are talking about when we use terms like *underlying fields*. Is such talk more hocus-pocus or what? Before we make the big journey of descent down the white water of the standing waves in our metaphorical river, we need to address the important questions of our inner scientists and skeptics. Otherwise, these wary voices will sabotage our journey.

The Question of Fields and Field Guides

In the latter years of the 20th century, an unexpected piece of the modern scientific story jolted us. The focus of evolution shifted from seeing ourselves as chemical reactions in hard core Darwinism to identifying humans and all living things, indeed, the Universe Itself, as pulsating energy emanating out of a process scientists called fields (Feynman, 1998) *Startling discoveries in quantum physics bent the scientific story back toward the view of ancient shamans.*

Let us see how.

Einstein acted as an early field guide, followed quickly by quantum physicists like Bohm (1995), Feynman (1998), and Puthoff (1989). From their visionary perch, these newer scientists tell us that something far more fundamental occurs in evolution than a series of chemical reactions. A pushing and pulling tugs at us, an interactional dynamic of force fields such as we explored with Kekule earlier.

Fields, these newer scientists tell us, provide the forces that literally move, inform, and form life.

Fields Defined

Earlier, I advanced the notion of *fields as regions of influence* (Feynman, 1998). Now, we delve into more specific scientific understandings of fields and how they are connected to the Primordial Mind/ Heart, source of Wild Wisdom, speaker of the original language. We shall see how this template tongue speaks to us in the form of *fields*, specifically, *eco-fields*. But first we need to delve into the meaning of *fields* from a scientific perspective.

Fields as Non-Material

Biochemist Rupert Sheldrake defines fields as non-material regions of influence (Sheldrake, 1995). The *non-material* descriptions add an entirely different dimension to the discussion because it liberates us from the confines of earlier science, a dreary chapter of the story which left most of us with the impression that material things are more real than the non-material (Hoyle, 1983). Most of us grew up thinking tables and chairs are more real than visions, premonitions, dreams, and intuitions. Not so quick with that assumption, according to the newer sciences.

Reality is not as it appears to the modern rational mind.

Not at all.

For example, the gravitational field is all around us, includes us, and moves through us. It is not material, but, nevertheless, quite real. Is it not? It is more real, more fundamentally real, than a rational understanding of matter, as we shall soon see. The gravitational field pervades the entire universe but varies in strength (Einstein, 1940).

Gravity itself is merely a word, invented for our story not by Isaac Newton but by Descartes, to describe an allurement between objects (Descartes, trans., 1988). If you stand on a chair and then jump off, you will experience an allurement, a powerful and non-material attraction between yourself and the floor. True: it happens so quickly you don't usually think about it. But slow down the action, implores newer science, and you will see something very different from what you have thought.

Gravity is not a material thing but an unseen force.

Information between you and floor is imparted in what scientists call a *gravitational field*. The information as to how fast you fall varies according to where you are. A few miles up in space, the non-material flow of information (which we call gravity) is still there, but the information is different. Now, you and the floor are told a different rate at which you will meet.

What? You mean the field is talking to us? A hidden Mother Tongue? Literally true.

Important qualities of fields in general emerge as we inquire into gravity:

- Objects can influence each other even though they are not in material contact. Recall an elementary school experiment of placing a magnet under a piece of paper with iron filings on the topside. What a marvel to see how you could move the iron with the force field of the magnet. It was like magic. It defied common sense. An unseen force, a region of non-material influence took over. Even with simple experiments like this one, we find ourselves under the spellbinding influence of interacting fields (Tiller, 1993).

• This non-material influence varies according to a number of factors. As mentioned above, simple elevation changes the influence and the information between you-on-the-chair and the floor. Change the elevation, and Nature's base vernacular tells you something different.

• Actual information is passed between yourself and the floor, using fields as the transporter or medium of the information.

So far so good in our story of the scientific understanding of fields, but our rational mind is about to be stretched to the breaking point. This stretch is necessary if we are to become fluent in the rudimentary information exchanges pulsating beneath our usual thinking.

Fields as Nonlocal

Recent experiments uncover a remarkable condition in larger fields, an action physicists label as nonlocality. Nick Herbert, a physicist known for translating complicated tenets of the newer sciences for non-physicists, puts it like this:

> The essence of nonlocality is unmediated action-at-a-distance. A nonlocal interaction links up one location with another without crossing space, without decay and without delay (1985, p. 51)

Henry Stapp (2004, p. 30), arguably one of our more important living scientists, states that nonlocality is "the most profound discovery in all science."

This discovery is a game-changer in our story.

What are these scientists referring to in describing fields as having a nonlocal quality? The linkage between one location (you on the chair) and another (the floor) happens faster, much faster than the speed of light. This pervasive linkage means that the information passed in the medium of the various fields goes really fast, so fast that our common sense rationality falls down on the floor and screams, "Foul!"

It means that Lisa received information about the fire at the ranch at a pace faster than the speed of light. In an instant she knew what was happening and what to do, imparted by the field, though her choices were involved and slowed the action.

It means that the information about the car wreck in the previous chapter came to the observer at the swimming pool faster than can be imagined. So fast his friends thought him mad. This nonlocality gives us a clue as to how the Onge People knew about the tsunami in time to move to higher ground. The newer sciences are teaching us the language of nonlocality, key syntax in our recovering the Mother Tongue, spoken so easily by the animals at the Malla Natural Preserve in Sri Lanka.

Now, let's proceed to another part of the story that includes other *fields* at work in the Universe as we now know it. In addition to what we call the gravitational field, there are three other fields now accepted by mainstream science: the electromagnetic field, the strong nuclear field, and the weak nuclear field. All of these forces or powerful, non-material influences were operating at full speed a millisecond after the Big Bang (Einstein, 1979; Feynman, 1998).

They did not evolve in our story. They were speaking with primordial or field syntax immediately at the moment of the great flaring forth, 13.7 billion years ago. Is that original conversation still available to us? It would seem so. Let us look deeper into the nature of these fields by examining briefly the electromagnetic field.

The Electromagnetic Field

The electromagnetic (EM) field is another field or region of non-material influence gaining the attention of the newer sciences (Becker, 1990). Many of us do not have a clear notion of what the EM field is, and, yet, we know that the EM field operates powerfully during many facets of our lives, including thunderstorms. We know that our bodies can become tuning devices or lightning rods. In fact, being struck by lightning provides a common, if frightening, example of how humans have the ability to access or tune into a region of non-material influence, the EM field. An estimated 240,000 people per year are struck by lightning around the world.[1] One man, Roy Sullivan, a National Park Ranger, has been struck eight times over a thirty-five year period. To underline how unaware we are of the working of the EM field, consider these facts: around the Earth there are 100 lightning strikes per second, 6,000 per minute, 360,000 per hour, and 8,640,000 per day.[2] And lightning strikes are just a tiny aspect of the work of the EM field.

Lightning Strikes as Dramatic Tuning

Drawing on the process and reality of the EM field moving through humans in lightning strikes, consider these facts brought forward by Robert Becker, a foremost researcher into the EM field (1990):

- Men are struck four times more often than women. Does testosterone assist as a conduit of tuning? Height?
- Humans are powerful links between the EM field and the ground, even more so than bronze statues. Even without a piece of metal like an umbrella or golf club, a human is more apt to conduct the EM energy force we call lightning than a bronze statue.
- Moreover, geographical location is a key. If you stand in the open during a storm in Florida, Texas, or Colorado, you are more likely to tune into or conduct the lightning strike than other locations in North America (pp. 76–89).

Do you get the picture here?

All of these factors indicate human choice and practice as being important in the experience of what we call being struck by lightning. You can tune into the EM field simply by choosing where, when, and what you hold in your hand during a thunderstorm. Such a basic experience strongly suggests that we can develop abil-

[1] weather.gov/os/lightning/overview.htm

[2] newton.dep.anl.gov/askasci/wea00/wea00239.htm

ities to tune into fields in many ways, as indicated by the examples in the previous chapter. These visions, dreams, and premonitions are not just New Age gibberish. Tuning is not only possible but part and parcel of our lives. Information does pass through the fields, from the unseen to the seen.

As the EM field passes through us in a process we call "being struck by lightning," it imparts important information. This primordial example leads us to explore more deeply the informational character of *fields*, as our story unfolds.

Fields Transmit Information

What, then, is the relationship of fields, information, knowledge, and wisdom? Let us start with the EM field and the lightning bolt just mentioned. As the EM passes through the human in the form of lightning, significant information transfers occur. For example, the strength of the particular bolt, the resistance of the specific human body, and the distance of the lightning strike from the human, to name a few bits of information imprinted in the movement of the EM field through a person in a lightning strike. Each of the eight times Roy Sullivan had the EM pass through him different communications from the EM field occurred. Let's hazard a guess that these *tunings* through lightning strikes reshaped Roy's identity or understanding of the world, for good or ill. Or maybe Roy did not learn to speak in the language of lightning, and this failure resulted in continuing strikes.

Or return to the gravitational field for a moment. If you drop an apple from six feet at the equator, the field tells both the apple and the ground how fast the apple will fall. Different information will apply if you perform the same experiment atop Mt. Everest. By the same token, if you take a tumble on Mt. Everest, your fall rate is different than at the Equator. At the risk of belaboring my point in our story, I continue to underline the reality of the field imparting information to all its parts at a speed faster than the speed of light, a dimension of the field story that knocked Einstein's socks off.

These simple instances of information exchanges in the field point to much larger considerations. When we review the developments in the newer sciences, we can easily apprehend that matter is not the essence of reality as reductive researchers advocated in the last century. Rather, non-material energy exchanges are everywhere in the form of fields. Einstein's discoveries make this notion a common fact: matter and energy balance as part and parcel of each other (Einstein, 1940).

But wait.

That's not my main point.

We are now discovering the astounding transmission of information in the energy/matter equation. After exploring the landscape of the newer sciences, Ervin Laszlo, systems researcher, concludes:

> There is not only matter and energy in the universe, but also a more subtle yet real element: information in the form of active and effective "in-formation" (2004, p. 46).

Laszlo's point is that information actually passes between energy and matter and—this is my next important point—*forms everything in the field as it informs.*

The Mother Tongue shapes us as it speaks to us.

The field passes information between its parts and forms as it informs.

We ourselves—I the writer and you the reader—are being shaped by information exchanges each moment of every day, including the writing and reading of this book. The EM field (through lightning and myriad other transfers) shapes us through its delivery of information. Gravity as a field shapes us with its information as we jump off the chair. If struck by lightning, your identity will shift significantly through what passes between the bolt and your cells.

And, as you and I exchange information through the fields, we shape each other.

The Big Bang Gives Us a Basic Syntax

This information exchange we are exploring in the syntax of fields happened from the first moment of the Universe, the Great Flaring

Forth. At the birth of the Universe consider these facts. If the expansion rate of the early Universe had been "one-billionth less than it was, the universe would have re-collapsed almost immediately; and if it had been one-billionth more, it would have flown apart so fast that it could produce only dilute, cold gases" (Laszlo, 2004, p. 64).

How did the Universe know how to behave at that first moment? Where did it receive the information? Random chance? Or was the presence of fields a Primordial Mind/Heart speaking through the language of fields? In the beginning was the Word, and the Word became the field and dwelt among us, full of grace and truth.

The Mother Speaks in Microwaves

After that first moment, the Universe emitted microwave radiation at about the 400,000-year mark, an instant in geologic time. Even though the microwaves were going in opposite directions at the speed of light, they still were operating at a uniform level (Feynman, 1982). How do we know? The cosmic background radiation is uniform for billions of light-years in every direction, even at this instant. This behavior of the expanding microwave radiation, along with many other examples beyond the scope of this book, continues to raise the question—what is the origin of this coherence?

It is no longer, in my estimation, sufficient to state dogmatically—*God*—without being informed by the newer sciences as possible revelations of the Primordial Mind, quantum intelligence speaking through the active voice of *fields*. Our inner skeptics and scientists may reject *God* as a source, but be at home with *quantum fields*. After all, the word *God* is derived from the German word, good or g̲u̲t̲, and we all know that this sacred subject is a bit more complex than good.

The Primary Voice of the Field

It seems to be the case that our Universe is making itself known as an evolving, coherent whole, operating with intelligence and information exchange at the very beginning point and continuing to our current moment. Could this coherence be due to information filtering up from these underlying fields we have been exploring, as well as linkages between eco-fields?

It appears so.

Einstein called the underlying field: the Unified Field Theory (1954).

Sheldrake called it the Morphogenetic Field (1995). Laszlo spoke of it as the Akasha-Field (A-Field), the Zero Point Field, or the Quantum Vacuum (2004).

This storyline of an underlying field is pivotal. These fields are full of information exchanges with all other fields. According to my story (and that of the ancient world), this unifying field emerges out of the Primordial Mind/Heart. It is not the Primordial Mind/Heart but rather expressive thoughts of that Intelligence.

Hence the term: the Mother Tongue, or Primordial expression.

As scientist Sir Arthur Eddington noted, "The stuff of the universe is mind stuff...the source and condition of physical reality" (Eddington, 1984).

The Shamanic Era, The Mother Tongue, and Fields

I want to pause here and make a brief but salient point for our story about the connection of the science of fields and the shamanic era. We find in traditional shamanic teachings the ability of humans to access or tune into information proceeding directly from the Primordial in Nature.

In my lifelong explorations in this shamanic area, I have acquired many approaches which yield direct access to the underlying fields, but these learned skills only scratch the surface of what is available in the standing wave of evolution Beck called Purple (2000). We will make that grand journey down the river to the shamanic in Chapter Eleven, but for now I want to emphasize how the primordial people of that era had many skills we have lost with our Western Civilization overlays.

In many profound ways the ancients were far advanced—I repeat in many different ways—beyond where post-moderns are today. While the newer sciences are brilliant in their discoveries and descriptions of the fields, they—and thus we—are quite clumsy in the tuning skills and abilities to know the primal nomenclature.

These shamanic methods I call *tuning devices*. Such practices are based on intuitive knowledge, persistent practices, and thus profound wisdom. At the heart of these abilities is the archetypal experience of community, the crucial soil that grows the tuning devices into the fields. Indigenous people in general, and the tribal training I had in particular, focused on tuning into specific landscapes. My tribal training taught me that the first job of the shamanic worker is to build bridges between humans and the larger environment.

If we can tune into gravity's information download by traveling from sea coast to mountain, then we have the possibility of tuning into vast fields just waiting to inform and form us. If the EM field can reach out to us 8,640,000 times per day in lightning strikes, then a different field can reach out to us each night in dreams. The Onge's warning of the tsunami becomes less strange. The Toltec reception of information about building the Teotihuacán pyramids from beyond the stars, not so bizarre.

Listen to a family story of these ancient tuning skills. Like all family stories it is partly fact and partly fiction pointing to a more basic truth.

The year is 1830.

The place is the Ohio River Valley.

My great-great-grandmother Tilitha lives in a Shawnee Town frequented by the noted shaman, Tecumseh. The story is murky here. It appears she was forced into a relationship with a slave trader from Texas that resulted in the birth of Louiza, a half-breed daughter. The two women were then dragged to Texas as slaves.

Many aspects of Tilitha and Louiza's story are missing, but one fact I know: Tilitha's local landscape was snatched from her. Her underlying relationship with her immediate eco-field was torn away. When in Ohio and Illinois, she and her tribe tuned into the local eco-field—they called it the Sacred Web—as a pharmacy for daily ailments. When she arrived in Central Texas, she was forced to use her tuning devices to establish a relationship with the new landscape, including the plants, animals, and people. Either that or die.

It took years for her to establish a coherence with this local eco-field. At this point in the narrative, Tilitha fades into the mists. We do know Louiza married a local white man who died and left her to live in a prejudiced culture as a half-breed woman with twin sons, one my grandfather.

One version of the family story in its next phase goes like this: a local tribe, the Tonkawa, gifted Louiza with a conch shell. She used this shell ceremonially and also practically to call my grandfather, Lee, in from the fields. Slowly, she discovered that the sound of the conch shell gave her a resonance with her surroundings, a tuning. Even as the gravitational field told the apple the rate of speed to fall at the equator versus Mt. Everest, so the landscape of the Texas Hill Country, the *eco-field*, told Louiza how to use the conch to heal herself and her neighbors in Texas versus the Ohio Valley.

One facet of her new environment was the local juniper forest. Known locally as cedar trees, these plants spewed forth powerful pollen in January of each year as part of a mating ritual. What we call allergies prevailed. Louiza called it cedar fever. Nasal drip, fever, sore throat, and itchy eyes debilitated her and her world, even as it still afflicts people in that area.

Perhaps, the trees themselves gave Louiza a cure, or maybe a hummingbird, or a vision quest, or perhaps a Tonkawa shaman who was aware of her challenges as a half-breed, female rancher. Possibly he gave her the cure to assist her in healing ways. In any case the eco-field spoke to her in an ancient speech telling her to eat two or three juniper berries a day, beginning in late November. She was told not to swallow the berry but rather to suck on it, much like tobacco, for a minute or so. Then, she learned to spit it out. That part of the informational download was important because juniper berries are, according to Western medicine, poisonous. Suck too long, and you might die.

Although the story contains few substantiated facts, I somehow received the conch shell and the cure. That much I know factually. When I moved to the Texas Hill Country nearly twenty years ago in a return to my home range, I immediately recalled the cure as I tasted the juniper berries, just as Louiza prescribed. I have used it with countless students. (Don't try it without guidance.) One such student was so beset with cedar fever that he had to take prednisone shots to obtain relief. The first year he tried the cure spoken to Louiza by the forested hills, he was totally healed, restored to harmony with the local eco-field. It seemed like the juniper forest now embraced him, and he thrived.

Thus, we see that the ancient shamans, like the newer quantum scientists, knew that the underlying fields pass information aimed at the evolution of the total landscape. Gregory Bateson (1979), seminal anthropologist, stated that the environment is a self-healing tautology, including humans when they return to their natural place.

Now, let's see where we are in the larger story of the book. I have mentioned the phrase eco-fields many times, and I am aware I have not explained myself. You know about my take on gravitational and EM fields, but what do I mean specifically with the term *eco-field*. That part of the narrative constitutes—at least in my version of the current human story—the key that turns the lock that may liberate us from the jail of Western Civilization.

Let us proceed to that part of the narrative.

CHAPTER SEVEN

The Eco-field Hypothesis

The story now turns in an unexpected direction.

For the first decade of the 21st century something nibbled at the edges of my mind until I realized there was a chasm in my understanding and experience of my environment. On the one hand, I thought of my environment as full of life, and the sciences of ecology and biology offered considerable support of this notion. On the other hand, the newer science of quantum physics and field theory inched its way into my mainstream and became a passionate interest as a central factor in my ecology, as I indicated in the previous chapter.

All well and good. But I could not bring these two maps of our planetary existence together, so I inched along, feeling the tension between the two.

June 2010

I attended an intensive seminar in a redwood forest setting at a retreat center on the flanks of Mt. Tamalpais in Northern California. We sat in a circle of twenty-five students and faculty discussing dissertation writing. In a lapse reminiscent of my elementary age schooling, I spent most of the morning gazing out the window at the lush forest and the mountain set against a late spring sky of brilliant blue.

The seminar faded to the background of my awareness. That's the kind of behavior that might attract a diagnosis of attention deficit disorder were I still in elementary school. The seminar conversation hummed in the background, and I tuned in every once in awhile, feeling not quite awake and not fully asleep. Let us be generous and say I learned in a hypnogogic state.

Late in the morning and without warning, I blurted out the phrase, *eco-field*. I blinked, realizing I was coming out of a trance state, a bit embarrassed at my outburst. The person next to me looked wide-eyed at my inappropriate utterance. The group directed its corporate attention in my direction, questioning the relevance of my comment to the discussion, but without judgment. Graciously, they listened to me as I explained how I yearned to put these two domains of ecology and quantum fields together. I asked them if anyone had heard of this term, *eco-field*, that coursed through me like one of the lightning strikes previously mentioned.

None had, nor were they too impressed.

And this was an extraordinary circle of brilliant students and world-class faculty, not to be taken lightly. Still, I was not discouraged. Like a detective with a new piece of evidence, I hurried to Google to see if anyone else on the planet was thinking in this direction. Expecting the usual long list of references, I found only one relevant source: Almo Farina of the *Istituto di Biomatematica*, at the University of Urbino in Italy.[1] Once on that site, I found, much to my surprise, a group of scientists at the University of Urbino performing important research in a new branch of science they labeled as eco-fields. In their hard-nosed research into landscape ecology, they had encountered serious limitations in biologically based paradigms. As they studied habitats for various species, the data they collected seemed to demand a larger perspective than just ecology. Terms like biosphere did not adequately describe what they were uncovering. These curious scientists followed the evidence until they fell off the end of their ecologically based map. They needed something larger to guide them.

---

[1] www.uniurb.it/biomat/farina

74

Farina's Eco-field Hypothesis

In 2004 they published a ground-breaking paper entitled, *The Eco-field: A New Paradigm For Landscape Ecology* (Ecological Research, 2004, 19:107–110). Their thoroughly objective research did not coincide precisely with mine, but their fresh hypothesis, coupled with my research, provided me with an important development in our story—one that follows.

At the beginning of the 21st century, Farina (2000) turned the attention of ecological thinkers to connecting niche theory with habitat paradigms, with particular attention to landscape attributes. As the data poured in, Farina and colleagues concluded that a local landscape had an underlying field, linked together non-locally in overlapping exchanges. Within this underlying set of fields, messages were being passed back and forth not only between creatures within a species but also in interspecies communication.

And that was not all.

The plants seemed to be sending messages to the birds and mammals.

And that was not all.

The soil seemed to be speaking to the grasses.

And that was not all.

The rocks seemed to be speaking to the soil.

In Farina's own words, we researched "the spatial attributes of the perceived landscape...and created a new cognitive paradigm called *eco-fields*" (2007, p. 32). In other words the landscape seemed to have cognitive qualities. A particular locale was thinking. Not as humans think *per se*, but thinking nonetheless. Such a possibility was not new to the ancient world, but, in the domain of postmodern science, it was astounding. What had been intuitive and implicit to ancient wise people was now becoming explicit through this newer science. The fresh take on the matter offered me an expanded view of local reality.

Farina and his colleagues borrowed heavily from von Uexkull (1982) and his vision of the *subjective surrounding* or *Umwelt*. The importance of the proposal that an environment has a subjective and intersubjective dimension cannot be overstated. All landscapes contain both an interior and exterior, not just an inert material existence as 20th-century reductive models proclaimed.

The Startling Nature of This Hypothesis

To fathom the jolting nature of this hypothesis, look out the window to your backyard, or go to a near-by park. According to the Urbino's group scientific research, your backyard has an interior as well as an exterior dimension. What is out there is not just a collection of things. Nor is it just a self-balancing system. *It is actually thinking, far beyond self-organizing.* To consider how paradigm-shaking this hypothesis is, mull these questions:

> Does a common rock actually have some form of ability to send messages?
>
> Or, does the soil actually engage in a primordial conversation?
>
> Or, does the grass speak in a dialect lost to the modern mind?

Defining the Eco-field Hypothesis

Farina (2007) went on to define the eco-field

- "as the space configuration/meaning carrier,
- under the epistemological umbrella
- of the individually-based landscape." (p. 32)

Implications of the Hypothesis

The story really gets exciting at this point, considering that you have a group of world-class scientists in Italy observing landscapes and suggesting that a particular ecology, now more precisely an *eco-field*, transmits *meaning* as well as *information* between its various parts. And this transmission occurs through the medium of fields.

Although Farina does not explore the implications of his research, it is there, like a pink elephant in the room with peanuts on its breath. Not only does a rock have an interior awareness at some level, it also transmits some form of meaning that couples with the entire field for an interwoven message and corporate intelligence. According to the eco-field hypothesis, every function that a species uses needs a specific spatial configuration innately and intrinsically recognized by the cognitive dimensions of the species.

"A species settles where such a configuration exists" (Farina, 2007, p. 32).

Implications jump out at us.

There is an intelligence within a landscape that forms and informs a specie and tells it where to settle, and English and Mandarin Chinese are not the languages of the landscape. *The landscape actually speaks with intelligence available to the different parts, and evolution accelerates when the parts are able to speak that language fluently.* Generally speaking, humans are the only participants in the eco-fields who not only do not speak the local language *but also believe no language is being spoken except their own.* Human researchers are genuinely surprised when they discover that plants and animals converse with complicated reasoning, albeit forms of reasoning and speech not channeled through the neo-cortex of the brain.

Beyond Ecology and Quantum Fields: Reciprocity

In one fell swoop this hypothesis leaps beyond reductive forms of Darwinism and also expands our understanding of quantum fields. A particular locale does not run primarily with the engine of the survival of the fittest, though that is a small aspect of the intelligence or cognitive capacity.

A landscape operates with meaning transfers moving through the medium of the fields reflecting a local cognition. Yes, cognition.

Darwin noticed a dynamic of the field in the form of survival. Good enough. The problem arose when he focused mainly on that dimension. Quantum physicists observed a responsiveness in the sub-atomic particles, an interior within the particles, but did not notice the meaning transfers between particle and scientific observer. Quantum physicists are aware of their influence on the wave-particle continuum, but they have not yet become aware of the influence of their experiments with the wave-particle continuum on their own marriages, or shopping lists, or banking habits. More on this limited view of fields in a moment. First, though, consider how does this hypothesis work on an experimental level?

The Skylark Experiments

Farina's scientific team engaged in numerous experiments with landscapes and eco-fields, and one of their most exhaustive studies was that with skylarks and their relationship with eco-fields.

Here is how the experiment begins.

A skylark searches for seeds to eat, and the seeds can be found in any number of environmental contexts from woodlands to open prairies. Even so, skylarks choose only open prairies, and this choice fascinated the Farina team. They discovered what they called a searching mechanism within the skylarks by recording sounds over extended periods of time. I came to call this searching mechanism a tuning device or channel selector. By whatever name you label the tool, the skylarks used it to locate themselves in a collaborative space ideal not only to survive but also to thrive.

In the midst of the mounting data of the longitudinal study, Farina (2007) began calling the landscape itself a *meaning carrier*, an ecological system which has an interiority and the ability to make choices about the interactive parts (p. 35). The experiments now progressed to the point of revealing an exchange of not only information but also meaning in a complex of eco-fields. The skylark not only needed the prairie, the prairie needed the skylark to provide a co-operative space for the evolution of the area.

The intelligence of the prairie eco-field spoke in a language that included both co-operation and competition. Farina's (2007) research catapults our understanding beyond Laszlo's (2004) idea of information in the field to *meaning exchanges in the field*. The research also transcends but includes the interspecies communication paradigm in that the Mother Tongue includes all aspects of the eco-field—its biology, geology, and physics.

So-called inanimate objects like rocks and soil become animate subjects. Other scientists (Federle & Bassler, 2003) pushed the research to discover that rocks and soil in their interactive cycles work together with a species for the exchange of both information and meaning, and not randomly.

Let's follow that cycle for a moment.

The skylarks have a relationship of meaning exchanges with the insects they eat. The insects need a particular kind of grass, which in turn thrives on a distinctive soil. The soil emerges from the rocks in a given area. Every step of the way, information passes not only from parts to other parts but also seems to be guided by an underlying field which grasps what is good for the whole. This intelligent intersubjectivity is not—to master an understatement—present in earlier evolutionary theories.

The experiments expanded. The prairie needed the shade of the mountain (another eco-field), and the mountain forest needed another form of rocks. Farina (2007) concludes from these detailed observations that "a species requires several eco-fields that in general exist in the same geographical space" (p. 35). There seems to be a strategy of the quantum field to embrace both random data and precise rules in balance with all the interacting connections of a specific locale.

In short, the eco-field hypothesis "states that a species is the summation of the different eco-fields" (p. 35). The fit between species and landscape is key-to-tumbler in an exquisite precision (Franklin, 2002). The simple location of a skylark in the open prairie rather than in the woodlands follows a coherence much like the expansion of the Universe a moment after the Big Bang (Feynman, 1998).

Just as the Primordial Mind/Heart spoke using an elaborate lexicon and *told* sub-atomic particles to expand at a precise speed that allowed the material world to form, so the skylark knows (a new epistemology?) its precise place in the interlocking eco-fields through exchanges of meaning I am calling primordial expression.

Implications of the Eco-field Hypothesis: Buffalo

Later we will explore in more detail aspects of my research on the restoration and healing of Deer Dancer Ranch. For now I note our organic experiments with buffalo over a fifteen-year period. The

Earthtribe gifted Judith and me with a young buffalo just weaned from its mother. It was a lone buffalo, a female, on a ranch without others of its kind, so it bonded with our human community called the Earthtribe. Over a period of two years we discovered that it was not acting like a buffalo, so we purchased a buffalo companion, a male.

The change was remarkable; soon they produced a small herd. We concluded that a buffalo is not a buffalo without other buffalo and an environment for roaming and feeding. The field transmits meaning not primarily through individuals but through communities, herds, and flocks. The whole is not only greater than its parts but also transmits through a field to its parts, imparting identity.

A buffalo is the summation of interlocking eco-fields and needs crucial elements of the landscape (such as others of its kind and freedom to roam) in order to flower in its unique identity.

Implications of Eco-fields: Humans

If such is true for skylarks and buffalo, how about humans and our place in a set of interlaced eco-fields? Is there a meaning exchange between all elements of an eco-field, including humans? Especially communities of humans? Strangely, Farina and other eco-field scientists do not address this issue. So, at this point, I am expanding their hypothesis.

If humans are an aspect of the eco-field (as surely we are), then sensitivity to environmental variables is foremost in current consideration.

Is this lost sensitivity, the tuning ability, at the fulcrum of Earth's climate crisis as generated both by humans and other causes (Taegel, 2010)?

Return to an aim of the last three chapters: to address the inner scientist and skeptic. In Chapter Five, I cited a number of human experiences of receiving information from the exterior to the interior—including mathematical formulae, premonitions of natural and personal disasters, and 9/11 dreams. Generally, humans think of such occurrences as coming "out-of-the-blue mysticism." In eco-field research we encounter post-modern, scientific paradigms indicating that eco-fields have a corporate intelligence in and of themselves.

Events happen in reference to that intelligence, which knows how to evolve coherence out of chaos. Out of the chaos of what appears to be undirected, natural selection arises a collaborative pattern, fractal after fractal. Such a notion is very close to the shamanic view that a meadow in itself is an intelligent being filled with spirits seeking a reciprocal relationship with humans and all systems. An eco-field is the Primordial Mind/Heart speaking in Its local drawl but also in scientific precision. While the Eco-Field Hypothesis does not prove the Self-expression of the Primordial Mind/Heart, it does give us a brilliant and arresting post-modern story, one that may appeal and speak the language of our inner scientist and skeptic.

Turn now to some of my human/eco-field research in this area.

Eco-field Transfers of Meaning: Human Communities
August 2008

Judith Yost and I were faculty in Wisdom University's intensive, *Nature, Trauma, and the Soul*. During an afternoon learning experience, we took the group deep into the redwood forest to a small creek. As a group we created a ceremony whereby we selected stones that symbolized the burdens we carry around with us as a result of our various traumas.

Students and faculty selected rocks the size of their inner burdens and then placed the rocks at a small waterfall. After laying down the burden or stone, a ceremonialist poured pure water from the waterfall over the head of the student for cleansing. Meanwhile, the larger group chanted ancient songs on a ridge just above the stream. In this manner, we facilitated a profound linkage between humans, stones, stream, and redwoods through ancient sounds passed down through the generations.

These burdens we attended to were not only our individual burdens but also the burdens of larger Earth. We stated we were there to establish a relationship with the forest and with all beings, including the rocks we carried. We offered prayers and entered meditation through the week to support this endeavor. These ceremonies were experiments in opening channels in the local eco-fields as we sought mutual healing in the field.

Our method?

We aspired to become meaning carriers and receivers.

As I stood in the waters of the creek assisting individuals with laying down their burdens, a student pointed to a bird flying low over our heads to perch in a large redwood tree.

Later, we identified the bird as a spotted owl.

Then, to our amazement, another owl sailed in to settle near-by, followed by two more younger birds who still sported fluffy down. These owls stayed with us for sometime, maybe an hour, as we continued with the ceremony, only now the owls were the center of our attention. In a sense they took over as ceremonial leaders, and we became followers.

Exchanges of meaning flooded the eco-field far beyond our native tongues and previous thought-forms. Something profound was happening in a transrational vernacular, transcending anything any of us had experienced to that point. To our amazement the owl family of four followed us as we walked along the trail in our return to our lodging, and they did not leave us until we left the forest for a paved road.

The next day some of our students went into the forest individually to sit in circles to meditate on the trauma of Earth and her inhabitants, as well as to seek personal healing and awareness expansion. Again, the owls came to the students and remained with them the entire time. In discussions that followed, we searched the Internet for pictures to identify the spotted owls and learn about them.

We gave thanks.

We researched the connection between owls and wisdom in indigenous people.

We gave thanks.

I felt strongly that the owls had come to connect Wisdom University with its sacred core. In previous intensives some students had asked the question, "Where is the spiritual core of the university?" The owl visitation pointed us in the direction of that question and others, as well.

How could we be wise, the owls seemed to say, if we did not consult them?

How could we claim to be a wisdom learning circle without a totem?

How could we be a university focusing on spirituality without a profound connection to all manifested by Spirit?

In 1990 I had written about owls being a shamanic totem since my childhood (Taegel, 1990). In the early 1980s an owl had guided Judith and me in the establishing of the Earthtribe, our longtime spiritual community. The bird had been a trusted ally for decades. Now, at this crucial moment in the life of Wisdom University, the owls returned.

It might seem that I would see this event as entirely natural and without metaphysical implications, and in a sense I did. I readily acknowledge an inner skeptic and scientist who does not easily sail on the ship of mystical occurrences. In addressing the questions of the skeptics both inside and outside myself, I investigated a research project by Hunter, Gutierrez, & Franklin (1995) concerning the daytime roosting habits of the northern spotted owl. The investigation revealed a strict correlation between such varied aspects of the eco-field as non-vegetated entities such as rocks, biological aspects such as herbs and grasses, and large plants such as both mature and old-growth redwood trees.

They further researched daytime and nighttime flying habits of the owls, as well as their breeding sites. From this fiercely objective research, I discovered that the behavior the spotted owls exhibited that day was highly unusual. It was rare for spotted owls to fly in the daytime, rare for them to light near humans, and certainly rare for them to follow us as we walked. To return for a second day stretched the known habits of the owl to the breaking point.

Like the magnets and the iron filings of the earlier example of the gravitational field, we humans, the owls, the rocks, the stream, and the redwoods had experienced a profound, unseen linkage through the eco-field and its non-material influence. The two dozen humans involved in this experience knew a profound meaning transfer had occurred. This ongoing visitation of the owls constituted an innate and phenomenological happening even if we did not have ready translations of the messages.

Interpreting the Meaning Exchanges

The meaning of the owl visitation was not immediately apparent. However, we shall see as this book unfolds and as we continue to view Wisdom University as an experiment in our organic inquiry, that the owls would lead the University in a very new direction. We shall discover that the eco-field that day anticipated the role of the Wisdom U. community in the larger climate crisis. One thing we knew: the Era of Natural Consequences demanded something radically different from our little university, and the owls came to show us the way even though the language of the landscape was still foreign to us.

The experience was both mystical and scientific. Farina's analysis of the spotted owl data points to significant information exchanges between owls and the entire landscape, including humans. Or, as his team put it, several "codes are contemporarily active" (Farina, 2007, p. 38). Farina's use of the term *code* is important because it anticipates larger codes present in the standing waves of all human eras, but especially in the shamanic era. We knew we would have to descend the spiral of the human story to the ancient wise people in order to gain a speaking knowledge of the profound spiritual meaning of our encounter. Science assisted us, but its language was not sufficient.

Eco-field Acoustics

Before I leave the domain of Farina's eco-field hypothesis and my elaboration, I want to explore briefly a branch of those studies called *acoustical ecology*. Acoustical ecology is a recognized branch of the science of ecology that studies the interaction of all sounds, including human-produced sound, in a given eco-field.

Much has been written about air and water regarding a particular environment and its wildlife, but studies are just now emerging concerning the implications of sound in the eco-field. In fact, "song has been proved to increase the information landscape" (Schaub, Schwilch & Jenni, cited in Farina, 2007). The role of song in teaching second languages is well known in human educational circles. Is it true, then, that underneath any human language is another array of sounds, a music of the spheres? With over three hundred different languages, Native Americans developed basic phrases that were basically two syllable sounds that were cross-tribal. The greeting, *Ah Ho*, would be an example.

This research tracks the ability of migrating Eurasian reed-warblers to attract other warblers to a given ecology, and not only the warblers to each other but also the underlying intelligence of the eco-field itself. Using tape-luring at stop-over ringing stations, these scientists found "a significant increase in captures during the tape-luring night" (Schaub, et. al., In Farina, pp. 40-41). The studies by Schaub, et. al. (Farina, 2007), also note the influence of human-produced sound pollution, especially in urban areas, as a source of health problems in both humans and wildlife.

Could the opposite also be true?

If humans use sounds learned from the shamanic era, could these sounds have a beneficial effect on the eco-field, including the spotted owls? Is there something happening here beyond the survival of the fittest? The survival of the most co-operative? The most resonant? The most fluent in primordial sounds? We sang ancient songs that day in the redwood forest in tribal tongues, as well as vision songs given to our spiritual community, mainly through vision quests.

We blew the venerable conch.

We beat a Siberian drum softly at the rate of our heartbeats.

Was there a resonance between humans and owls?

Had we, almost inadvertently, tapped into the Mother Tongue?

The students and the faculty continue to benefit from the guidance of the owls and the setting of that redwood eco-field as the story unfolds. It is also probable, given the eco-field hypothesis, that the owls benefited from our human sounds. Were we in a small way telling them and their species that not all humans seek to destroy their habitat? Were we making amends for our species' profligate and arrogant behavior?

This acoustical healing facilitated a mutual transformation, I propose, in the eco-field. In the words of systems scientist Gregory Bateson (1974), we as a community became a "self-healing tautology" (p. 230). If such a proposal has validity, then it opens an entirely new dimension in environmental recovery. Are we transcending but including environmental activism? Does this small experiment point the way for a deep resonance between humans and more-than-humans in an eco-field? One that heals all?

If so, and I believe so, then we humans are poised through the eco-field hypothesis and its implications to return to the circle of life. Such a return opens vast possibilities through speaking with the verbs of the forest. Before I leave this chapter, I want to acknowledge the inner skeptic, as well as the limits of an epistemological map at any given moment. We spoke glowingly of the spotted owl visitation and download to faculty and staff of Wisdom University. It would take us two years to shift our consciousness enough as a community in order to follow the directives of the owls to give up our unquestioning allegiance to Western epistemology, emphasis on *unquestioning*. A spirited debate has spread throughout the University as to the relationship between industrial and eco-field epistemology. The University advances no orthodoxy of knowing, but we do put the new epistemology described here in dynamic tension with Western Civilization's approach to reality.

Before I address that crucial point, I move to plumb in more depth the role of eco-fields within standing waves.

CHAPTER EIGHT

Eco-fields Within Standing Waves

We stand at the head of the white water river, scratching our heads as we look at the map of the way down the river. Danger lurks. We need more knowledge of the map before we start the descent. We have seen that the field guides to the standing waves—Graves/Beck, Gilligan, Houston, Kegan, and Fowler—all saw only one element in the river waves.

Then, we entertained the Eco-field Hypothesis (EFH1) as presented by Farina and expanded in the previous chapter by my research (EFH2). Our two research approaches are noteworthy because of the eco-field's ability to scan the wave with wide angle goggles and see many different forms of information and meaning in the waves of environmental development. Thus, donning the lenses of the Eco-field Hypotheses (EFH1&2) allows us to see that cultural memetic codes exist within the standing waves and provide a virus-like source of information while, at the same time, noting that these memes are a small aspect of the wave.

In order to grasp the larger map of EFH 1 & 2 fully, we need to spend a few moments discussing Beck's use of the term *meme*. The aim of our discussion is to underline why we need a larger map than he presents (Beck, 2002; 2006). He limits himself to human values, and that limitation is precisely what will overturn our canoe on the river journey.

Memetic Codes in the Standing Waves

Clare W. Graves did not speak of *memes* in his original research referred to in Chapter Two (Graves, 1971). Richard Dawkins is generally credited with introducing the term *meme* to popular usage in his 1976 book, *The Selfish Gene*. Richard Brodie expanded the usage of memetics in his 1995 book, *Virus of the Mind*.

Dawkins used *meme* as an embryonic concept for discussing evolutionary dynamics in explaining the spread of ideas and other cultural phenomena. He did not know about eco-fields, but he sensed powerful exchanges occurring in culture beyond traditional biological models. The etymology of the term relates to the Greek word, *mimestos*, for something imitated. Dawkins uses examples throughout his work such as melodies, catch phrases, hoola-hoops, religious beliefs, and clothing fashion, all examples of strange and viral-like human imitations (Dawkins, 1976).

According to Dawkins, *memes* self-replicate and respond to selective pressures from culture. In his model we can expect the contagion of the wave to enter us like a virus, and we then pass it on to others, all happening outside our awareness. Dawkins reaches for something important in his scanning of the wave, but does not quite get there.

Spiral Dynamics and vMEMES

With the publication of *Spiral Dynamics*, Beck and Cowan (1996) greatly expand the meme map of the river. Beck in particular draws on both Dawkins and Brodie but adds a distinctive flavor. Imagine a *meme* as a virus within a standing wave or level of development that replicates behaviors, concepts, ideas, and values. Then, as you pass through the wave, the virus enters your system.

But there is something far more important than melodies and hoola-hoops being imparted. In each wave, argues Beck (2002), there is a template source of informational downloads he calls a vMEME. The small *v* stands for human values; thus, the vMEMES are our basic values in a given wave. As these values touch our skins and innards, they spread through us like a raging virus, leaving traces of information as they pass through (2006). Our values, then, are not usually chosen with awareness but rather contagiously imparted, like a disease.

For example, consider the wide-spread use of both biblical literature and pornography in our culture and how the mixture of vMEMES is promoted by even conservative Christians. A confusing contagion occurs when you enter a Marriott Hotel room in the form of a picture of a prominent Mormon on the wall and the *Book of Mormon* and the *Bible* in a drawer along with the adult movie channel guide. Various viral downloads seek entry into your system as you unpack your bags. The biblical virus seeks to infect you as does the pornography.

Eco-fields Contain Memetic Codes

Researchers encounter a massive rock in the river—the jagged limits of the biological model. Biology is the science of life and does not address the Universe before life emerged on Earth (not to mention other possible life forms elsewhere) about four billion years ago. That leaves about ten billion years of the Universe outside the lens of biology.

As such, biology does not speak the language of rocks and soil, glaciers and lava, earthquakes and weather systems, all large contributors to pre-biological syntax. Memetic studies, biologically and psychologically based as they are, simply miss much of the important information available in the waves in which we will be splashing as we journey down the river. Human cultural values are important, but they are a tiny sediment in the waves. *We humans simply are not as important as we pretend.*

At this moment in the Era of Natural Consequences, maps that pertain exclusively, or even mainly, to humans will not suffice. The rocks of the wild river will tear our boats apart. Look at the tsunamis and tornadoes. These weather forms are living, energetic beings, but beyond the lens of human, memetic codes.

On the other hand, Farina's (2007) Eco-field Hypothesis (EFH1), with our elaboration (EFH2), broadens the conversations from behaviors, thoughts, and values of humans to interspecies communication and then to aspects in the landscape previously thought to be inanimate. EFH2 goes even farther and broadens the lens of our goggles to include meaning carriers between all aspects of Earth's terrain.

Here is the crucial addition to the hypothesis: this larger view of the eco-field includes reciprocity between humans and all other aspects within the waves.

We need an EFH2 type map for our trip since we, as post-modern humans, are quite vulnerable, possibly facing extinction as a species. Ancient peoples had intuitive access to the full possibilities in each of the waves, but we do not. We are post-moderns bereft of the skills necessary to tune into the eco-field waves. As a group we do not know how to use the broad bands needed to download what is crucial to survive and thrive. As you notice in your reading thus far, I introduce terms like *tune in* without telling you what I mean or how that might happen. In the next chapter, I want to sort through what I mean by this phrase in order to keep my agreement with you to be as clear as possible.

III

The Descent:
Journey Down the River

CHAPTER NINE

The Inner Council of Selves as Tuning Devices

Our story moves to the actual transmission of bytes of information and hopefully of wisdom within the standing waves of the white water river.

Shift metaphors for a moment. Suppose that you visit Earth from another planet or Star system and find yourself in a typical North American home. You notice a contraption called a television set. Your field guide to planet Earth tells you that visual movies and various programs come through the set. The guide explains that these waves float around in something called a field all the time and that, given certain actions on your part, will come into the television set for you to view. If your visitor asks for more specifics, you might tell him that your TV set has electronic circuits that decode broadcast signals sent from a transmitting source.

Fine, the extraterrestrial might say, but how do I turn the set on? And how do I get to certain channels? How do I learn how to decode the signals?

We have an analogous situation as we behold the standing waves of the river roaring before us. As we enter the waves, how will the information enter us? Does our choice enter as an active participant? In short, how do we tune in to eco-fields? An important dimension of EFH2 is the tuning device of the council of selves, a notion so important that I shortly will make a significant proposal regarding the council. First, though, I speak briefly to how the inner council of selves works.

The Inner Council of Selves

Like the early colonies of 1776, our inner world holds many sub-divisions. In earlier works I label these sub-flows of patterns within the personality as sub-selves or simply selves (Taegel, 1990, 2000, 2010). Our interior world contains many forms of energy described by the term selves. A few of the common selves are: the critic, the pleaser, the perfectionist, the victim, the persecutor, the pusher, and the rescuer (Stone & Stone, 1989). These are the selves created by our dominant culture, and, as you can see, the council is missing some crucial players if we are to survive and thrive, namely the wild heart self, fluent in primal discourse. We will get to that sub-self in a moment.

The organizing force within the inner council of the person is called the operating ego because that dimension of the personality is in charge of driving the person down life's road (Stone & Stone, 1989). Also prominent within the inner council are the vulnerable selves, which usually originate in childhood and are prime attractors within the standing waves, as we shall soon see.

Hidden from awareness in the depths of the unconscious are the shadow selves (Jung, 1969; Stone, 1985). The shadow selves are aspects of our inner life pushed into the dark recesses of our interior by our usual operating egos. We disown these selves because they are not acceptable to the values we hold or the patterns of our lives. The disowned or hidden selves are also powerful attractors of energy forms within the standing waves. In our dominant culture, the wild heart self, so crucial for our journey, is a shadow self for a vast majority of us.

Finally, within the ego is an aware space created in an ongoing way through our awareness practices such as psychotherapy and meditation. When this aware space opens up, it can attach to the ego to make an aware-ego, a channel selector that has access to numerous bytes of information in the waves as we pass through.

EFH2 and the Council of Selves as Tuning Device

I am extending Farina's EFH1 to include the reciprocal dimension of the eco-field between humans and more-than-humans (EFH2), something landscape scientists and quantum scientists have been slow to do. Over a thirty-five year period of research, I have considered the body, the brain, the soul, or the mind as the tuning devices into these waves.

Sometimes, I have thought of a physical form such as a conch shell, a sacred pipe, a shaman's drum, a phurba or the red stick (*baton rouge*) of the Muskogee/Creek as useful tuning devices that increase the broadband signals for greater bandwidth as related to the underlying fields. I have experimented with biofeedback equipment, entheogens, and other drugs. I have considered ceremonies such as vision quests and sweat lodges, buildings such as cathedrals, and sacred places such as Machu Pichu, Stone Henge, Teotihuacán, Göbekli Tepe, and Enchanted Rock. Then, there are dreams, therapies, yoga, meditation, imagination, extra-sensory perception, to name a few means of expanding consciousness.

My research reaches two conclusions evidenced in this proposal #1.

First, there is no escape from the many selves of the ego. Most of the world wisdom traditions state directly or imply that it is possible to escape the ego on a more-or-less permanent basis. You might agree with these traditions.

You would be wrong.

At least in the light of EFH2 based on the research of the Earthtribe and our therapeutic community that is the case. I personally have never talked to anyone whose enlightenment means they escape the confines of the ego's many selves. According to Huston Smith, both he and the Dalai Lama have angry selves popping up occasionally (personal conversation, 2000). Mother Teresa wrote of her many doubting selves in her diary. Gandhi discovered a repressed sexual self at age seventy-six. Ramana

Maharshi—thought by many to be the most enlightened person of the 20th-century—was so upset by arguments in his kitchen by the cooks that he refused to go in the kitchen for the remainder of his life. And my own personal experience with Martin Luther King, Jr. revealed both his saintly and not so saintly selves.

Meditate all you want. Choose whatever path of enlightenment that floats your boat. You can meditate, vision quest, ingest LSD or peyote, do yoga, and participate in tantric sex in order to tune into the sacred and profound. You still have to face your many selves everyday. If you do not, they will pop out in the most unexpected places, even as Gandhi's sexual self surprised him shortly before he died.

(As an aside, you might be thinking I am justifying my own limited enlightenment. You would be right.)

Second, this council of selves is, along with your body, a most important tuning device into the eco-fields, indeed, the outside world. Perception is everything. The inner council broadcasts to the field and invites the bytes of information into the inner world and then sends forth its interpretation or signals of reality. Usually this interpretation is seen as "truth."

EFH2 Proposal #1

Now, for a concise statement conveying the first of three aspects of the Mother Tongue Hypothesis in its EFH2 form.

The information and potential meaning from the eight (or so) standing waves of the 200,000 year human evolutionary story enters the individual through the council of selves. These selves are tuning devices picking up the codes inherent in the standing waves, both from human and more-than-humans.

Most important: the Primordial Mind/Heart enters primarily through the natural or wild heart self as that self is catalyzed by an Earth-based community and its local landscape, or eco-field. The primal enters the inner world only through the selves oriented to the base language of both humans and more-than-humans.

How the Council of Selves Tunes into the Fields

Let's say you visit your family of origin. It is Christmas. You step into the house. The smells. The sounds. The family phrases. All enter your system and pass through your inner council. One of your parents says something ever so slightly critical of your appearance. The utterance floats in the field like an old horror movie just waiting to come in through your movie channel. Your inner critic can either act as a channel selector and bring it into your consciousness as a central actor of the moment, or you can listen briefly to that old tape and choose not to allow it to dominate.

Or, you go to Peru and partake of an ayuhuasca ceremony, a potent natural drug and tuning device. In the altered state experience, you see dimensions of reality you did not know existed. You are enlightened. Then, you return home after your trip to a difficult family situation. Your new enlightenment will have to pass through your inner council. How that council tunes in and integrates determines the direction of your expanded experience. While you can have an initial tuning into the field through any number of methods, the tuning ultimately has to be channeled through the inner council.

This proposal assists us in understanding ancient shamans. In my late 30's, I worked for a decade in training with a traditional shamanic circle (the *Ahe-chay-cha*) led by Bear Heart Williams, a Muskogee/Creek medicine person. At the time I was a member of a professional group, the American Academy of Psychotherapists, and I introduced many of its members to Bear Heart. One psychologist came to us with the sudden onset of crippling arthritis.

Being a professional and post-modern human, the client had sought the best psychological and medical help available, but to no avail. Bear Heart immediately diagnosed him as possessed by an evil spirit. Although I was an apprentice in the *Ahe-chay-cha* medicine circle of shamanic healing, my inner scientist was skeptical, especially about Bear Heart's diagnosis. At that time, *evil spirit* as a description of the human condition was not in my vocabulary.

My mentor patiently explained to me that a foreign force had entered our client sent by evil medicine persons, an explanation shocking to my scientific sensibilities. As was often the case during the decade of my training, I was pushed to enter a state of willing suspension of disbelief in order to learn from the circle. The training challenged me to confront squarely the notion that my graduate degrees made me superior to my elders.

How wrong I was!

We employed a form of shamanic soul retrieval unique to Bear Heart to bring back the man's essence which had been lost in the spell cast on him. Within an hour or so the presenting client was better. Within days he was totally "cured." We both were shocked—the client and I—but Bear Heart, steeped as he was in shamanic practices, considered the cure a matter of course.

Using EFH2 proposal #1, I now see that there was a foreign force that invaded our client. The debilitating information came from the eco-field as an influential quantum packet, most likely through the tuning of his inner critic. The force field filled him with debilitating information that contracted his system into convulsions of pain and suffering. The internal critic was both the tuning device drawing in the dark energy force and also a gateway for that field to impart a viral load that told his system to be inflamed on a cellular scale.

Moreover, I cannot rule out Bear Heart's perception of an even more profound force that he called an *evil spirit*, a description beyond my comprehension at the time.

EFH2 Downloads and Historical Persons

Buddha

Stories that surround Buddha's enlightenment address the issue of external powers seeking entry into his life through his personality. For example, he sat under a Peepul tree for forty-nine days. The stars reached out to him, as did an earthquake. (Information transfers from the stars seem to crop up time and again.) Nature all around appeared to move through him, assisting in his enlightenment process (Smith, 1991). Some Buddhist storytellers also speak of evil spirits floating around him (Kyokai, 1966). In a number of accounts, there are five maras or tempters seeking entry into his depths. Buddha's refusal to allow a plug-in from the tempting spirits is essential to his enlightenment (Smith, 1991).

How does Buddha's condition translate into EFH1? He sits connected to the field through a tree. He experiences meaning transfers within the landscape. Information laden energy forms enter his inner council through his nature-based self, one I call the wild heart. Buddha's path is similar to the wilderness quest common to all primordial cultures.

But what of the five evil spirits? Stories that speak of miracles and evil spirits are often embarrassing to modern Buddhists. Many Buddhists dismiss these accounts as folk tales, as does Ken Wilber (2003). In this sometimes casual dismissal, much richness is lost. In EFH2, energy forms from the eco-field seek entry through Buddha's various sub-selves. In addition the ancient stories seek to convey an obscure reality, and I do not reduce Buddha's remarkable events solely to EFH2.

The underlying field speaks in many ways; indeed, the intertwined eco-fields may well harbor within the matrix of complexity energy forms well-described mythically as *demons*. Bear Heart taught me to proceed respectfully and not to be too quick with my scientific musings. Also, when I am ensconced in the cleverness of my own explanations, I tend to have bad dreams.

Jesus

Jesus journeyed through a similar process detailed in the oldest story we have about him (Mark:1). Mark's account is brief. Jesus fasted for forty days and nights in the desert in a vision quest typical of tribal peoples. Such a quest leads me to refer to Jesus as a shaman (Taegel, 1990, 2000). During this time, dark forces appeared and tempted him, much as happened with Buddha. Jesus refused each temptation; the devils departed; angels came and brought nourishment. It is almost as if Jesus and Buddha used the same inner council channel selector.

Larger Discussion

What we have in both of these stories is an ancient shamanic wisdom. An exterior form emerges in the eco-field as a broadcast signal, seeks entry (through the inner council), and the venerable quester either accepts or refuses. Powerful forces are stirred as the two wise persons leave their dominant cultures and experience a birthing of their wild hearts within the wilderness. Then, epochal forces from the eco-fields seek entry through that wild heart sub-self.

In one of the major tragedies of industrial civilization, both Buddhism and Christianity have largely ignored the wild birthing of this essential wisdom in their founders. As quickly as possible, the organizations that emerged from these visions covered over the lexicon of the wildness with distant and increasingly abstract language that pushed away the sensuousness of the experience. In their codified books these institutions wandered far away from the fire of the direct access of their wilderness founders.

Speaking of drifting too far and distancing from the texture of the essential, I verge on that mistake in communicating with you. Shift gears for a moment. We pause from the psychological rigor of this chapter and move to direct access of eco-fields through the senses.

CHAPTER TEN

An Eco-field Love Affair

It began as a summer romance.

We met casually at a Joan Baez concert on a warm August evening with a soft breeze, sweet smelling honeysuckle, and busy hummingbirds as our companions. Although I was with my spouse, Judith, a seductive feminine beauty caught my eye from behind the stage. The haunting songs of an aging Baez quickened my heartbeat. This was not our first meeting, of course; we had known each other casually for quite some time, a few summers as I now recall. Yet, this night with its music and delicious, picnic aromas excited a new romance.

And her name?

Umpqua.

She not only was named after a river. She was the river. She flowed behind the half-shell stage in this outdoor concert setting in South Central Oregon. Dressed in alternating garbs of lacy white water and cerulean blue pools, she dominated the scene. Or, maybe that dominance was not true for locals, who were fascinated with Joan and inoculated to Umpqua's beauty. But I could not take my eyes off the comeliness of the river in the fading light of dusk.

Actually, I did not feel unfaithful to Judith as I contemplated an affair with flowing water. The romance with Umpqua would catapult us to new domains of intimacy. Strangely, I wondered if my attraction to Umpqua constituted a betrayal of my love of the Blanco River back in the Texas Hill Country, but the feeling passed. My summer love of this new river was not an intimacy of monogamy.

One afternoon during a golf game, Umpqua caught my eye from the perch of a tee box, so much so that my playing partners had to call me back into the game. During that moment between golf swings, the eye of the river locked in, and my consciousness shifted. The seeds of love planted in the Baez concert sprouted in this unlikely and tame setting.

On the last hole a blue bird flew up in front of the face of my playing partner. The fluttering lasted long enough to interrupt the play once again. The encounter opened us up, so that our talk about the event took precedence over keeping an eye on the ball. The blue bird's appearance rubber-banded me back to an early vision quest where its wings gave me medicine, and, in this state of mind, I sensed something was about to happen.

Little did I know.

Our foursome walked slowly toward the river. Off to my left I glimpsed a movement in a blackberry bramble. A few steps later, the movement increased, revealing a brief YouTube moment; a creature something like a black lab dog bounded toward us through the underbrush. Then, a flash of white signaled from the tip of the tail of the mammal immersed in the bramble. I walked closer and tugged at my partner for his attention as we held our breath in silence. An animal I had never seen before trotted out of the vegetative entwinement. A coyote? A dog? A small bear?

Once it moved, I saw clearly that it appeared kin to a fox, yet was black as a desert night, not the red or gray I associated with a fox. I could not place it in the framework of my experience. Perhaps, I mused, the animal was, like me, a mongrel. It had an extended slim body with long legs, a protruding snout, and a thick, elongated, fluffy tail. The white tip on the tail threw me. As I relaxed and looked closer white, maybe gray, flecks stood out from the face and rump, as well as down the underside of the tail.

But the tip of the tail? Snow white.

What could this animal be? Its eyes held me for a long while, imparting a series of messages that slipped under the radar of my usual logic. That evening I told my tale to Judith, and we Googled the term, *black fox*.[1] Jumping out of the computer came vivid images of the black fox, just as I had seen it hours before, white tip on its tail and all. Sightings, the article explained, are extremely rare. In some parts of the world the black fox hovers near extinction because of the human sport of fox hunting.

Still vibrating with the sensuousness of the visitation, I drifted off to sleep. I dreamed and saw three kits, baby black foxes, just outside the gate of Judith's and my house. Excited, I rushed to tell Judith to come outside and enjoy the sight.

Thinking she would be in her office, I threw open the door to encounter two adult foxes. Immediately, I recognized the vixen and reynard, as they are called, and they sat regally in the middle of the room. Their black coats and white tipped tails touched me just as they had in my waking moments, and I spoke,

"What are you two doing here? How did you get in Judith's office?"

Their reply came in a telepathic message,

"We can enter where we wish, when we wish."

(Did they mean, enter my house or enter my dream?)

"What is the meaning of your visit?" I asked them.

They sat quietly, a cellular wisdom radiating in their presence. To my astonishment even in the dream a language beneath language spoke clearly.

Two commands:

One: "Go swimming in the Umpqua River and immerse yourself in the arms of her waters, allowing her molecules to move through you. Relax into the field of her dreams."

I could do that.

Two: "Meet me in the ancient desert."

---

[1] www.quidoo.com/TheBlackFox

Ancient desert? I had not a clue as to what that instruction meant. In time I would know, and that knowing would lead me to question the very foundations of industrial civilization.

Translating The Underlying Message

Weeks followed with my easing into a daily swim in the Umpqua and periodic hikes in the rain forest along Umpqua's banks. While these activities constituted a delightful way to celebrate my 70th birthday, specific understanding of the two instructions from the fox as a representative of the local eco-field, escaped me.

Escaped me until one early September day my colleague, Jim Garrison, called to invite Judith and me to travel to Southeast Turkey, the heart of Kurdistan, to explore the archeological site, Göbekli Tepe. This exploratory trip, he explained, would be added on to a pilgrimage we were co-leading with Raymond Moody to the dream incubation sites of ancient Greece.

Judith and I looked at each other with a mixture of feelings. If we agreed to such an extension of the pilgrimage to Greece, we would have to cancel a hiking trip to a remote Cyclades island and a romantic getaway for which we had already paid. We agreed to dream into the possibilities that night. I woke up the next morning after more fox dreams with the firm conviction that we must travel to both Greece and Göbekli Tepe, and Judith agreed. Our celebratory getaway would have to wait. Images of the black fox returned time and again, as if to create in me a longing for something larger, unnameable.

Bear Heart's Translating Tool

Then, a few days before my actual 70th birthday, my mentor, Bear Heart, now living in the ancestral world, reminded me in a vision of the most important tool a person can have in translating primal utterances.

"Remember," he coached me, "The first tool I taught you when you were a young whipper snapper?"

I did not.

He chided me that I wrote about this foundational tool in an earlier book (1990), laughing about the whole notion of books.

Even with that hint I could not recall until finally it emerged from the mists. All translations are contingent on a silence impregnated with *waiting*. Bear Heart had taught me that the essence of vision questing was developing the inner muscles of *waiting*, something that was much bigger than but included patience, not my strongest point. Waiting on the meaning of the fox visitation would continue until a hot afternoon in Turkish Kurdistan, and that part of the narrative itself will have to wait until more of the story unfolds.

"All things in good time," Bear Heart taught me.

CHAPTER ELEVEN

The Descent into the Scripture of Nature

At long last we are prepared to embark on the journey down the white water river of the human story, eco-field maps in hand and our inner scientist and skeptic on board. My hope for us is to become aware of instagrams from eight major standing waves in the river, the eco-fields. Likely, the information-laden standing waves will bounce our canoe around on our perilous journey, and this point deserves emphasis.

As we journey through the standing waves, they offer powerful, information filled forces that surround and enter through our inner council; often these energy forms dominate us before we know it. Once we reach the Purple and Beige waves on the downward journey, we will open the possibility of soul retrieval and conscious tuning into the eco-fields—the moorings of Earth Wisdom.

As we put our canoe in the water, I want to warn you that our usual use of English loses its ability to describe what we experience. So delve into field notes of the Spirit of the Depths for a moment, so we can better read the map.

Field Notes on the Descent: The Darker, The Better

Ah, yes. The lure of the descent!

In our current global civilization we are so enamored with ascending, progression, heaven, evolution, transcendence, and enlightenment that we have largely forgotten the mysteries and resources of the dark depths. Yet, our rampant cultural longing tells us something is missing, something we can no longer afford to cover over with compulsive substitutes.

Time and again Carl Jung traveled with his companion, the Spirit of the Depths, especially in his recently published notes in *The Red Book* (2009). His discoveries in the dark abyss were so jolting that his heirs refused to publish his field notes for forty-eight years. We cannot afford such delay in the Era of Natural Consequences. Unlike Jung, we need to be open about our fellow sojourner, the Spirit of the Depths, even if that openness offends. Such is our hinge of history.

In an extended conversation with David Abram (2011), the two of us found ourselves laughing and telling students in a video presentation: "We have to balance out enlightenment with *endarkment*. It is time to descend into the dark. That direction is not to be avoided. It is not what you think, or imagine."

"Everything is inside us, deep in our own roots, just waiting to be touched," writes Peter Kingsley (1999, p. 8). Notice the phrase *deep in our own roots*. Kingsley encourages us to make the journey to *The Dark Places of Wisdom* (1999), where we will find our own tendrils in the soil of the dark night, for in that soil we behold stars.

Descent Into the Stars

While it appears that I mixed metaphors in the previous sentence, I did not. All soil on our planet comes from the stars. In addition astronomers point out the reality that our planet hurls through space, spinning on its axis all the while. When we look into the night sky, we may be looking down or up. It is scientifically accurate to say we descend, as well as ascend, to the stars. As we are introduced to the language at the base of the known Universe, our left-brain English loses traction. What we thought was up, might be down, and vice-versa.

The stars themselves, which are in one sense light years away, also are the fibre of our bodies and the soil underneath our feet. In a strange twist of the newer sciences, our bodies turn out to be made of star dust. What we look at through the Hubble Space Telescope 50 billion light years away, we can also see in the freckles on the back of our hands. The wrinkles on our faces may be the best clue to the space/time continuum of the night sky. Star creatures in the ancient pyramids are not so strange to science after all.

We also can descend into the depths of the oceans, guided by the Spirit of the Depths. There in the darkest recesses of the waters we are actually looking at the stars since all water on this planet came to Earth through asteroids.

And in the darkest waters or nights we can best see the stars. We need to travel down to see up.

The ambient light of our industrialized cities actually keeps us from the darkness needed to see that we are the stuff of stars. No wonder we have trouble in noting our place in the eco-field—too much light, not enough dark. In order to have more light we need more dark. The shaman who creatively opened the doors to Western Civilization, Parmenides, never once traveled out of the darkness into the light. "When you follow what he (Parmenides) says (about light), you see he was going in exactly the opposite direction" (Kingsley, pp. 50, 51).

I am aware that I write these words to loosen me up and to open us to the rich possibility of the alphabet of the primal. Down we go.

Descending the Spiral: Down the Umpqua as a Metaphor
Late July, 2011

At the headwaters of the North Umpqua, the river rises from the snowmelt of the beautiful Cascade Mountains. Just a few mountains over from the headwaters, people still ski, enjoying snow fields that rarely retreat completely with the July heat. Flowing through steep canyons and surrounded by old growth forests, the river reaches out to me time and again. I am proud to be a lover of Umpqua, renowned for her sometimes jade green, sometimes topaz blue waters. She is still wild. She flows over 80 miles before meeting a dam to slow her down in Roseburg, Oregon. Locals tell me the

North Umpqua is the premier fly fishing river of the Northwest for anadromous fish.

Look around at our point of departure: the green eco-field wave, where Cultural Creatives and readers of this book are likely to dwell.

Green Eco-field

As I drive down Highway 138, I behold with disbelief a clearcut on distant mountains. The terrible sight of ignorant misuse of the forest sends waves of energy through me, emails from the green eco-field. Horror at human misuse of the forest jumps into my thinking in the form of judgments.

I see the abuse of the forest in a favorite game of mine, golf. These days I do not play much golf, even though I treasure the game. As I receive a green infusion, I judge golf courses as an environmental degradation, frequented by myopic capitalists dressed in funny clothes. Maybe, I will take up fly fishing. At this moment, I drive in our hybrid auto down Highway 138, seething about the clearcuts.

Green *vMEME* sound bites overwhelm my consciousness. And, alas, evoke my judgements. Only in retrospect am I aware of these green influences. During the drive these powers completely envelop me; indeed, become me for the moment.

In that envelopment of green, I am proud of my *getting* 50 miles per gallon with my new Prius. Really, more than proud, self-righteously proud of my vehicle and my hiking instead of golfing. Yesterday, I read that the Oregon State Police arrested three logging protesters perched high in two trees at a timber sale site in the Elliott State Forest northeast of Coos Bay. They are my green eco-field brothers and sisters. They go to jail for their green beliefs. If I had more courage, I would join them.

I cheer them on. At least when I tune into the green vMEME on NPR and its protest of logging. If you are reading this book, you most likely have a heavy dose of the green eco-field. Perhaps, you join me in making this wave a sometimes center of gravity. When we are in the green eco-field, we rest wonderfully in the sheath of interconnectivity. That is the good news. The bad news is that this green eco-field tends to be self-righteous and subtly judgmental, as you can see from my comments here.

A large old growth Douglas fir spreads out over Highway 138, pulling me out of the unhealthy side of green into a softer place. From that more heartfelt space, I see the irony of my being in an air-conditioned hybrid auto, living in a house made of wood from the forest while, at the same time, cutting myself off from those who clearcut.

Let's journey farther down the river as we experience the alluring guidance of the Spirit of the Depths.

Orange Eco-field

As I proceed down the mountain, I glimpse a prodigious house hanging over a cliff with a spectacular view of the North Umpqua. A day dream bursts into my mind and creates a desire for such a house. Something foreign has invaded me that prompts me to want to possess. Not just admire, possess! Like the clear-cutters of the lumber companies, I am ready to cut down trees to improve my view for my fantasy dream house.

What is this invasion of hankering and possessing?

The imaginary house I would build floods my mind and, strangely, my attention flits toward Costco and Home Depot, temples of the orange eco-field. An urge to go there and check out building supplies for my erstwhile house arises, and, maybe I will buy a flat screen television while I am there.

Curious and powerful urges.

Once in the orange eco-field, more scientific messages of orange human values also seek me out as I wonder about the rate of flow of the river at my favorite waterfall (12,000 CF/S), the elevation (8000′ at the point of departure), the geologic time of the eruption that formed near-by Crater Lake (7,700 years ago), the current temperature (62°F), and a ten-day weather forecast (too many variables). Linear thinking dominates. Bathed in orange, I am dominated by the vernacular of the consumer and the engineer.

Then, I am jolted from my orange daydream, jerked out of unaware orange thinking by the sight of an osprey sitting on its nest atop a pole put there by the Forest Service.

Awake, I am now aware of the orange advertising seeping in and then sweeping through me. In my inner council exists a consumer, birthed and developed by the dominant orange culture. The inner consumer attracts a wave with information that imparts in me a desire for a new house. My inner scientist and skeptic, never too far away, raise questions and take measurements. That's what they do when excited by program transfers. It all started as I tuned into the opulent house hanging over the cliff. This input comes through the waves of the eco-field just as surely as if I had tuned into The Shopping Channel or Discovery Channel on my television set, mostly without my being aware.

But the osprey on its nest wakes me up.

Blue Eco-field

My expanding awareness allows me to disengage from the orange instagrams for a few precious moments. Thanks to the osprey, I float free, liberated. I breathe without inhibition. I continue driving down the river.

Then, I stop for a better view at a scenic turnout. A sign jumps into my awareness space as I exit the car. Tacked on a tree posted near a rundown, double-wide home, a sign trumpets the Tea Party. I cannot help myself.

I look closer.

Like looking at a car wreck. A distasteful curiosity.

I move closer. The sign posts the Fifth Amendment of the U.S. Constitution, with interpolated thoughts on trespassing and conspiracies. The Blue Eco-field—steeped as it sometimes is in rules, laws, anger, and fear—broadcasts its wavelengths into my inner council.

Before I know it, an argument between the green and blue standing waves erupts in my inner landscape. In my mind's eye I shout at Rich Raynor, a local Tea Party leader, who just two days before this journey, led his group to crash a gathering of liberal Douglas County folks. Raynor said his Tea Party believed the gathering of Democrats was "a communist front and said he would not stand for America becoming a fascist nation." His Oregon Tea Party even followed the gray-haired, Democratic enemies to their homes to monitor their communist beliefs.

I shout back at Rich Raynor.

"What a dumb ox!" I rail at him, "You don't even know the difference between a communist and fascist. You denigrate the very liberties you espouse!"

Looking from the signs back to the river, I calm down and realize I tuned into the competing green and blue eco-fields, both filled with self-righteousness. This tiny conflict of the eco-fields in my council reflects the gridlock of the U.S. Congress. How easily I tune into different wavelengths that slip into my consciousness without my awareness noticing. Without awareness, the eco-fields tangle and bump into each other with very rough edges.

Really, *tuning in* does not adequately describe my experience. It's more like, they wash over me, engulf me as my canoe capsizes in the blue wave.

Red Eco-field

The green, orange, and blue transmissions of attitudinal scripts obscure my original purpose of hiking, and, typically, my thinking is not getting any better. This year I propose to visit all the major waterfalls of this watershed. But yesterday, I read about the dangers of hiking because of increasing marijuana production on private and public land in Douglas County. The Central Oregon Drug Enforcement (CODE) warns of heavily armed growers who set booby traps almost impossible for the casual hiker to discover. Hunters and hikers have been shot at, kidnapped, and threatened with violence.

Plus, under a law that took effect in 2010, loaded guns are now allowed into national parks and wildlife refuges. You might think that those of us who surround ourselves with green values would be exempt from terrorist mentality. Not true, for me. A stands-ground-and-shoot shadow hangs out within my inner council.

In Beck's map of the descent, the Red Eco-field abounds in today's world, seeking entry at every turn of the road. Terrorists are around the corner and seek the vestibule of our inner councils. Behring Breivik grew up in liberal and wealthy Norway with Christian values, and yet the dysfunctional side of the Red Eco-field took him over. He slaughtered seventy-seven of his fellows. Muslims have no corner on dysfunctional red. Breivik and Timothy McVeigh demonstrate Christian terrorism. The blood lust of the Christian crusades and American Puritans clamors to invade us.

As I drive and look for places to hike on the river, the news releases of the Norway murders flood into my consciousness through NPR connecting with my inner terrorist.

A few years ago Judith and I were hiking on property where we did not have permission, at my suggestion I might add, fence jumper that I tend to be. Massive elk hounds were loosed on us by a raging man guarding the area. Then he marched us off the private land bordering the Gulf of Mexico, all the while aiming his hunting rifle at us as his house mate shouted for him to shoot to kill us. Luckily, a police officer happened by and rescued us. Later, we found that drug smuggling was involved, and we had stumbled both on a marijuana grow and a point of entry on the dock of the bay. Had I a gun in hand that day my warrior would have had easy access to my inner microphone, and I do not know what my choice would have been.

Red and violent aspects of the eco-fields move faster than the speed of light seeking our interior doorways through memories and news releases. Without realizing it, I am in a war with the drug dealer, ready to shoot at a moment's notice.

Back on Highway 138, without being awake to the waves of information entering me, I find myself making plans in my daydreams for my hike. Do I need bear spray, not for bears but for dangerous humans? Should I carry a gun? Take karate lessons? A cool breeze wafts across my face that jolts me out of my waking red dream. I marvel at the power of the red vMEME to enter my consciousness without my permission. My own repressed inner violence acts as the tuning device to bring violent movies to my interior screen.

With all these tunings that bypass my aware ego, you might wonder if I will ever arrive at the trailhead for my hike. That is the way life goes for most of us. We are mostly dominated by the inflows of information. We think we are in charge, but really the vMEMES mostly do the choosing, utilizing our sub-selves as characters in dramas we create. We console ourselves by thinking psychological work with our inner dynamics will protect us from the waves of ego invasions. Not true, in my experience.

Nevertheless, take heart: the trailhead to the purple world is just around the corner, and help is on the way.

Purple Eco-field

As I drive, I am suddenly drawn to turn and cross a bridge to the far side of the river toward a place called Swift River Trailhead. You could say that place—in particular, the Purple Eco-field—called me out of the cross-currents of my mind to cross the bridge.

Once out of the car and on the trail, I dawdle over a sign indicating there are seventy-nine miles of trails along the banks of the river. A large snowfall over the winter unleashes torrents spilling over massive rocks. No wonder the Natives in their Chinook language refer to the river as *lemolo* or wild and untamed. Two translations of the Chinook word *umqua* are "thundering waters" and "across the waters." I smile as I walk because I have crossed the waters into another dimension, and I hear the thunder of the waters as I stride away from the trailhead.

The sound of traffic fades. A calm settles over me. I know I have descended far enough into the depths to be in the shamanic eco-field. I have traveled deep enough into the dark to see the stars. My mind talk clears.

Above me stretch towers of trees—hemlock, true fir, Douglas firs, and a mixture of hardwoods. In front of me I catch glimpses of radiant light streaming through the intertwined arms of the old growth forest, trees that are brothers and sisters of Siberian elms who held me so tenderly when I was a child in distant West Texas.

My awareness shifts its focus like a beam of flashlight on a dark night, moving first to one spot and then another. For an instant, or maybe an eternity, my interior is gifted by an animal presence, and I settle into being one among many forest mammals. The landscape takes me into itself, putting aside for this glorious moment the informational sound bites I received on my field trip down Highway 138.

Stopping, I sit on a moss-covered log, breathing. Wave-like emails enter through my soul from the forest depths.

Somewhere, I read we share 50% of our DNA with trees (Little, 1989), and I am totally in that 50% of myself swallowed by the plant community. No hierarchy exists in this state of consciousness, no sense of more or less. At ground base we are all equal—*all are my relatives*. From bacteria to majestic sequoia to human, we support each other, each with its own gift of Intelligence, Primordial Mind.

And, in such shamanic states, we all speak with a spirit voice and read the Scripture of Nature.

Moving deeper into the folds of mothering through the crunch beneath my feet and the gentle moisture floating through the fecundity of the intermingling of life all around, I become a simple utterance of the Forest's Holy Writ.

She says to me, "If there is ever any conflict between these utterances and your books of wisdom, always trust the direct hearing, seeing, smelling, and touching of this basic scripture."

As I walk, I notice I have covered a couple of miles of companionship with sugar pine, often six feet in diameter. Behind me are tiny waterfalls; before me a green gem of tumbling water called Fern Falls; even farther in the distance roars a larger falls. Pausing, a fallen sugar pine with a clean cut stretches out to my right with a sweet odor, and I notice a resinous substance found within the circle of its rings. Its stalactites of stickiness reach out to meet my now childlike fingers. I rub my hands with the joy of its pungency.

I extend my fingers and touch the dripping sap. The tree claims me as its own offspring with its mark of sap and dirt, a tattoo which continues to offer me its sticky gift every step of the way as I turn back toward the trailhead. Along the trail I glance down at animal scat. Mainly, it is composed of seeds, black berries, and other plant matter. Likely, a bear dropped it in the center of the trail in a tubular form, reminding me I am not the top of the food chain in these surroundings.

A few days preceding this hike, Judith and I walked briskly on the other side of the river. She broadcasted a message into the eco-field to connect with a central totem, the bear. We climbed past three major waterfalls, collectively called Fall Creek Falls, until we reached a trail higher on the mountain. Once above the falls, we walked easily along an old logging trail. On one side of the road, a forest ecology displayed resilience in a comeback after profligate logging, while on the other side the old growth forest thrived. Suddenly, on our left about fifteen feet away in the old growth hemlock, a large black bear stirred and looked our way.

For a highly charged, animating moment, we engaged each other as mammals. Our mutual paleo-mammalian brains vibrated and joined. Then, all too soon, the bear burst away with surprising speed, maybe 30 mph. While Judith remained in a shamanic pose, I turned to see a cub emerge out of a blackberry bramble and stand briefly on its hind legs. Immediately, I experienced the primal vulnerability of being between a mother and her cub. We slowly moved away from that eco-field to give her and her cub room to be with each other in that very distinct mother/child intimacy.

In such moments I become more congruent with my essential nature as mammal. Transfers of hidden meaning abound through the cells of my animal body, by-passing the intricacies of busy mind talk and academic research. An insight arises: before we can embrace an identity as human, we first must dive into being mammal. David Abram tells us to *become animals* (Abram, 2010).

I recall a comment by Carl Jung, "Sometimes a tree can tell you more than can be read in a book" (quoted in Sabini, 2008, p. 1).

And not only a tree, especially today, a bear.

A primal intimacy abounds.

Another Chinook word comes to mind, *illahee*. Regional tribes throughout the Northwest translate this word as country, earth, or soil, but also sometimes as river. The Chinookan language group consists of a cluster of tribes, mainly in Oregon and Washington states. I laugh at the contrast of the rich sound of the tribal word, *illahee*. It rhymes with a childlike, tee hee. In Black Elk's vision there was a great conflict between chaotic and coherent forces. When coherence won the day, the victory cry of his vision was Un-hee! (Niehardt, p. 27)

I chant:

Ilahee

Tee-hee

Un-hee.

The richness of these words seems so much closer to the bone of things than my newly discovered scientific word, *eco-field*. Later in the week I will dine at an excellent restaurant in the village of Glide called *The Illahee*. The organic salad with nuts and cheese transfer the meaning of the forest to my innards.

Back on the trail and off to my right, I hear the crashing calling card of Deadline Falls, a feature of the Tionga leg of the seventy-nine-mile hiking trail. The path to the falls beckons me as if pulling with an unseen hand. My intuitive response and choice to act on the dreamlike pull indicates the forest and river form a conspiracy aimed at mutual unfolding.

Angling down past moss-covered old growth double trees, I find myself standing before fast cascading water. It thunders forth loud music with the onomatopoeia of *bam*, *crash*, *boom*, and, not to be forgotten, *umpqua*. By now I am deep into my subjective descent into shamanic purple, an eternity away from the new Costco store back in town, the opulent house hanging over the cliff, and my inner Tea Party.

Tiring, I sit on a log placed there by Boy Scouts from the little city of Roseburg in 1993. Breathing slowly, I focus on the waterfall. Out of the corners of my eyes to the left and down, there sits, to my utter surprise, an apparition of the black fox, white tipped tail wrapped around its feet.

I wonder what his appearance means.

"To bring you here," he imparts, "and to let you know there is darkness afoot with a light on the tip of the tail."

White in dark. Stars in water. What channel am I tuning into through this forest field? My inner skeptic wonders what mushrooms I ate.

To my right appears Bear Heart, three years dead in ordinary life. He tells me to look at the waterfall for guidance. Behind him hovers Tilitha, my Shawnee ancestor, smiling but not speaking. Or is it another feminine goddess? Or a galactic mentor?

Bear Heart ushers me into the waterfall. Suddenly, a Chinook salmon jumps high into the air, sun splashing off his side, displaying a brilliant red near its tail as it tumbles to the bottom of the falls.

I blink.

Is the fish in my spirit vision or in the material world?

I do not know.

Another salmon jumps; this one makes it to the top. Through the foam and spray I see its hooked nose and gaping lower jaw as it stands on its tail, pitching upward, defying usual gravity. From the far side of the river, a fisher person shouts with glee at the sight. Definitely, the fish jumps in the world others perceive, not merely in my shamanic vision.

Or do the two merge into one?

In any case I know with pristine purity and transparent clarity this merger of man and waterfall constitutes a transfer of meaning from the eco-field, or more poetically, *the illahee*. The message imprints into my mind like a burned CD, only more so. What the code within the waterfalls means I do not know, nor do I have a desire to decode it at this moment, only savor. Details of the message of the Mother Tongue will arise later as I lean into it within a communal context.

I settle back, using the log as a backrest. My eyes fall on an informational sign provided by the National Forest Service. It reads simply and to the point:

> "Salmon are guided on their long journey from the Pacific to their birthplace and, often back, by the Sun, the stars, the Moon, and the magnetism of the Earth. They use keen odors as well, often returning to the very gravel beds where they were born."

The matter-of-fact statement of the sign tickles me. It assumes that we all know that the stars, the Sun, and the Moon send electro-magnetic impulses through all the creatures in an eco-field, leaving traces of the meaning of their message and guidance along the way. Just as we have learned to pick up signals through cell phones, waves from cell towers, or even GPS beams, so the stars send other wavelengths through the eco-field.

Thus states the usually reserved Forest Service, unaware of their reliance on star seeds of meaning transfers. Do they realize the implications of this statement? That the eco-field brims with innate intelligence? Do they realize that in a moment of inspiration they have departed from the reductive confines of Industrial Civilization and entered the purple of the shamanic? Do they realize they have joined hands with African wisdom keepers who speak of visits from star system Sirius?

Through tuning devices implanted over the eons by natural processes, these stunningly beautiful creatures, the Chinook salmon, reach up with electrical receptors to catch signals so clear they can travel hundreds of miles over waterfall after waterfall to the exact place where they were born. Like the moment after the Big Bang, there is a precision that bespeaks of an underlying field radiating intelligence, if not specific design.

I ponder.

What is missing in post-modern humans that we turn off the signals or are not aware that such signals exist? My thoughts wander back to an incident in the Portland Oregon Airport last summer. One of our Earthtribe participants had emailed that he was vacationing in Oregon, but we had not been able to connect. Nor had we talked in nearly a year. At a very busy gate in the airport our flight was announced, and I walked to the queue waiting to board the aircraft. Someone behind me coughed and cleared his throat, and I turned.

It was Brian, our vacationing friend, sand from the Oregon coast still on his shoes. We laughed and laughed, did the three of us—Brian, Judith, and me.

What a synchronicity!

"Let's have some fun," Brian offered, "and see if an Intelligence has arranged something else. Where are you sitting on the plane?"

"11A and 11B," we told him.

He looked down at his ticket and smiled, "I'm on 11C," and then continued, "I really am blown away. I needed to talk to you. I have been connecting with eagles and whales along the Oregon coast in a significant way. Somehow, my experience of the coast and its creatures have arranged our meeting."

The three of us struggled to find usual vocabulary; it just was not there. What passed between us was a sense of the primordiality of the river, the coast, the waterfalls, the bear, the salmon, the eagle, the forest, and the whale. In some manner beyond our usual rationality, an underlying connectivity, passed information in a nourishment akin to breast milk.

With such musings we leave this mysterious realm, the shamanic realm, and proceed to another trailhead, lower on the river.

Beige Eco-field

A few days later

No cars are parked at the Panther Trailhead.

The sign there warns of a trail with damaged walking bridges and a burned forest, down to the waterline of the Umpqua. I walk and see no humans. It seems no one wants to hike this devastated path. The marked opening snakes through the Middle North Umpqua River watershed, which contains 125,386 acres and includes thirty-four miles of the North Umpqua River. Highway 138 is the only paved road, and 149 people live in this vast acreage part-time. Forty-four streams pour into the main river and provide ideal habitat for salmon. Unaware logging has ravaged 32% of this riparian region where species struggle to recover. In contrast the remaining protected 68% contains excellent wildlife habitat.

A Beige eco-field prevails (see Chapter Four).

Major lightning strike fires in 1987 and 2002 are natural in occurrence. Yet, with the intense logging, the fires burn through areas now unprotected by the moisture of the rainforest, leaving a landscape akin to a post nuclear event.

The scene beside the Umpqua reminds me in many ways of Mt. St. Helens. When that venerable stratovolcano erupted May 18, 1980, it left a spectacular *beige* landscape. The impact of that event leveled 150 square miles of trees, sent the mountain's north face fourteen miles down the Toutle River and dropped a thick coat of gray ash over the acre of land we owned over 100 miles away near Bend, Oregon.

In such an event, beige in the eco-field speaks of destruction and chaos, but also of resilience, thriving, and rebounding. Many factors point to an underlying coherence, including the early morning timing of the eruption, the late arrival of spring in 1980, and, more importantly, the amazing ability of insects to parachute into the field once recovery was underway.

Islands of coherence sprouted everywhere, surprising the science of the time and its vaunted computer models. Some species managed to survive amidst the earthquake and eruption while others scraped by at the edges and, quite literally, crawled back into the pulsating heart of the eco-field. I should say interlocking eco-fields because there are many. Near the volcano a blowdown zone destroyed trees for about 143 square miles. The scorch zone covered about 42 square miles. The pyroclastic flow raged out of the volcano's mouth at a speed of up to 125 mph with temperatures of 1200 degrees Fahrenheit and created a pumice rock plane of about six square miles.

The varying effects of the eruption created different eco-fields or local landscapes, each having its own intelligence for recovery. Let me explain what I mean by coherent intelligence. I mentioned earlier *the timing*. Because the eruption occurred at 8:32 a.m. PST, many nocturnal creatures were already burrowed in for the day and were, therefore, protected in their homes beneath the surface. It appears now these nocturnal creatures were essential for the astonishing rebound.

The seasonal timing also fit with precision to provide recovery. Even though it was May 18, spring was late in coming that year, so drifts of snowfields covered crucial areas of the understory of the forest. Because of the unseasonable cold, migratory birds and salmon had not yet returned and were thus protected.

How to explain such *coincidences*?

Typical of orange science, uninformed by quantum fields, Charlie Crisafulli, a research ecologist, commented on the timing, "You just don't think about that (the timing); that's a chance event."[1]

Chance event?

---

[1] earthobservatory.nasa.gov/Features/WorldOfChange/sthelens.php

That is one way to look at it. But with EFH2 an exchange of meaning between the magma, the earthquake, the eruption, the season, the wind, the twenty-four hour journey of the day, the understory, the snowfields, and countless other variables come into play. This intertwining collaboration reveals an underlying intelligence, according to this hypothesis, and finds convincing support in Farina's careful research (2007). Are we seeing in EFH2 a middle ground between reductive Darwin and so-called intelligent design?

At my feet, as I walk on Calf's Path away from the Panther Trailhead, is a beautiful osprey feather. I stop and place it in my medicine bundle, alongside a sacred pipe. Then, I break out the ceremonial conch shell passed down to me from my ancestors. I blow the conch to confess our sins in logging and human-started forest fires, to celebrate the field's resilience, and to express my joy at the view of the whitewater river paradoxically made possible by the thinning of the trees in the fire.

Two rafts of whitewater adventurers pass by, and look up to hear the sound of the landscape, the blowing of my conch. One paddler raises his tired arm and lets out a yell of joy. They made it through the whitewater. They survived. He also seemed to speak for a still recovering forest. That's the Good News of the Gospel of Beige: our eco-fields can transcend surviving. We also can actually thrive. Even when the eruptions and fire leave apparent chaos.

Comments at the Base of Highway 138

In Proposal #1 of EFH2, I suggest we need to descend to purple and beige, the shamanic dimension, in order to retrieve the skills necessary for decoding the meaning transfers through the Spirit of the Depths. In this standing wave we can reclaim the ability and sensitivity to join the salmon, the bear, and the forest with the task of decoding the messages of the electromagnetic and eco-fields as passed through the Sun, the Moon, and the stars.

Field guide and scientist Almo Farina researches the terrain through his reporting in the studies of the reed warblers and their ability to transmit signals (Farina, 2007). Carefully, he and other researchers record the remarkable ability of the reed warblers to communicate, tuning into eco-fields that transmit information faster than the speed of light. On occasion we humans too can join an intimacy that ties into vector lines of energy in such a way that the Onge tribe moves to high ground, Tilly Short saves lives in Sri Lanka, and Lisa Dvorak listens to the warning signs of fire at Deer Dancer Ranch.

Every step of the way the messages and Scripture of Nature reach out to awaken us out of the stupors of unaware cultural vMEMES imbedded in the eco-field. But only when we immerse ourselves in the Spirit of the Depths found in purple and beige can we create enough power through our inner wild heart to enter a tension with the civilized selves. I complete this chapter with the continued emphasis on the importance of said tension that challenges our civilized selves through an aware and antinomial stretching. Such antinomial stretching makes possible solutions for the Era of Natural Consequences.

But something is missing in the journey down Oregon Highway 138, and to that missing piece we now turn.

CHAPTER TWELVE

Riding the Waves in the Vessel of Community

Spring of 1981

A gathering of the *Ahe-Chay-Cha* training circle assembles in far Northern New Mexico, led by Bear Heart and other traditional medicine people. These indigenous people do not use the term *shaman*; indeed, most have not even heard the term. Each tribe represented has its own description of a Nature-based practitioner. For example, one wise woman, a Comanche, who spoke little English, refers to the medicine person as a *puhakut*. That translates as *one through whom the Sacred Wind, Life's breath, moves freely.*

A Lakota elder speaks of our work and training as *wichasa wankan*. When I inquire as to a translation, none is forthcoming. Another apprentice tells me the translation is simply *holy person*, a description that fits Black Elk's teaching (Neihardt, 1959). Even the name of the traditional training circle is elusive, but usually we refer to ourselves with the Muscogee/Creek description as *Ahe-Chay-Cha*, a term that likely emanates from Mt. Cheaha and Chief Shinbone in current day Alabama. (This connection I recently discovered when I visited the holy place with a Wisdom University intensive.)

Part of the training is to enter this ancient tradition with humility and with a discipline of not speaking of one's self as a shaman or medicine person or, actually, any spiritual title. This apprenticeship constitutes a very different education from what I am accustomed to in the form of orange Ph.D's, state licensure for the practice of psychotherapy, or ordination in traditional religion.

"It's OK," the traditional wise persons instruct me, "for others to refer to any of us by names of honor. But we are not to speak that way of ourselves. You don't need to. People seeking healing and teaching will know to work with you by the way you carry yourself, by the way your spine aligns with the Earth, and by the way Grandmother's breath and life flows through your body and being. Energy and Spirit speak for themselves. Being traditionally trained means walking in this way."

I soon would see that the point of shamanic training was not about me, or about my obtaining a title or advertising brand. It was bigger, much bigger.

Mandate for Community

In the ceremony of their gifting me with a Sacred Pipe to aid in tuning into the Great Mysterious, the elders instruct me to return to urban Houston and be available for the emergence of a Nature-based community, or tribe as they call it. They kid me about starting a group of hybrids, referring to the rich mixture of my blood. These older wise persons risk much in terms of criticism from fundamentalists in Native ways who do not want anything shared with non-Indians or even mixed bloods. But this circle of wise people know prophetically that the ancient wisdom is needed to meet the challenge of the coming era. Possessiveness in any form simply does not work. There is, they explain, no time to waste in hoarding secrets. Too much is at stake.

In conversations that last through many nights around numerous fires, we talk about the loss of the experience of *tribe* both in the dominant culture and in indigenous peoples. Most of these men and women are part of tribes who no longer practice ancient ceremonies of vision questing and sweat lodging, or, if they do, it is not the focus of their tribes. They may be the last of their kind in tribal ways, as well as their native tongues. Bear Heart himself is one of the few medicine persons to speak fluently his native tongue, Muscogee/Creek. They teach me ceremonial elements of their various languages, and I speak the words out loud, feeling their rich resonance as close relatives of the creatures of the sacred web.

Brief examples:

Puha!

Mitak Oyasin!

Hozho!

Hey Chanupa, Ay te cacila!

Ahe-Chay-Cha

Try speaking these words aloud to feel their resonance.

The words underline the importance of using ancient languages which can call forth the sense of community stored in the memories of our cells. The apprentice circle discusses the beginning of gambling casinos and how tribal energy moves toward the orange vMEME and thus away from the sources of the shamanic era. My mentors express concern about this movement and the use of their ceremonies by their students without deep, ongoing ceremonial community.

The Hopi in our circle tell of Prophecy Rock and The Great Turning from one world cycle to the next. The only way to make this turning will be in the building of ongoing tribe. The fast-food mentality of workshops in dominant culture just will not be able to travel the sacred spiral with any long-term impact. With every fibre of their being, these elders emphasize that the community they want me to establish will include humans and more-than-humans, a return to vibrations of Wisdom's Web.

I protest!

Where can we find such communities? I know of none anywhere. Plus, I had tried for years to start such communities, and the tribes would begin with a bang and wither with the heat of conflict within the group. I confess to my mentors: I have been a failure as a community leader, and I do not see how I can, in good conscience, utter a vow dedicated to building circles of awareness, love, and respect. As I look into tanned faces, I experience a profound vulnerability in the open face of the task.

The Prophecy of Community

Not to worry, they instruct me. We peer into the fire, somewhere between 2:00 a.m. and 4:00 a.m. One of the Hopi in our circle begins a story, his voice rich with a deep baritone. He begins.

The year was 1958.

A Methodist minister named David Young drove across the desert of Eastern New Mexico. Young stopped to offer a ride to a Hopi Elder, who accepted with a nod. After riding in silence for several minutes, the wizened wise person, spoke:

> "My people await the Pahana, the lost White
> Brother from the stars. All our brothers and
> sisters in the land wait, looking to see the White
> Brother appear."

Then, the Hopi elder proceeded to delineate for Young an amazing array of prophecies which came mainly from the Hopi, but included wisdom the hitchhiking elder had gathered from many tribes in a recent cross-country sojourn.

As soon as the Hopi storyteller mentioned David Young and the geographical area where he picked up the Hopi hitchhiker, it immediately captured my attention. The setting of the prophetic story was not far from where I vision quested at about the same time on an island in Lake Conchas, Tucumcari, New Mexico. Chills ran up and down my spine at the coincidence. The Hopi elder in my training circle continued.

Young wrote down the prophecies, and then pondered what to do with them. Certainly, the adults in his congregation would not be interested in these esoteric utterances. Then, it dawned on him to present the material to his youth group, called the Methodist Youth Fellowship, or the MYF. He mimeographed the prophecies on one of those machines that leaked purple ink all over the pages and his hands. The youth read the material, mesmerized. They loved it. Soon, it circulated underground throughout Eastern New Mexico and West Texas youth groups, a presage of the 1960s revolution.

As the storyteller continued, my mind wandered to a vague memory of discussing such prophecies from a mimeographed document at McMurry University, a small Methodist school I attended in 1959 as a curious freshman. Four years later, the renowned anthropologist, Frank Waters, published *The Book of Hopi*, a book which—I discovered later—may have relied in part on these tattered mimeograph sheets (Waters, 1963).

Then, a piece of the memory jolted me.

At that time I dismissed the prophecies as mumbo jumbo. They did not fit my eighteen-year-old world-view, dominated as I was by Abrahamic religion. Lost in my thought, I almost missed the message of the elder speaking to me. He jolted me by striking his drum and repeated something he had already spoken:

"My people await the Pahana, the lost White Brother from the stars. All our brothers and sisters in the land wait, looking to see the White Brother appear."

The elder paused and looked at me.

With my chin on my chest, I avoided his stare.

I knew I was not the Pahana.

Yet, the connection to the brothers and sisters from the stars stirred something deep within.

Silence.

"How does this story relate to me?" I asked when I recovered.

Bear Heart spoke, "There are nine signs in the prophesy of the major Turning. You are part of the eighth sign. We are sending you to create little lodges that can become a network of love all around Earth. The White Brother of the stars is not an individual but rather these communities as they connect with the wisdom of the Milky Way. These tribes of mixed blood people, these rainbow communities, will be the Pahana of the stars."

I breathed a sigh of relief. I was off the hot seat.

Or was I?

The shamanic elders in New Mexico nodded in resonance with the star prophecy. These communities, they explained, could form canoes for riding through the great waves of destruction and purification so clearly predicted in the prophecies given to Young.[1] About the stars I knew nothing, and the Pahana star prophecies would incubate for fifty-two years before I would have even the smallest hint of the meaning.

Bear Heart spoke for the group: "Go back to Houston. Sit under a tree at sunrise, everyday. Meditate. The right people will be attracted to you to form the nucleus of a new kind of tribe."

So, I sat under a magnolia tree at 1107 Marshall in Houston as people scurried by on their way to work. Holy breath passed through me mixed with CO_2 from the urban traffic roaring by my tree.

I sat for a year.

No one appeared or expressed interest.

Then, slowly, ever so slowly, a few brave hearts were attracted to the tree and slowly knitted together. Bear Heart continued to guide me through a decade in mid-wifing a series of nature-based communities whose roots reached deep into the loins of Earth. Later, the communities would, loosely speaking, be called *Earthtribe*. I sought to integrate my profession as an evolutionary psy-

---

[1] www.crystalinks.com/hopi2.html

chologist and family systems therapist with the shamanic training. It did not always go well.

Bear Heart and I disagreed often about the dynamics of such a tribe as I sought to integrate my scientific and shamanic training. Understandably, my mentor was cautious about "mixing psychology with your medicine ways." During this time Bear Heart's wife died, and he went through a dark night of the soul, including the loss of his son. Later, he married Reginah Water Spirit, a skilled practitioner of Voice Dialogue, an approach to the Inner Council of Selves. Eventually, Reginah provided a welcome bridge between the two of us and the integrating of these two resources of psychological innovation and ancient wisdom. After an extended hiatus, Bear Heart and I had a deep and joyous reunion before his journey to the other side. Meanwhile, the Earthtribe grew stronger and sprouted other communities.

Over the decades the Earthtribe—and other Nature-based communities—offered models for vessels navigating the standing waves within the eco-fields emerging at the turn of the 21st century. In my mind Wisdom University's embracing of the Earthtribe and developing a concentration in Earth Wisdom and the Primordial Mind fulfills part of the prophecy of the Northern New Mexico circle so many years ago.

Now, after three decades of experience with the Earthtribe and many other communities, I am prepared to speak of how such communities offer hope in the Era of Natural Consequences, this historic moment predicted by the wisdom teachers of my training. Whether these tiny communities constitute the seeds of the prophetic Pahana, the mixed blood brothers and sisters of the stars, I do not know. I do know Earth-based communities are the only hope I see for the human species. Such hope provides a context for offering the next proposal for EFH2.

EFH2 Proposal #2

The vessel for the descending journey through the standing waves to the shamanic era (purple) and to the survival era (beige) lies in Nature-based communities. The Nature-based component is the crucial element because it provides the milieu for the wild heart to flourish. In such a matrix the Mother Tongue can return. More usual forms of community are not sufficient for the day.

Communities that practice on a regular basis the development of sensitivity to more-than-human elements of the eco-field are uniquely positioned to recognize the skills of beige and purple. The more-than-human elements of the eco-fields offer information, skills, and wisdom for the human community. They alone can create in us a healing intimacy so crucial for the birth of a new day. Like the insects and the nocturnal mammals of Mt. St. Helens, they can form islands of coherence.

The ascending movement up the river (spiral) after the descent will be addressed in Proposal #3 of EFH2, but first we need to look deeper into the qualities of the tribal vessel.

CHAPTER THIRTEEN

Qualities of the Communal Vessel

Travel down the wild river is exhilarating and dangerous. We need the safest possible vessel to carry us. Whatever communal vessel you ride in currently, take it out of the water and examine it with me. Can the vessel make the next leg of the journey, the one where we bounce around in the standing waves in the white water? Keep that central question in mind as we appraise the qualities necessary for building a vessel of community to make the descent and ascent on the river time and again. Following are the qualities we aspire to in our vessel.

Community Begins with Inner Council

Earlier, I spoke of the inner council of selves. (Chapter Eight; Taegel, 2010, 1990). It is enough here to state that community begins with an ongoing, aware assessment of the inner council of selves. The practice of including the various members of the inner council no matter how destructive, punitive, angry, afraid and wounded they seem on the surface constitutes the origin of community. This inclusion means a form of listening that does not allow the parts to dominate the inner microphone.

The Community Council of Landscape

The council of more-than-human creatures is necessary to save us from the narcissism of post-modern culture. The more-than-human in the eco-field comes to us in the form of the council of allies: bacteria, rocks, rivers, plants, trees, insects, reptiles, birds, mammals, wind, weather, and countless aspects of the eco-fields surrounding us. The wisdom of the Ahe-Chay-Cha Circle revealed itself in the primal instruction:

Go, *sit with a tree at sunrise.*

And not only that: sit until you become an attractor force in the eco-field. The powerful truth of the shamanic dimension of the eco-field is that the linchpin of community starts with recovering the permeability between humans and more-than-humans in the local landscape.

"You," my mentors seemed to say, "are not the attractor. It is the tree, the sunrise, the city, and you as an individual blended into a web. Together the component parts form the attractor force that will be a core of the Pahana tribe."

This teaching that the individual is not the fulcrum of the field constitutes a valuable cure for our rampant personal and cultural narcissism.

The Council of Ancestors

More-than-human includes not only all aspects of the material world but also the unseen or ancestral domain. Accessed by dreams, visions, meditations, ceremonies, and entheogens (sacred plants), the ancestors are available to guide and interact as dimensions of community.

In the shamanic training circle, we begin many prayers with the phrase, *Grandmothers and Grandfathers.* In the Earthtribe we have eight directions. The first seven—East, South, West, North, Earth, Sky, Relations—include the council of what we can perceive with our five senses. The eighth direction—Ancestors—allows us access to what we can perceive through our sixth sense.

The council of ancestors develops through practicing skills we retrieve from purple/shamanic, the sixth sense. Christians call on the ancestor Jesus, or the Cosmic Christ. Many Lakota call on Sitting Bull and Crazy Horse. Buddhists call on Gautama. Jung was guided by Philemon. Bear Heart continues to council many of us as an ancestor. Many tribes call on representatives of the Star Nations. We need all of the energy forms from the domain of the sixth sense to build the form of vessel for this journey.

The Community Core: A Partnership Council

Once the profound connection to the more-than-human aspect of landscape is established, attention turns to a basic human relationship as the foundation of the community. Often this core of community emerges in a marriage or a long term partnership/ friendship or both. For a community to flourish participants need to feel the soundness of a relationship that has structural integrity and tested intimacy.

Here are a few qualities of structural integrity. The core partnership demonstrates the ability to:

* work through conflict,
* take care of vulnerability,
* explore shadows,
* offer sexual safety,
* be honest and forthright in financial matters,
* engage in emotional and physical health practices,
* explore the edges,
* expand awareness space,
* plum spiritual depths,
* demonstrate grounded stability.

In developing these qualities the partnership core of the community transcends an individual and moves toward a sense of a *relationship* or *set of relationships* as being leader. A new form of sacred leadership emerges, one advancing relationship as the value and the locus of influence. The core partnership becomes the basis of a council leadership model.

The Council of Trans-human Relatives

In another narrative (Taegel, 2000) I describe in detail the mind shattering experience twenty-five of us had on a mountain side in New Mexico. There, a seven-foot tall energy form emerged out of the mountain forest in such vividity that it imprinted itself on our consciousness for decades to follow. And that imprinting was true for atheists in the community as well as Christians, Jews, Buddhists, and other spiritual traditions.

Through the years this *Warrior of the Meadow*, as we came to call her/him, appeared from time-to-time to lead us along the way. In the Ahe-Chay-Cha circle, nature spirits are called *little people* or *spirits of the land*. Celts seem to be describing a similar energy form with the term *faeries* or nature devas. Students of the Greek traditions know *Pan* as a nature deity.

Do these descriptions fit the form appearing to us? Or is it possible that this energy form was a representative of the Pahana of the stars? The Star Nations of Native America speak of such apparitions as *relatives*. Once, I described this apparition to a Lakota holy person (*wichasa wakahn*), and he firmly instructed me as to how the form was a star person in full regalia. In a recent dinner conversation with Nassim Haramein, he listened carefully to this appearance and suggested the visage was likely a teacher from the stars.

Whatever the descriptions for such an experience, the vessel of community for our river trip must include these spirit manifestations of the eco-field that are embedded within the material world but appear as energy or spirit forms, knowing they manifest for the purpose of evolving the eco-field. Embracing the reality and council of these relatives is a central task of our vessel.

The Ceremonial Community

We humans are communal animals. We hunger for community that fosters our growth, and a sense of balancing safety and adventure is also crucial. Ceremony offers the possibility of safety as both a cradle and challenge.

But not just any ceremony.

This era requires nature-based ceremony in order to foster the inclusion and flourishing of the wild heart and the speaking of primal grammar. Ancient ceremonies foster sitting on the earth, fasting from excess, listening to the muse of landscape, and making contact with the ground through bare feet. The close contact with the raw elements of weather act as an emotional corrective and introduce a reality not present in dominant culture. During the Era of Natural Consequences it is necessary for our communities to travel light, to owe no money, to live as simply and organically as possible, and to be able to be flexible with the crashing of waves all around.

Community as Tuning Device

The notion of the community as an attractor force in the field would seem to be self-evident. It is not. At least, we as a species seem to have forgotten—especially in industrial culture—the power of the community's ability to tune into the field as demonstrated in the Onge tribe in Sri Lanka (Chapter One). If the medium is the message in Marshall McLuhan's system, in EFH2 the shamanic community is the medium itself (McLuhan, 1967). If you recall, the actual title of McLuhan's best known book is *The Medium Is The Massage*. McLuhan adopted the term *massage* to denote the effect each medium has on human sensorium as the various broadcasts are absorbed. Radical at the time, McLuhan's view of the impact of television pales beside the Internet. Nevertheless, in EFH2 I propose that neither television nor the Internet is the powerful broadcaster for our day, except as these technologies undergird the power of community as medium.

As we recover our lost sense of the intricate communication system of the fields and integrate that language with the language of the Internet/technological system, then we hold in our collective hands a powerful tuning device, a dowser beyond dowsers. My proposal then: a shamanic community can best offer the healing *massage* and *message*, the laying on of communal hands for the curing of the human sickness currently ravaging Earth.

The Community as Broadcaster of Intention

Much has been written about the power of intention to shape reality. Skeptics justifiably raise the question as to why intentions often do not work. We are discovering the following about broadcasting intention into the eco-field:

- Intentions need to be clearly and explicitly stated.
- Intentions need to pass through the aware space of a communal aware ego.
- Contractions in the body need to be released so the full language of the fields can move freely through the physical and corporate body of the community. An example might be the purification of the body in the sweat lodge ceremony or acupuncture.
- Aware choices by the community need to be made, witnessed, and revisited.
- Aware practices within the community need to support all of the above steps in the broadcast of the intention so that conflict in the broadcast can be reduced.

When the above steps of the Mother Tongue are followed in the context of an intentional Nature-based community, the eco-field seems most responsive. As my colleague, Teresa Collins, puts it: "The Universe seems to respond to intention, passionately stated, with unconflicted behavior."

The Community as Interpreters

As questers return from visionary realms, the process of interpreting the visions begins. Farina (2000) points out the importance of tracking meaning exchanges in the more-than-human dimension of eco-fields. I translate his work into EFH2 to include the human factor. As these meaning exchanges occur through various downloads—including vision quests, meditations, prayer, and other non-ordinary states of consciousness—a question looms of translating meaning transfers into thought forms and action that make for a more healthy species and planet. The importance of this translation of primal utterances into current language cannot be overstated. In this translation the word becomes flesh and dwells among us, full of grace and truth.

The translation of the primal communications shifts states of brilliant consciousness into traits of character. The focus: turn states into traits.

Thus a central function of the council of presiding elders in the Earthtribe is to "bring in the questers and listen to their visions." We encourage visitors to other realms typical of the shamanic era first to trust their own inner council as the foremost authority for their visions. Upon return they sit before a council of elders whose primary function is to witness the visions, not tell the quester what the vision means.

In our post-modern culture the first task of community as interpreter is to listen without projecting onto the quester a personal or even a tribal map. The vision and/or dream is valued in and of itself, a *das ding an sich*, thing in itself, or, better, an event-in-itself. Through the next period of time, months or years, the fitting of the vision/dream into the larger tapestry of the tribal, then global tapestry, occurs.

A second interpretive function of community lies in the telling and retelling of the visions over a number of years. In this practice the tribe learns to recover the oral tradition. Each time the vision or meaning transfer passes through human words, another aspect of the unutterable shines through and asks to be included in tribal consciousness. In the multiple narrations of the visions/dreams/visitations, the downloads of wisdom continue. The function of the tribe is to provide a safe and encouraging setting for the exploration of meaning transports.

In short, the task of community at this point is to be a witnessing presence to the coherence building throughout the interlocking eco-fields. Next, the community provides an ongoing setting for the integration of the downloads and the container for continued telling of the visions. The river-worthy vessel of community, then, becomes a mediator between dimensions of reality.

Community as Participatory Eco-field

The above qualities of community unveil a radical model of participation in the eco-field. David Abram (1996) quotes anthropologist,
Lucien Levy-Bruhl in his focused use of the world participation:

> ...the animistic logic of indigenous, oral
> people—for whom ostensibly 'inanimate'
> objects like stones or mountains are often
> thought to be alive...and powers may be felt
> to participate in one another's existence, influ-
> encing each other and being influenced in
> turn" (p. 57).

Both Abram and Levy-Bruhl conducted their research before
the EFH1 or EFH2 as scientifically based research was formed
(Farina, 2007: Taegel, 2010). Yet, their statements concisely illus-
trate the reciprocal nature of reality. The interface between all
aspects of the interlocking eco-fields create in-depth reality. Thus,
the role of community is to become participatory or reciprocal with
all aspects of the eco-fields.

The role of the shamanic elder in our river-worthy vessel is
to be an:

+ ...intermediary between the human community and the
  larger ecological field,
+ ensuring that there is an appropriate flow of nourishment,
+ not just from the landscape to the human inhabitants,
+ but from the human community back to the local earth.

(Abram, 1996, p. 7)

This definition of the shamanic community is crucial because
it varies considerably from both Eliade (1964) and popular shamanic
teachers like Michael Harner (1980). Eliade restricted the use of the
term *shaman* to persons who enter trance and address the tribe
through a visit to the spirit world and then a return with helpful
and healing information (Eliade, 1964). Harner, too, emphasized
altered states of consciousness through drums and hallucinogens
in soul retrieval.

Both Eliade and Harner have contributed to the understanding of the shamanic standing wave; however, they largely ignore what I consider to be the most important aspect of the shamanic community—the mediation of meaning between the human and more-than-human dimensions of the eco-field.

Many researchers (Abram excepted) miss the notion that the ongoing, Nature-based community itself is *the* medium of soul retrieval, not the individual seeker or the shaman herself. The shaman "derives her ability to cure ailments from her more continuous practice of 'healing' or balancing the community's relationship to the surrounding land" (Abram, 1996, p. 7). Soul retrieval begins with a balancing of the current eco-field with particular attention to all the more-than-human creatures. It is difficult to balance the eco-field of rocks, soil, grass, trees, insects, birds, mammals, wind, and rain if the central teaching occurs in the air-conditioned space of offices and conference centers.

Soul-retrieval, the ballast of our vessel, occurs best through the mediating space of *community*. The Nature-based community becomes both the medium through which healing passes and the corrective for individuals whose altered states of consciousness may or may not serve the larger whole. The task of the community vessel we seek for this journey must learn the subliminal language in the dimension outside human control.

Community and Emerging Intimacy

Intimacy with a natural area can be likened to a first-date romance, as in a Spring picnic on an ideal weather day. It seems to be the case that the eco-fields provide us with certain magical days that are akin to a first kiss. But the form of intimacy required for the return of our species to the eco-field insists on a long-term marriage of sense and soul. You can learn a few words of natural sublimity on a beautiful-day-picnic, but to become fluent in the language of a given landscape requires years—through pleasant and unpleasant weather conditions.

Think about it.

The forests and landscapes we have destroyed demand that we sit with them through all kinds of circumstances in order to establish the trust necessary for profound intimacy. The more-than-human has to learn to trust wayward humans. Let's look at a specific case of a community of humans and more-than-humans finding a common language.

A Community Experiment in Landscape Language

For thirty years now in the Earthtribe, we have sought to take the fleeting moments of awareness of being a relation among relations and turn them into our basic identity. The practice of moving beneath our literate selves to the Primordial on a regular basis presents a major challenge, but the rewards are great.

In 1990 Jack and Allison Jensen purchased a 500-acre ranch nestled in an outbreak of the Southern Pine Forest about two hours east of Austin, and one hour west of Houston, near the rural town of Columbus, Texas. Clearly, the eco-field within the ranch had once been a place of enormous beauty and sacred power, but it was a paradise lost, much like Earth in general.

The Earthtribe needed a place to gather since our previous ceremonial grounds had been surrounded by suburbia, and neighbors were complaining about the noise we made. In effect, we had been evicted from our ceremonial grounds because our worship was not civilized enough. Graciously, the Jensens extended an invitation to gather in a meadow on the ranch.

Majestic pines and hardwoods spoke of an ancient story; indeed, many of the trees were old growth, an unheard of occasion in the Southern Pine Forest where such stands are rare because of the lumber industry's profligate use of the forest to supply our building booms.

The first day we arrived at the ranch about thirty strong, we found the meadow to be overgrazed to the point that hundreds of acres were completely devoid of native grasses; all that remained was a skinned gravel-like ground. The once pristine creek running through the ranch to a large lake was filled with old tires. Beer cans were everywhere, along with piles of human trash where the former owners dumped their remains without regard for the land. Iron stakes had been driven into old growth trees, and sap ran out of the open wounds. Once clear ponds were now dark and murky. Several hundred acres to the south of the meadow also had been grazed until no grass remained; in fact, few weeds could even be seen, though there is little distinction between weeds, grasses, and flowers in a restored eco-field. The main lake was brackish and trashed.

To get to know this tired eco-field, I spent four days and nights fasting and praying in a circle, seeking entry into the depleted space. On about the third day of fasting, I experienced waves of energy coming toward me in the middle of the night from the heart of the damaged eco-field. The imbedded message I kept receiving was that I needed to go to my urban home and clean out my closet.

What a odd message!

Was this the sum total of a four-day vision fast? If so, it did not seem very spiritual to me. As I thought about telling my vision to elders at the end of my fast, I was frankly embarrassed. I felt no meaning transmittal was happening; an interval of tortured time passed before I would connect the dots. There were personal dots that led to a major move out of my urban home, once I cleaned out not only my closet but my attic. But the larger message was this:

"Will," the terrain pronounced, "if you love us, help restore us. In return we will nourish your little group of humans and give you big visions."

We were being invited into reciprocal healing.

As the years passed, we received expanded murmurs from Grandmother Earth through her local eco-field, the ranch. She aspired to restore this aspect of her being as one of Her many eco-field projects around the globe. We were not alone. She was manifesting plots of ground all around the planet, islands of health within Her system.

Meanwhile, the Jensens invested heavily in the ranch and its restoration. Eco-field cleansing and balancing blossomed. Month after month we held ceremony, cut and trimmed trees, picked up cans and tires. Ranch hands, ecological scientists, and biologists directed us. Most important, we loved the landscape. Animals returned—migrating birds, great horned owls, occasional eagles, hawks, songbirds, white tail deer, red deer, bison, ravens, axis deer, fallow deer, and predators, as well.

Grass was planted, but mostly reseeded itself. Soon acres of grass sprouted as if it had just been waiting for the proper human partner, and soon healthy grass communities covered what was once red gravel. In the middle of the ceremonial meadow, we planted a large red juniper dance pole, a large tuning device and Earth Dance pole. At about the five-year mark the meadow was once again green and vibrant, so much so that the five-acre meadow where we danced had to be mowed each month before our sweat lodge ceremonies.

At the ten-year mark, we began having vision quests on what was now called Deer Dancer Ranch. Ancient, ancestral archetypes rose up out of the loins of the eco-scape and filled the vision circles of questers with powerful visions. These visions were not primarily psychological in nature but presented themselves in energy forms of ancient ancestors. Buffalo pawed the ground as we entered sweat lodges. Red deer followed questers around.

It had taken ten years of monthly ceremonial practice, and the land had begun to trust us humans. We had vision quested in New Mexico, Colorado, Montana, New England, and Washington, all wonderful and powerful places. Yet, this once bedraggled land was now yielding most amazing visions as its sparkling health, power, and vibrancy returned. What began as a restoration of the landscape ended up as a restoration of us humans to the landscape.

Not all the time, but occasionally, more-than-humans and humans engaged in profound intimacy. Fluency requires decades of dedication, as with any language.

Council as a Means of Communal Governance

Before I leave our exploration of the communal vessel, I want to touch briefly on the very large subject of tribal governance. Our experience with Wisdom University, the Earthtribe, and other educational partners is that communities often begin with strong individuals as founders, move to partnerships as described above, and unfold into a council or councils as a means of governance. Once we open our inner councils to hear a wide range of inner voices, then it becomes necessary to create communities whereby a spectrum of voices can be heard.

At Wisdom U. we are experimenting with administrating the University with a CEO of three persons, a model we have followed for a number of years in the Earthtribe. This experiment materializes out of an unfolding of our little university from the strong individual leadership first of Matthew Fox and then of Jim Garrison to a more communal model. We will see momentarily that forms of governance and leadership require the ability of an organization to descend and ascend the spiral and be fluent in each standing wave.

Multilingual Communities

Once a community grounds itself in the Mother Tongue, it then has the task of becoming fluent in each of the eight standing waves. Return for a moment to one of our seminal river or field guides, Clare W. Graves. Graves found himself astonished when he uncovered individuals who could move up and down the eight stages of cultural evolution in terms of what they valued (1974). Don Beck described the moment of Graves' discovery like this: "He (Graves) found in his interviews a 'whole different breed of cat,' people he didn't know existed" (Beck, 2006, CD 1). Later, Beck described the quantum leap from the 1st Tier of human development to the 2nd Tier as landing in a more individual wave (yellow) and then in a more communal wave (turquoise) (Beck, 206, CD 6).

Here is an astonishing result from the seminal researchers I considered (Chapter Four): none of these field guides could find communities that had the ability to ascend and descend the river of standing waves.

Individuals? Yes.

Communities? No.

♦ If we humans are to flourish as a species, we will need to coalesce into communities that are linguistically grounded in the primal but also are culturally multilingual. Here are the language requirements for thriving in the world to come:

- A beige language of resilience and survival
- A purple language of the shaman
- A power language of red
- A structured and traditional language of blue
- A scientific and consumer language of orange
- A systems and technological language of green
- An integral language of yellow and turquoise

In this book I explore only briefly and anecdotally two communities yearning for and sometimes practicing a base Mother Tongue, as well as the multi-lingual abilities mentioned above. A more thorough research is needed as global communities are sprouted by the Grandmothers and Grandfathers.

Summary Comments

Recently, in a faculty/staff gathering at Wisdom U., I found myself outlining three different vessels I see trying to float the turbulent river. Interestingly, the vessels seem to compete in a colorful regatta with each vessel viewing the other as inferior.

If that continues, all three will sink into the roiling waters.

First, I notice a large contingent of communities majoring in altered states of consciousness. These communities vary from Holotropic Breathing, to peyote churches, to ayahuasca pilgrimages, to vision quests, to fire walking, to trance dancing, and to dowsing. The theme of these communities is to achieve an altered state of consciousness as a way to become a tuning instrument into the transformational possibilities in the waves. Carlos Castaneda, Stan Grof, and Michael Harner are leaders in this domain. The advantage of such communities lies in the vast resources beyond the usual, rational mind and the utilization of altered states as the energetic juice that powers the vessel.

Second, I notice shamanic communities that emphasize the return to the landscape through the senses. Dave Abram has written magnificently of the use of the five senses as opening the portals between humans and more-than-humans. The advantage of such communities rests in the powerful, reciprocal healing available to the eco-field when humans return to more-than-human subtleties of information transmittals.

Third, I notice shamanic communities that are sound, well-grounded psychologically and also have pushed themselves beyond the psychological into the transpersonal. These communities typically consist of people who have had considerable therapy and yet have transcended the limits of that approach to the human condition. The advantage of these communities lies in a sense of integrity, clarity of communication, resolution of conflicts, and emotional safety.

In order to journey up and down the standing waves in the Era of Natural Consequences, our communal vessel will need all three of these emphases. To shift metaphors, think of a stool with three legs. You need all of three of the legs to sit upright. In just such a communal vessel, we are prepared for the return ascent up the river.

IV

The Returning Ascent on the River

CHAPTER FOURTEEN

Looking Up from the Bottom of the River

We have built a vessel worthy of the descent and the ascent. That done, look up the river at the standing waves of eco-fields. Gravity brought us down the river, but now we must turn to the Sun and other stars for the power to propel us up the river. Maybe we can install solar panels on our vessel to power us on the ascent.

Let's see what I mean by that statement.

Lost at the Bottom of the River

Upon our return to our usual lives from ceremonial experiences in a specific eco-field or standing wave, Earthtribers discovered many pitfalls. The first challenge arose in the return to daily life after dwelling with the Spirit of the Depths.

For example, on many occasions car drivers would make a wrong turn and find themselves lost as they returned to Houston from Deer Dancer Ranch. They would arrive at I-10 in an altered state and not know whether to turn left or right at the freeway junction, an easy awareness in their usual state. Instead, as they were ensconced in an altered state, they turned the wrong direction and found themselves half-way to San Antonio before they snapped back to an inner council member who knew the way home to Houston.

How did this loss of direction happen?

We realized that transfers of meaning within the eco-field of the ranch—entering our lives through altered states of tribal ceremonies—did not apply to immediately practical issues like driving directions. A persistent question arose: how could we integrate the profound and wild wisdom of the depths with our lives on freeways? The sounds of birds and music of the spheres did not easily translate into freeway directions.

The Lure of the Depths

Another challenge in the profound experiences of the depths resides in the simple desire to dwell with the beloved community in the beauty of the cherished eco-field—in this case, the ranch. Fantasies of building a remote commune far from the madding crowd persists. Like the students of Jesus, we want to become permanent residents on the Mount of Transfiguration, the mountain of visions. Yet, we surmise the solutions for our planet can arise only if we travel on all levels of human existence and speak all the languages. We could not live permanently in the standing wave of the shamanic era and be fully servants of Earth in the current crisis. The power of re-enchantment is strong, yet there is another call: that of the heights, so we have a tug in both directions, a major dilemma.

The Dilemma at the Base and Top of the River

Most of the world's spiritual traditions aspire to enlightenment, the upward call of the headwaters, which often means pushing away from the sensuousness of the eco-field. The seduction of the heights of the spiral pulls us to escape Earth and go to Heaven, Nirvana, pure Reason, or the Absolute outside Plato's cave (Bloom, 1968).

The ascenders find joy in the heavens and cast aspersions toward the descender's enchantment in the Earth, which I discussed above. Neither extreme works for the Era of Natural Consequences; we need to journey up and down, connecting the Primordial Mind with modern mind as we learn to use the base language of all the communications of the standing waves of eco-fields.

So, how do we resolve the tension of ascending and descending?

Help and Hindrance with Wilber's Pre/Post (Pre-Trans) Fallacy

Does the good cosmic map maker, Ken Wilber, offer us help with the ascending/descending tension? Well, yes and no. He writes, referring to the stages of human development (or, as I prefer, *the standing waves of the river of life*):

> In any developmental sequence—pre-rational to trans-rational, or sub-conscious to self-conscious to super-conscious, or pre-verbal to verbal to trans-verbal, or pre-personal to personal to trans-personal—the 'Pre' and 'trans' components are often confused, that confusion goes both ways.
>
> Once they are confused, some researchers take all trans-rational realities and try to reduce them to pre-rational infantile elements (e.g. Freud), while others take some of the pre-rational infantile elements and elevate them to trans-rational glory (e.g. Jung). Both that reductionism and that elevationism follow from the same pre/post fallacy. (Wilber, 2006, p. 52)

Wilber's insights assist, and I am chief among those needing help. Earlier, in my training in shamanic ways and in the forming of the Earthtribe, I noticed a blessed confusion. Maybe I exaggerate blessed. To be more accurate, call my early state of mind *troubling and chaotic.*

Clearly, we in the Earthtribe were experiencing something in mystic moments beyond the scope of modern rationality; the eco-field downloads stretched us beyond common sense and the scientific method, far outside the bounds of rationality. And, yes: there was an enticement to glorify the pre-rational of the pre-writing era of the shaman. Abram (1996) argues so brilliantly for the reawakening of the animistic dimension of perception and feeling that he teeters on the edge of renouncing rationality and intellectual analysis altogether.

For some time, I teetered with him.

I cannot read Abram's stunning analysis of our current alphabet without wondering if we humans took a wrong turn in embracing a form of writing that disengages us from the natural order and leads more and more into abstraction, as does the Greek alphabet and our current English alphabet (1996, pp 145-147). Perhaps, this reading of Abram's teetering is my own projection because I fell into the enchantment trap for a number of years.

That said, I would rather be enchanted by the sensuousness of Earth than lost in the Absolute and dry Reason of Wilber. (Please allow this voice to speak in my inner council.) Nevertheless, soon enough in the Earthtribe story, I felt a call to ascend the river. By this time I was traditionally trained in ancient medicine ways, but I was also a competent psychotherapist and aspiring scientist. The call to remain in oceanic bliss was strong, but a disturbance in the field called to me, a questioning.

Most of our Earthtribe participants at the time were either psychologically trained or clients or both, so we returned from our ceremonial settings to the questioning rationality of modern psychology, after sojourns in sweat lodges, trance dances, and vision quests. The call to walk in the two worlds was persistent. One world was and is not sufficient.

The mystical experience in Nature is like plucking the string of a guitar. Once plucked, though, the type of amplifying box of a given guitar determines the sound. The amplifying box can be beige, purple, red, blue, orange, or green. It can be pre-rational, rational, post-rational, or trans-rational. It can be pre-personal, personal, or transpersonal.

Thank you, Ken Wilber. He outlines brilliantly the standing waves of our river.

The Trans/Pre Fallacy: 1.0

So far so good with Wilber; now for his hindrance.

Upon a further reading of Wilber, it is clear that he is much more at home with his Buddhist and Neo-Platonic flights to the heights and not so much with what he calls, somewhat dismissively, *nature mysticism.* He correctly sees the sequence of development or movement through the standing waves:

* Nature mysticism to
* Deity mysticism to
* Formless or unity mysticism to
* Nondual mysticism. (Wilber, 2006, p. 93)

That said, his post-modern prejudice prevails as related to the profundity of nature mysticism and manifests in a question put to him by an interviewer:

"Is it possible that ancient shamans from the archaic era (purple in Beck's map) could practice the highest form of mysticism and meditation?"

Wilber: "Probably not... Because the structure of consciousness necessary for nondual mysticism had not been laid down yet, and, if the shamans had achieved that level we would have evidence of such states in cave paintings and the like" (Wilber, 2003, Disc 8).

Is he not at this point assuming that later developments (trans) are better than earlier ones (pre)? We shall see how this fallacy in his map is indicative of a major error in most of post-modern thinking: the trans/pre fallacy—*after this, therefore better than this.* Let's see what I mean by this statement.

Evidently, Wilber is not aware of the archeological site, Göbekli Tepe! Currently, a shocking shift appears in archeological paradigms stimulated by discoveries in the last decade. Archeologist, Klaus Schmidt, and the German Archeological Association have been uncovering evidence that shamanic era humans had well within their grasp the ability to think abstractly. Schmidt writes of the Göbekli Tepe culture, "The people must also have had a highly complicated mythology, including the capacity for abstraction" (Schmidt, 2008, p. 14).

Why is abstraction so important to our discussion?

Schmidt was referring to a substantial community of people whose world view reaches back into the Neolithic Period, some 12,000 years ago and whose practices hint at an exquisite symmetry between humans and more-than-humans. While at the same time, they demonstrated the ability to stand apart or abstract themselves from their situations and think in the third dimension.

How do we know?

Their three-dimensional sculptures of their animal allies are startling and reveal a shamanic ability to be held by both the Spirit of the Depths and the Spirit of the Heights. Put another way, they had the meditative capacity to engage in a state of consciousness called, the *Witnessing Presence*, a state Wilber holds does not manifest in the human story for another 8,000 years. Wilber maintains that nondual mysticism does not appear with the human species in any significant manner until Plotinus and Nagarjuna, circa 200 CE.

It now appears Wilber is mistaken in this aspect of his map.

Phrased in my parlance, the nondual mystic is the person situated in a Nature-based community who has the ability to journey up and down the standing waves of the wild river, speaking the language of the Mother Tongue, as well as the language of each standing wave. I will return shortly to my experience of the Göbekli Tepe people in my actual visit there.

For now I point to Wilber's hindrance—his own lack of experience with the standing wave where primordial mysticism is freely spoken, the language between humans and more-than-humans. I single out my good brother Ken, (if I may be so bold as to speak of a man I have not met in person), simply because he, as a Neo-Platonist, is typical of post-modern prejudice with regard to Primordial Wisdom. Such a post-modern predilection I call the *trans/pre fallacy, the tendency to think "after this, therefore better than this."* We are now experiencing the planetary consequences of such arrogance and prejudice against the capabilities of our ancestors.

After a lifetime of immersing myself in the ancient eco-fields, I—like Wilber—am guilty of the arrogance for which I hold Wilber accountable. We in the post-modern era live with the virus of our culture, which somehow thinks of itself as being more advanced in most ways to the ancient world. It is precisely this bias against the descending current that has gotten us in the predicament of the Era of Natural Consequences. Simply put:

If we are not intimate and speak the language of more-than-humans, we tend to abuse our environs, or, at best, be indifferent and ignorant. Or to state our particular form of spirituality or mysticism is more evolved than these ancient resources. Such a reasoning has given us conscious and unconscious permission to rape the environment, all the while thinking we have consent.

In our governance and life styles, we are like the rapist who tells himself that she really wanted it, only the object of our violence is Earth Herself.

Closing Comments at the Bottom of the River

When I immerse myself in the intellectual snobbery of our reductive and overly rational culture, I lose the juice of emotion and the intuitive and felt sense of the primal. When I stand with the morning sun warm on my back, toes digging into the grass and soil, my shadow cast across flowers carefully tended by my friend and mother-in-law, Eldora, I enter a deep sense of relaxation and alpha meditation. A hummingbird sounding forth its winged music in the lost language at my ear, a surge of the energy of the Spirit of the Depths moves through my sore muscles from hiking the previous day.

In such intimate exchanges, we humans can find the fuel to propel our vessel up the river, and, I will propose momentarily, it is only with this nature mysticism that we can obtain that fuel unique for this particular era.

CHAPTER FIFTEEN

The Return Up the River

Winter, 2011, the Texas Hill Country

I am jostled awake during the pregnant night time of 2:00 to 4:00 a.m., the moments when the veil is thin between realities. I am aroused by the sound of great horned owls. Blinking in a half-awake, half-asleep state, I walk out onto surrounding acreage I share with the stars and the owls. I feel drawn to think about Kurdistan as a context for navigating our canoe to the purple wave wherein dwells shamanic wisdom.

The Power of Pre-historic Wisdom

Autumn, 2010, Kurdistan, Southeast Turkey

In this altered state, vivid images arise of Wisdom University's visit to Göbekli Tepe, Turkish for potbelly hill, in Southeastern Turkey. In that part of the world, they call the area Kurdistan, or the land of the Kurds. We had just completed a pilgrimage with Raymond Moody (2010) to Greece where we visited the Oracles of the Dead, so we were primed for a plunge into the Spirit of the Depths, literally a dig into Earth Herself.

Four of us on the faculty from our seminar in Greece flew into remote Sanliurfa (simply Urfa to the locals) to see firsthand what all the fuss was about concerning this new archeological dig.

The purpose of our trip was to explore the possibility of an academic and spiritual pilgrimage to the site. At first blush our travels constituted a comedy of errors where we rented a car, nearly ran out of gas, got lost in the desert, and blundered through Urfa, attracting occasional attention as the only Westerners on the streets.

Finally, on an early November day we wound our way Southeast of Urfa about twenty miles to the archeological dig, a short distance from the Syrian border. At first glance it was not the most auspicious of places; in fact, it resembled the hot and windy semi-desert of my childhood. Only there was nothing "semi" about this desert: it was the real deal. Klaus Schmidt, the lead archeologist, was not there to greet us, a setback in our plans. Actually, though, this disappointment turned into a benefit because an indigenous guide took his place, and his guidance would turn out to be crucial.

In 1994 a local farmer was plowing his field, and the plow dug into a large stone, exposing the tip of what turned out to be a prodigious monolith weighing about seven tons. The most important archeological discovery, perhaps ever, started with his rusty plow, not a Western scientist. To give us a context of time, the monuments at Göbekli Tepe are almost twice as old as the Pyramids of Giza in Egypt.

This very farmer, who had toiled in his field and unearthed the first megalith in 1994 with the clank of plow on ancient stone, met us at the foot of the hill. His name, buried somewhere in my notes, escapes me. Accompanying him was his thirteen-year-old grandson. The grandson and I made a good connection even though he did not speak English, nor I, Turkish. Rather, we sent messages in the language of landscape. The grandson graciously and enthusiastically guided us around the site, and we were presented a perspective the more academic Schmidt likely could not provide. After all, the grandson was an aspect of the eco-field of generations of farmers and herders who lived in situ with all the dimensions of this stark landscape, a long way from Schmidt's verdant Germany.

As we trudged up the deceptively steep road of the potbelly hill, we were not prepared, even with Internet images fresh on our minds, for the massive pieces of spiritual art weighing from two to seventeen tons. Excavations of the numerous giant megaliths revealed a complex configuration of forty-three T-shaped standing sculptures arranged in three adjacent circles, all surrounded by high walls.

The standing megaliths feature eco-acoustic architectural features seen at other megalithic sites like Stonehenge, but keep in mind that these sculptures are 9,000 years older than Stonehenge. Plus, there are only seventeen standing stones at Stonehenge, and at Göbekli 43 stones have been uncovered thus far with 95% of the site yet to be explored. One of the stone sculptures is thirty feet long, and the tallest is thirteen feet high. Impressive, to say the least.

Two of the massive blocks immediately garnered my attention as they depicted the unmistakable forms of nonlinear standing waves. Researcher, Alex Putney, describes the scene like this:

> "One example shows the giant *standing wave* arch drawing down from the sky toward an animal that seems to be rising off the ground by the acoustic levitation effect of infrasound resonance ... Atop another *standing wave* stone, psychoacoustic animal symbols are carved along with three different sizes of *standing waves* connected to three block forms representing the temple's resonant stone foundations.
>
> The three *standing waves* and the three blocks are specifically rendered in Fibonacci ratio with one another, overtly referencing the tri-frequency acoustic signature of nonlinear *standing waves*." (as recently rediscovered and mathematically modeled by Cervenak, et. al. in 2003)[1] (italics mine).

I noted the impact of seeing *standing waves* in the form of stones, and the sculptures appeared to me as rivers of stone as they flowed on to another. The beauty and flowing nature of the megaliths jumped out at me and inspired me to employ the standing wave

---

[1] www.HumanResonance.org, May 4, 2011

metaphor throughout this book. Soon, the undulations of stone energy moved through me, and a low-toned sound vibrated, tuning and opening my heart. Was it the wind? My imagination? Memories of my childhood on the windy Southern Plains of North America?

As I puzzled, the farmer's grandson approached me, motioning for me to follow. The path took us up a knoll to a solitary mulberry tree. Our guide explained that this hardy tree on the highest hill in the area had been sacred to the locals for as long as he could recall. This tree suggested to archeologist Schmidt that he might be onto something important to the scientific and spiritual history of the place, and maybe the planet. We sat beneath the tree, looking down from the hilltop at the concentric circles of stone sculptures below us. The power of this vantage point was palpable, or as Schmidt put it when he first felt the presence of the tree, the desert, and the stones:

"Within the first minute, I knew that if I didn't walk away immediately, I would be here the rest of my life" (Schmidt, 2008, p. 33). And years later this site is still his primary place of work.

The youthful guide tugged at my shirt and pulled me around the top of the circle to a northwest point on the circumference of the area. There he motioned for me to sit down. After a while, he pointed to a specific megalith, down and slightly to my left. My eyes struggled to focus in the bright sun and blowing dust, finally resting on an incredibly beautiful relief sculpture of a *fox*.

Not just a fox; rather, the Spirit of Fox.

To grasp the impact this living image had on me, return to my description of the black fox appearing to me on the Umpqua River at the edge of a golf course thousands of miles away. At the time fox visited me, I had no idea about traveling to Göbekli Tepe. Then, fox appeared to me again in the rain forest of Oregon when I sat by a waterfall on my 70th birthday. At that time I queried the dream/vision of fox, wondering what its presence meant. In the ensuing months dreams of fox cascaded my night times. Now, two and a half months later the energy of fox was jumping out at me from these 12,000-year-old monuments with such force as to take my breath away.

Coincidence, *archetype*, and *synchronicity* are inadequate words to describe my feeling at that moment. The meaning transfer moving between fox, mulberry tree, teenage boy, and myself lay within the inexpressibles of the Great Mother. I knew a profound shift was taking place within me, but I did not know what the meaning transfer within the eco-field was. I will reflect on that theme in a moment, but first let me continue with the story.

A few nights later, the four of us faculty members decided to go out to the archeological site at night for the experience of opening to shamanic packets of wisdom. Specifically, we wondered if the ancestors of the stones might be willing to make themselves known to us. When we arrived at the bottom of the potbelly hill, we discovered a closed gate. But, we noticed, there was a space between the iron gate and the fence.

Should we enter?

Common sense and even ethical directives said, "No."

Still, we decided to explore farther. Slipping through the gap we walked a short distance up the hill to a limestone shelf. For many reasons, including respect for the boundaries and our own well being, we decided to go no farther. That was a good idea because we later learned there was a large dog and a human guard with an AK-47 protecting the site. And rightly so. The treasures of this place need protecting, even from well-meaning folks like us.

Nevertheless, we decided to lie down on the limestone shelf where our ancient ancestors of Göbekli Tepe had reclined to prepare themselves to enter the holy shrine. Not far from where we were resting was the purification basin where the ancients held a cleansing ceremony before they entered the holy of holies, *the sanctum sanctorum* of fox and standing wave stones, as well as other sculptures alive with spiritual vitality.

As we lay on our backs, the desert night sky reached out to us, enfolding us. A shooting star blazed across the horizon. I thought of my relatives who lived in the same village with Tecumseh, the Shawnee Chief and Shaman. At his moment of birth a shooting star soared across the night sky, hence his name, Tecumseh, translated as *Panther-Across-the-Sky*. Star people abound. A profound connection beat in my heart between this sky, the sky of my primal ancestors in the old and new worlds.

Then, it happened. An information transfer.

Four.

That was all.

Four.

Like many eco-field packets: the immediate meaning escaped me then, as it does now as I write. In the car traveling on our return trip to Urfa, the four of us processed our various experiences. I told the group of my strong impression—four. Jim Garrison offered the possibility that *four* meant we have four years to make the great turning. That would put the human story at 2014.

Perhaps.

It would take time to divine the meaning. That, and the continuing mentorship of the night sky. The difference in the eco-field of the Göbekli desert night sky and the night skies in the Western Hemisphere startled me. The stars of that sky expanded my heart in ways I had never experienced. It seemed the Göbekli ancestors were speaking through the stars in this manner,

"Do you see why it all began here? This is the place of the garden story. This is where our tribes took a turn that led you current humans where you are today. We are here to assist you. Listen to us. Listen to our peaks and valleys—our successes and, most of all, our mistakes. Many advanced civilizations have come and gone at the very point where your civilization now stands."

Although my Earthwalk neared seventy years, these pivotal moments in the innards of the dig would lead me to questionthe very foundations of civilization's knowledge and my previous understanding of the human saga. Since this was the shamanic sky that inspired the visions of the Göbekli people, Abraham, and Jacob, its mentoring seems especially auspicious to fuel us on our ascending journey to see what my Göbekli-inspired questions uncover. Connecting our communities with all the ancestors, and particularly the Göbekli ancestors, provides the kind of shamanic power needed for an ascending birthing of a new era.

Proposal #3 of EFH2: Fuel for the Journey

The Göbekli narrative also prepares us contextually for Proposal #3 of EFH2. Fueled by such units of information I just described from beige and purple (using Beck's map colors but not his strict framework), we begin the ascent up the river of standing waves. This ascent is very different from the ascension promoted by the mystical traditions of Greece, Buddhism, Hinduism, Judaism, Christianity, and Islam.

Why?

Addressing that question will occupy much of the rest of this book, as I just hinted. First, though, let me review my proposal for fuel for the thrust upwards.

- *Proposal #3: This ascent moves with the power of the Primordial/shamanic as the fuel and energy for the tribal vessel.*

- *No community can ride up and down the currents of the river (spiraling as it is), given the Era of Natural Consequences, without high grade shamanic fuel.*

- *Without this fuel the community fades, loses its power, and dissipates in the face of fierce environmental pressure.*

The Strategy of the New Ascent

Look at our little vessel. We have described its qualities. We have confidence in its energy to move up the river. The shamanic fuel is taken from the Sun in the solar panels of community that hold and disseminate the new hydro-carbons. The vessel is set to pause at each standing wave and to allow the intermingling of downloads from each standing wave. In that canoe we all speak the Mother Tongue, but we also can speak the language of the particular standing wave. In these conversations we can select the best and healthiest from each wave and move onward and upward to a communal dialogue at the highest reaches of the river.

In the tension between language of the wild heart and all the other vernacular of the standing waves resides the potential for solutions which move us, I hope, to think of our time as the Era of Natural Birth. As we travel upward through the remaining six standing waves, the downloads from each eco-field (vMEME) will enter through a sub-self within the inner council of selves (Proposal #1). Interestingly, we have discovered through the decades of research in the Earthtribe that each of the standing waves has within it a Nature-based energy form that can enter the inner council through the wild heart that has been retrieved in the shamanic wave.

No matter where you travel, no matter the standing wave, the language of survival is spoken through trees, birds, water, and blue sky. Other energy components seek entry as we paddle through the waves as well, and they also enter through a corresponding aspect within the inner council.

The Ascending Current of the Stars

Before we embark on the next leg of the journey up the river beyond the shamans of Göbekli, the question of ascending the river returns to haunt me. I am clear about the power that pulls us down the river: the gravitational field. But, I know from experience that much energy is required to forge upstream. In the previous Göbekli narratives, I advance the notion that the stars themselves pull us up the river. At first, such a proposal seems preposterous, but return to the salmon's journey up the river I described earlier (Chapter Eleven). The scientific description for salmon is anadromous, a term derived from the Greek *anadromos, meaning running upward.*

The salmon offer us strong clues for running upward.

That they can smell and taste a river, even a particular pool in a river, has been scientifically substantiated. The salmon speak to us in the lost language where olfactory and taste syntax are crucial for the journey, but there is much more. How can taste and odor be the pivotal factors when sockeye salmon navigate thousands of miles of open ocean, far from specific river vernacular?

Speaking to this issue, recent research demonstrates that the fish are remarkably sensitive to and in tune with the Sun's azimuth and altitude. They combine this information from the Sun with the electromagnetic field not only to guide them but also to provide the impulse to move upriver and even to propel them headlong up multiple waterfalls.[2] In some ways the power of the stars with the salmon is more remarkable than the pull of the gravitational field when they headed down river on the descending current.

We know about gravity and its power, but now we can recover the language of the salmon and the stars themselves to make our returning ascent. Like the salmon, we have been afloat in a sea of chaos and like these fish, we too have the ability to find our way upward. We, too, possess in our cells the anadromous capacity. We too have the capacity to hear the voice of the electromagnetic field.

These lengthy comments conclude our movement through the shamanic wave (purple). Now, our vessel takes us to the next wave of development.

The Red Eco-field: Facing Aggression and Using Power

As we depart the shamanic era, the next standing wave we encounter on the ascending journey is the red eco-field, holder of the red vMEME (Beck, 2002). The red vMEME within the eco-field contains potential downloads of violence and aggression, but also—thank goodness—the inspiring archetype of the warrior.

The issue of violence and aggression jolts any student of human nature and is especially troublesome for those of us who value Nature-based communities. Let's cut through my words here and confront a bothersome question:

If the ancient expressions of the Mother Tongue are so pregnant with possibility, why are violence and aggression a prominent feature of the ancient peoples?

The idealism of Thoreau and other nature romantics seems to ignore the practice of violence and aggression in tribal peoples.

[2] www2.gi.alaska.edu/ScienceForum/ASF6/691.html

This romantic tendency shows up throughout my books as well. For a moment, then, I seek to open my eyes to the aggression present in the red wave. Integrity demands this opening.

Examples? What about the feminine based Minoans? Are they not an exception to this aggression? Much evidence supports a peaceful Minoan society; however, it must be confessed that "type A Minoan swords were the finest in all the Aegean" (Roebuck, 1998, p. 65). Was this so-called peaceful society the weapons manufacturer of the ancient world?

It would seem so.

When I visited the Knossos palace with a research and spiritual pilgrimage seminar, I noticed the prevalence of the double-edged hand-ax. This ax was the invention of an ancient Minoan culture rich in feminine spirituality and fluent in primal expression. Forerunner of modern weapons of mass destruction, this ax was revolutionary at the time because the warrior could slash as she swung in two directions, thus producing twice the mayhem. And many substantial Divine Feminine women today wear a symbol of this ax around their necks. Arguments among archeological scholars as to the extent of this Minoan warlike tendency continues, but the fierceness of the women warriors cannot be denied.

The same can be said concerning the indigenous peoples of the Great Plains of North America. I grew up in a culture greatly influenced by the Comanche; in fact, a distant uncle was a marginal protégé of renowned Comanche Chief, Quanah Parker, one of the most important of America's indigenous shamans. A great healer, Chief Quanah was also a fierce warrior, given to excesses of torture in conflicts outside the bounds of his tribe (Fehrenbach, 1974). The Comanche were astonishingly tender within their bands but merciless toward humans outside their own circles. A list of their torture techniques—many of which they learned from their civilized European invaders—cause any romantic view of hunters and gatherers to blush.

These starkly violent YouTube-like scenes from the red ecofield cannot be taken lightly or covered over with superficial spirituality. Rather, we must face this dimension within our inner council so as not to project our own violence onto the world. One of the principal causes of war is our inability to embrace our inner warriors with awareness. Since our own killer instinct is repressed in dominant culture, it is projected outside ourselves. The U.S. Congress, for example, inclines itself to make war, but projects its inner warrior onto the largely poor youth of our country and sends them to die. Because Congress does not own its shadow, it makes war.

But not just our Congress. We the people ignore our youthful warriors when we send them forth to kill and also when they return. The My Lai Massacre of Viet Nam and the recent massive killings in Iraq and Afghanistan reveal a distorted warrior. At this writing, eighteen combat vets per day commit suicide upon their return. Principally because we disown the red inside ourselves, we give no context for returning warriors. The returning warriors sense our disconnect from the meaning of war, and, therefore, our attempts at welcoming them back are hollow.

My colleague, Ed Tick, expresses the possible aware embracing of the warrior succinctly in his book, *War and the Soul.*

> Plains people had elaborate ceremonies for every aspect of the Warrior's life—war and peace, victory and defeat, leaving the village and returning, and special dances for other occasions. Among the Lakota, sacred dances included the Scalp Dance and the Dance of the Dead (2005, p. 137).

The ancient warrior communities, still fluent in the Mother Tongue, embraced the ceremonial practice of initiating young people into adult responsibility and identity through vision questing. Missing in post-modern vMEMES is the role of the elder in initiating the young person in bringing the warrior into the inner council.

The Role of Community in Transfers of Power

While ancient tribal ethics of compassion did not often extend beyond their circle to other tribes, the tribe did utilize the community as a container for aggression and violence. For example, I have written elsewhere extensively about the role of women in deciding when the Iroquois League went to war (Taegel, 2010). Typically, with Native Americans, the community was intimately involved in any decision about war and actively utilized ceremony in the integration of the war experience into the life of the community.

As Ed Tick (2005) points out, the tribe was intimately involved in any violence and war through dances and ceremony. The chiefs had to participate in the fighting because the tribe required it. (Compare this practice with our political leaders whose idea of going to war means watching the Super Bowl). The women and children often were near the lines of conflict, so the awareness of power, war, and aggression was fully in consciousness. It seems crucial that in many tribes the wisdom of females—creatures who give birth—would have a deciding voice for possible maiming and death.

In the Earthtribe we have sought to devote a monthly ceremonial practice aimed at bringing into our consciousness shadow aspects, including our anger, aggression, and violence. On occasion we have initiated young people into this practice; however, we have not been able to extend this practice to larger numbers of adolescents. This failure has been one of the many limitations of our experimental community thus far.

A hypothesis that has emerged out of our ceremonial practices over a 30-year period is that a major cause of war is unconsciously initiating young people into adulthood through going to war. According to the implications of EFH2, every generation in Western Civilization generates war to initiate its youth at an unconscious level.

The hypothesis continues: we will continue to go to war as long as we do not initiate our young people ceremonially into the aware embrace of anger, aggression, and violence. This integration of the warrior makes such a hypothesis possible, and we can pull its energy into our vessel as we continue up the river to the next standing wave.

Rules on the River: the Traditional (Blue) Eco-field Wave

The next wave we encounter I call the blue wave. Here are the headlines of this stage of our journey: the blue wave gives us rules for community living, beginning rationality, and then architecture. I warn you in advance that appreciating the blue wave is a challenge for me. As soon as I recognize a gift of this developmental phase, another question occurs to me. Keep in mind my bias as we splash into the blue of the wave.

Though it arose at different times around the planet, the traditional or blue dimension of the eco-fields emerged in the human story for Western humans circa 600 CE with Parmenides. Known generally among Greek scholars as a Pre-Socratic, Parmenides is more precisely described by Greek scholar, Raymond Moody (2010), as well grounded in the shamanic tradition. That Parmenides entitled his only known work as *On Nature* confirms his deep relationship with the cycles of the natural order, a key shamanic trait (Parmenides, Coxon, ed., 1986).

Here is how I see the structure of blue consciousness rising to the fore: Humans had developed survival skills, had developed shamanic abilities, and had unfolded the warrior value of "might makes right," an early expression of survival of the fittest. In order to take the next steps in the human journey, humans needed some form of more structured consciousness to harness both the primordial spirituality of the shaman and the instinctual aggression of the warrior. As a shaman on the cusp between the standing waves of red and blue, Parmenides opened himself to the push and pull of Spirit in moving to the next wave of human development.

The richness of his shamanic journeys is reflected in his poem, *On Nature*:

How the earth and the sun, and the moon,
And the ether common to all, and
The milk of the sky and the peak of Olympus,
Yea, and the fervent might of the stars
Were impelled into being.

Circling the earth with its wanderings,
A borrowed, a night gleaming splendor.

(Paremenides, Bakewell, Ed., 1907,
Davidson, trans. lines 130–134)

173

According to Moody (2010), Parmenides entered a shamanic state of intoxication with Nature and journeyed to other dimensions of reality where he encountered the goddess, Alethia, known as the divine holder of truth. At first glance Alethia's instructions on logic as given to Parmenides seemed innocent enough. Evidently the goddess gave him the foundations for the systematic study of inference and precise reasoning. These were the rules of the new game meant to manage the aggression of the warrior. Simple enough, right?

However, history turns on this one shamanic journey, the content of which would provide the basis of mathematics, science, semantics, philosophy, and computer science. In short, the goddess unfolded for humans a form of reasoning that would become the basis of Western Civilization.

What happens here?

A Divine Goddess gives us the basis for the overly rational patriarchy?

What powers and intentions are at work in this paradoxical download into the blue standing wave?

At this point in the story, there seems still to be a balance between the feminine principles inherent in the shamanic journey (purple) and the masculine rules of the game in logic (blue). The rationality provided a map for the deep spirituality of the shaman while at the same time inviting the warrior to the negotiating table.

"Come let us reason together, rather than fight."

But, then, something went terribly wrong with this gift of the goddess. An imbalance would occur and develop the severe patriarchy known as industrial civilization. Was this perversion of Parmenides' shining vision what the Göbekli elders saw as the final direction of their discovery of agriculture? Did the download of reasoning and questioning dominate the inner council so as to repress the sublime Mother Tongue?

Speaking of questions, here is a difficult one for progressive, Cultural Creatives: are bright blue fundamentalist Islamists and Christians calling our attention to the excesses of post-modernism? Do they sense, albeit often unconsciously, that something is dramatically flawed with dominant culture? Have we lost our discipline, intention, and persistence?

The Form and Flowering of the Axial Age

But I get slightly ahead of my story. Before we explore the ramifications of emergent rationality as a structure for primordial spirituality, I want to touch on physical architecture as a gift of the blue eco-field to hold the raw fires of the shaman and the aggression of the warrior. Let's set the stage for emergent architecture. What makes this period time—800 BCE–200 BCE—so pivotal? It is often called the *Axial Age* and marks the transition from archaic, to traditional, to modern in an astonishingly brief span (Beck, 2002; McEvilley, 2002).

At the fulcrum of this great turning (*axial*) in the human story is Dodona. Ancient Greek tradition considered the Oracle of Dodona to be among the oldest in antiquity (Herodotus, Godley, ed, 1920), and archeological excavations have confirmed that Dodona functioned from the Bronze Age (2600 BCE) to the end of the fourth century BCE (Hammon, 1986).

Raymond Moody (2010) holds that shamanic worshippers around the ancient oak tree of Dodona extend backward in time even farther into prehistory, perhaps to 4000 BCE. Worship took place in the open-air, around the sacred oak tree in which lived revelations of the god Zeus and the goddess Gaia (sometimes known as Dione).

The shamanic figures, *hypothites*, are known to scholars today as the priests of Zeus; however, their names in prehistory are unknown. They lived around the tree in this mountainous area, going barefooted year-round because they wanted to maintain their direct access to Earth (Easterling & Muir, 1985). Were they using the skin-to-Earth as a tuning device?

It appears so.

Newer scientists confirm this ancient wisdom by pointing out our lack of having our feet literally on the ground in industrial culture (Ober, Sinatra, & Zucker, 2010). Through our practice of being insulated from the grass, soil, and rocks with our rubber soled shoes and air-conditioned houses and offices, we are electron deficient. Much of our sickness, pain, and inflammation results from this estrangement. These newer scientists note this direct contact with dirt as a conductor of the electromagnetic field as Nature's original anti-inflammatory (p. 15).

The Dodona shamans interpreted divine will for the local tribes by listening to the rustling of the leaves of the massive tree and the flight of the wild rock doves that nested in its foliage (Herodotus, Godley, ed., 1920). In this shamanic standing wave the sojourners who came for healing camped out under the stars, and the shamans slept under the auspicious tree. The practice was prevalent in spite of the weather, which can be quite cold in this area of Greece, reaching zero at times.

Barefoot in the snow, the local healers plied their shamanic skills for all who journeyed to the great oak tree. As we consider such a site, we behold a shamanic, communal practice in full bloom around a sacred tree. These ancients seem at first glance to be primitive and uninformed by modern standards; yet, intuitively, they knew about electromagnetic downloads and inflammation.

So far, this Dodona narrative sets the stage for us to apprehend how the Axial Age moved the human story from the purple shaman and red warrior to the structured ruler.

The Blue Eco-Wave Manifests Architecture

From the beginning of the fourth century BCE, buildings began to be erected on the sacred site of Dodona as the people we call *Greek* replaced the indigenous people who walked in the snow. The first of the buildings was the Hiera Oikai, supposedly the residence of Zeus. The Greek builders also erected a temple for Gaia or Dione, as well as Herakles, Themis, and, not to be forgotten, the sensuous Aphrodite.

I suspect Aphrodite did not appreciate being crowded into a building, bereft of the sights and sounds of the outdoors, but, then, humans have a tendency not to discuss such matters with the gods. We tend to tell the gods what to do, and then call it their will. Put another way, we humans tend to ascertain what we think is best for

176

humans and try to impose our limited view on the eco-field. In the process, we often ignore the larger intelligence of the field.

After the Greeks took care of the gods by giving them shelter, they created monumental structures for themselves such as the theatre, the bouleutrion, the prytaneion, and the magnificent stadium. Soon the nature-based campsite that had served the indigenous people through the millennia around the oak tree became known as the sanctuary of Dodona, and the buildings became the focus of life by the end of the third century BCE. At that time Dodona gained a position as the preeminent cult-center of the Greek world. This important status was so noted by Plato in the *Phaedrus*:

> Socrates: They used to say, my friend, that the words of the oak in the holy place of Zeus at Dodona were the first prophetic utterances. The people at that time, not being so wise as you young folks, were content in their simplicity to hear an oak and rock...
> (Plato, Rowe, trans., 2005, p. 62, 275b5)

This conversation recreated by Plato occurred outside the city of Athens in the countryside, and Socrates seems to be inspired by the natural setting to recall the spirituality of the oak and its attendant shamans. Also notice Socrates' sarcasm as he poked fun at Plato and other students, and perhaps himself, for thinking they were more advanced than the Dodona shamans.

Or, can we take Socrates literally as poking fun at the simplicity of the shamans for listening to oak and rock? Was he assuming his dialogical methods were superior to listening to the rustling leaves? In either case this ominous bit of dialogue points us to consider a perilous direction for Western Civilization.

The Trans/Pre Fallacy: 2.0

Let me digress for a moment to the *trans/pre fallacy* which uncovers a modern pride in rationality, questioning, dialogue, and transcendence to the detriment of pre-writing wisdom. As earlier indicated, in the use of the phrase—trans/pre—I turn Wilber upside down. In doing so, I refer to this ever-present tendency in post-moderns (*trans*) to think we know more than the ancient speakers of the Mother Tongue (*pre*). That fallacy created a felon we call the Industrial Age, and we are currently experiencing its consequences through the literal trashing of our landscape, all the while holding tightly to our post-modern maps.

As scientists delve more deeply into the human story and its origins, the rich complexity of the soil out of which we current humans emerged stands out. No longer are we so cock-sure about a linear view of evolution. Take, for example, the research of a team of paleontologists lead by Louise Leakey and her mother Maeve Leakey. This team found two fossils in Kenya that have shaken the human family tree, rearranging major branches previously thought to be in a straight ancestral line to Homo Sapiens.[3] Scientists who dated and analyzed two specimens—a 1.4 million-year-old Homo Habilis and a 1.5 million-year-old Homo Erectus—reported that their findings challenge the conventional view that species evolved one after the other. Apparently, these two early ancestors lived side-by-side in Eastern Africa for a half a million years.

Underline 500,000 years.

That these two hominid species lived together for such a long period of time and yet retained their individuality raises many questions. Did the eco-field tell them something specific related to the larger story? Were they co-operative? Could they have been more advanced than we have thought in previous models? Does the size of the brain cover the vast arrays of intelligences? What mix of incubation occurs in the present day out of which will emerge still another species, perhaps Homo Universalis?

Such findings bring to mind an experience I had as a group of us studied the rock art found at the confluence of the Rio Grande and Pecos Rivers on the Texas and Mexico border. This outbreak of shamanic art may be the largest collection of shamanic art in the world, certainly the Western Hemisphere.[4] Compared with rock art in Europe, this rich window into the deep soul of ancient wisdom and its artistic language is little studied (Taegel, 2000).

[3] www.nytimes.com/2007/08/09/science/08cnd-fossil.html

[4] www.rockart.org/introduction.html

The usual scientific understanding of migration from Asia to North America posits a land bridge at about the 10,000 year mark. Humans poured across, goes the evolutionary story, and populated North America. That impulse of human migration no doubt happened, and that is why many Native Americans have Mongolian features, as depicted in Hollywood's movies. Simple and straight forward, right? Much like Wilber's view of spiritual development in humans: nature mysticism to deity mysticism to causal mysticism, to nondual mysticism. Straight lines. Little complexity.

Only, there is a fly in the ointment.

Anthropologists at the University of Texas uncovered remains of humans living near the Cave of the White Shaman. They reconstructed the skeletons and made representative statues of each. One, as you might expect, was short and had Mongolian features. The other, however, was tall and appeared to have European features.

Who were these people living among the transplanted Asians? Forerunners of the Pahana? The mythic stories of the Ahe-Che-Chay passed on to me say they originate outside current theories, influenced by the Stars, perhaps, as Plato suggested, from Atlantis or Lemuria. In any case, we confront another situation where very different forms live in an eco-field, as the ancient hominids did for 500,000 years. How did they communicate? I propose through a language of Mother Earth. And it is very possible that we have been through rich spirals of development, waves upon waves of deep communication forms waiting to be re-discovered.

My digression suggests that we cannot be as certain about our map as this blue wave indicates. Even so, this phase of the trip offers us many gifts.

The Gift of Architecture as Container

Our brief examination of Dodona reveals the architectural forms or containers provided by the ancient Greeks in the service of the profound spirituality of prehistoric peoples in that area. They meant well. Simply put, the Greeks took over from the prehistoric people, built magnificent buildings and came in from the weather. As we might say, "They had sense enough to come in out of the rain."

And, as the shamans became priests they put on shoes and moved the seekers into dormitories. Thus, the primary function of the blue standing wave is to provide structure and safety from the unpredictability of Nature, both in the form of logical thinking and brilliant architecture.

But are such developments advances? That is the crucial question I raise in the *trans/pre fallacy*. See: I can't help myself. I keep returning to the questioning state.

Certainly, we are moving up river in this blue standing wave, but the structures of logic and architecture also distance the human journey a few steps away from direct access of the rock, soil, and the oak tree. As we shall see and as all human history makes clear, the movement away from the Primordial in Nature can be dangerous to the welfare of the human species and to thousands of other species as well.

At this point, we might well ask, "Where did we in the human epic take a wrong turn? Or have we?"

The *conscious* use of architecture provides a progressive step, but notice the word *conscious* or aware. It appears the Greeks lost their fluency with the Mother as they acquired facility in the language of logic and architecture. Dominated by logic and material building, they misplaced their awareness, as have we.

How?

Estrangement from the oak tree, which speaks in the rustling oak leaves, occurs when buildings and logic become more important than the direct access to the mysteries felt under a blue Greek sky and the successor to the oak at Dodona.

Instead of listening to the rustling leaves and the waterfalls, we listen to the pale substitute called The Weather Channel, or even Plato's works. Or consider the apex of human architecture, which in my opinion is the Chartres Cathedral in France. Notice how that magnificent human architecture pales beside a simple waterfall in an old-growth forest. If you had one last moment on Earth, would you choose a crown-jewel of human architecture or a simple walk on the beach? Or a clear view of the night sky?

Another Gift of Blue: The Strange and Beautiful Nekromanteion

As we splash around in this eco-field standing wave, we must consider the Nekromanteion, perhaps the most important of the *oracles of the dead* as we ride our communal vessel from purple to red to blue. The *oracles of the dead* is a phrase Greeks used to describe the shamanic work of practitioners who called on the dead through various ceremonies to assist them in their current life (Moody, 2010; Olalla, 2002).

Notice the contrast of these ancient practices of calling on the dead while we in our dominant culture do everything possible to avoid the reality of death as part of the process. I call to mind the famous Lakota utterance of Sitting Bull: "Today is a good day to die." To our ancestral grandparents, death was a principal source of wisdom, essential syntax of the Mother Tongue.

At the base of the spiritual center at the Nekromanteion is a cave situated on a high hill completely surrounded by nearby wetlands with mountains on three sides. An hour's hike to the West is Ammoudia Bay. The mythically famous Acheron River, a central feature of Homer, flows by the Nekromanteion just to the east side of the complex and eventually into the bay.

The Nekromanteion site is significant for our discussion because it clearly illustrates the movements from standing wave to standing wave as humans flowed in their vessel from purple, to red, to blue standing waves. The cave was used by indigenous people as far back as 2500 BCE (Olalla, 2002). Just as they had with Dodona, the Greeks protruded out of the mists of prehistory in the 16th century BCE and obviously recognized the power of this place. They entered the cave and eventually shored up its leaking roof with massive stone arches. Upon entering the cave in the Fall of 2010, I experienced it as a hybrid between the indigenous peoples and the Greeks. Let me explain by taking you on a journey with me through the cave.

As I enter the cave, I notice the walls are rich limestone, wet with a dripping spring. The floor is uneven and treacherous to walk on as I proceed around several small pools. The cave, only about thirty feet in depth, appears much like any basic limestone indentation around the world.

However, as I look up toward the ceiling of the cave, I see the massive arches which give a Greek architectural feel as it unfolds out of the primordial spirituality into traditional architectural forms. You could say the ancient cave, perhaps 250 million years old, produced Greek architecture through the need the spiritual sojourners felt to provide support to their beloved place of dream incubation, much as miners provide support for a mining operation. The blue and purple eco-fields blend beautifully into the cave's ceiling.

So far so good.

The structures and architecture are, indeed, gifts, but I also must further point to the dark side of this wave with the coming of the Christians. They built a chapel on top of the cave. The Christians were bright blue and ignored the richness of the primal wisdom of the cave; indeed, they aimed at controlling the shamanic instinct since that raw power was perceived as an evil threat. Recall this urge to stamp out the primal at the previous site we considered, Dodona. The Christians migrated into the Dodona area, assessed the power of primordial, nature-based spirituality manifested in the oak tree, perceived it as a threat, and, voilá, cut down the oak tree down. This excessive repression would repeat itself time and again until, today, we arrive at our current state of planetary affairs.

In the instance of the Nikromanteion, the Christians built a monastery called Aygios Loannis Prodromos. Fortunately, the monks did not destroy the cave as had their fellow Christians the old growth oak tree at Dodona. Still, the general approach of the Christians to the Spirit of the Depths was to cover it over with stone and concrete and thus to banish the Mother's potential to the basement of unconsciousness.

The point I make here is that both Greek and Christian architecture impose their containers onto the fire of the primordial. I do not want to over-romanticize going barefoot in the snow to receive vibrations of Grandmother Earth. Who would not want relief from the cold? Plus, the temples and monasteries provided refuge from the intensity of weather. When we journey up the river in our vessel of community, we can retrieve the close connection with Earth shared by the pre-Socratics while at the same time maintaining sustainable architecture that offers us shelter. It is not an either/or situation. A shift to simplicity in architecture can assist in the renewal of the eco-fields, give us direct access to Earth, and offer protection from the powers of weather beings.

Having affirmed the usefulness found in the blue wave (and also explored its dark side), I turn now to examine more closely the cave associated not only with the Nekromanteion but with Plato's famous allegory. In one quantum leap, upstream we move, for the moment, through the blue wave to the orange wave.

CHAPTER SIXTEEN

A Surprise in Plato's Allegory of the Cave

Consider Plato's Allegory of the Cave as a powerful force bouncing us from the blue to the orange standing waves. Humans would not reach fully into the orange wave until 1859 CE with the discovery of petroleum and a few years later with Darwin's publication of *The Origin of the Species* (Darwin, 2009). Yet, Plato was the first impulse toward orange, and the wave would become so powerful that, today, it threatens to smash our human boat to smithereens. We are now on the dangerous downside of that wave as we careen into the Era of Natural Consequences, hoping it will turn into the Era of Natural Birth.

The Massive Standing Wave of Industrial Civilization

Let us pause in our journey to survey the roiling waters around us: namely, the dynamics of the wave. As we can readily perceive, the red, blue, and orange eco-fields dominate the planet today (Beck, 2002). Understanding these vMEMES within the eco-fields is crucial for our survival as we learn to speak the various wave languages. Cultural Creatives (green and higher) are a minority, and, though they are growing, they still are a faint voice (Ray & Ray, 2000).

This converging of the red, blue, orange, and green eco-fields constitutes the making of a powerful vortex, a perfect storm as it were. Here are the four main forces in these stormy waters:

- The Abrahamic religions with their extreme emphasis on transcendence and thus the denigration of the environment,
- Charles Darwin's focus on the survival of the fittest,
- The rise of capitalism, building on Darwin's mandate to compete,
- The Post-Socratic Greek emphasis on the primacy of rationality, dialogue, and transcendence.

Taken together these forces converge to create a perfect storm of the industrial culture and its fierce denial of the Spirit of the Depths.

And, surprise, the pivotal player is Plato.

Plato's Surprise

Let us begin with the basics of Plato's extended metaphor as recorded in *The Republic* (Plato, Rowe, trans., 2005). Picture a group of people chained to the walls of our cave. Behind them roars a fire, itself hidden by a small retaining wall. Attendants in the cave use puppets or cutouts to cast shadows on the front wall, something like a puppet show (Moody, 2010). Meanwhile, outside the Sun shines brightly. Those are the headlines of what many think constitute the seed which sprouted Western Civilization. If so, the allegory merits our close attention.

According to traditional Platonists, the shadows represent an illusionary reality while the imprisoned people live in ignorance, thinking the shadows are reality. Plato even proposes dragging the participants out into the Sun, against their will if necessary, to introduce them to the bright light of the Sun, his metaphor for Absolute, Pure Reason.

Here are main points of the allegory:

- The cave wall is the screen onto which humans project their illusory reality.

- Outside is the Sun, symbol of Absolute Reality, to be approached as Pure Reason.
- The process of approaching reality requires the practice of reasonable and questioning dialogue. (Plato, Bloom, ed., 1968, 514a–520a)

All of Western thought turns on this simple story. No wonder this Greek period of history merits the label *Axial*! We turn on this era in West Civilization like an axle in a truck. With wondrous and inspired writing, Plato—this muscled ex-wrestler—commits us all to the upward path away from the cave and to transcendence. Plato values the absolute and pushes off of the relative, all of the material world.

Move away from the shadows from dark to light, he argues.

And who can resist that invitation. It is alluring.

Still, this split of the material and spiritual hounds us to this very day.

Thinking of this parable, Thomas McEvilley, author of a defining book on the shape of ancient thought, calls Plato's split of human thinking: "*the original mistake*" (2002, p. 57).

Like the Abrahamic religions of Judaism, Christianity and Islam, as well as Buddhism and Hinduism, Plato powers away from the sacred in the cave (material world) itself, from Nature, and also from the human body (Cohen, 2006). I am aware minority mystics in these wisdom traditions are sometimes Nature-based and nondual, but they have had little influence on the mainstream of industrial culture.

But Plato?

His works still drive us in one direction: upward. In this case upward may mean our downfall if we do not learn to ride the descending waves. As is the case with most human creations, Platonic teachings are projections of the tensions we humans feel inside. Plato's cave allegory may well speak of his discomfort with his own sensuality, his own body, likely his own sexuality (Moody, 2010). Martin Heidegger, in his commentary on the cave allegory, underscores the primacy of rationality and discomfort with the sensual in Plato:

"The intellect is where truth has its essential locus" (Heidigger, 1998, p. 180).

Then Heidegger concludes his essay on the cave with the comment:

"The story recounted in the allegory of the cave provides a glimpse of what is really happening in the history of Western humanity…" (1998, p. 182).

And what *is* "really happening in the history of Western humanity?"

Directed primarily by this Platonic impulse, the Western mind would not for the next 2,500 years be at home in the cave, gateway to the Primordial. Indeed, Plato's estrangement from the Mother Tongue has condemned us to speaking the language of orange, detached rationality and repressed sensuality.

How does this perspective show up in our dominant culture?

In my thirty-five years of the practice of psychotherapy, a majority of the men in therapy had at the base of their symptoms an estrangement from sensual, intuitive, and felt reality. A large portion of women had symptoms closely related to their separation from the instinctual and the wild heart. Both sexes in general (though there are isolated exceptions) manifested difficulties in intimacy that resulted from the absence of shared intimacy with Nature. One observer has noted men spoke the language of Mars and women, Venus; indeed, the book on the subject sold seven million copies (Gray, 1992).

And neither sex speaks the Mother Tongue, at least not in the dominant culture. In that regard, we are all offspring of Plato for both good and ill. Before we examine in greater detail Plato's mistake, consider his enormous legacy.

Benefits of Plato's Legacy

Alfred North Whitehead wrote, "The safest general characterization of the European philosophical tradition is that it consists of a series of footnotes to Plato" (Whitehead, 1979, p. 39). That quote summarizes my proposal—our basic approach to life and reality in the Western Mind is shaped by Plato in general, and this cave allegory in particular. Most interpreters of Whitehead think he was being complimentary of Plato, and he was. But I see an inherent question in Whitehead's comment. First, however, let me note some of the benefits of Plato's story before I move on to expand my more basic point of his difficulty.

Plato rebelled against a culture that was steeped in Mother Earth immanence, and he rightly saw the need to move to the Sky, Transcendence. The possibility of balance lay within our human grasp at that juncture. Spiritual traditions adopted Plato's suggestion of transcendence and developed the Witnessing Presence, the capacity to stand apart from the process of the many selves of the inner council and witness them. We shall always be in Plato's debt for opening the door to that possibility. Robert Kegan's research tracked the development of this capacity to observe self all the way to the top of the river (1982). Briefly put, Kegan's research revealed this basic: to evolve you have to develop the capacity to observe your own process.

To find yourself, you need to transcend yourself.

In its best version, Plato's story of the cave opens the way for the transcending impulse to unfold, or as Jung put it, to *individuate* (Jung, 1981). Through Plato's brilliance we are able to move into the possibility of extracting ourselves from the enmeshment of much of the shamanic era and enter into active-self-observation (Kegan, 1982). Moreover, a sense of human individuality has issued directly from Plato. In many ways you could say that American and European culture embody this fascination with individual rights and the pursuit of happiness.

I personally am indebted to Plato, Whitehead, and numerous Platonic scholars for this rich sense of rationality and individuality. With Plato we learn to lean into the questions and to know that truth is truth pursued. For much of my philosophical life, I have sat reverently at the feet of this giant of antiquity, not willing to allow my questioning of his perspective to flower.

Until I visited the actual cave itself.

A Visit to Plato's Cave, the Nekromanteion

Walking up the hill toward the Nekromanteion in Northwest Greece, site of the cave, I felt a deep sense of gratitude for the structure of rationality present in the cave story, one of the most sublime descriptions of reality in all literature. We entered the gate supervised by the Greek government and proceeded to the path leading to the cave. At the beginning of the path and off to the left were the ruins of the dormitory where pilgrims seeking healing stayed, sometimes for several months. Several months? That kind of dedication to healing in itself is healing.

Next, we duplicated a ceremony of the ancients by throwing a rock over our shoulders, an effort at leaving behind our usual personality patterns. Then, we walked on a path that led around to the mouth of the cave, located on the East side of the garden-like Nekromanteion with the Acheron River flowing briskly alongside the path as background music. With the sound of the river in our ears, we crawled through a maze with our eyes closed to prepare us for the mysteries of the famous site. At last, we came to a very steep stairway that led down into the cave fifteen feet into the darkness.

The descent was profound.

A fellow sojourner tied a blindfold snugly on my head as I stepped slowly downward and felt each step with care. The cave floor seemed to welcome me, yet it was slippery as moisture seeped down the limestone walls and spread across the floor. Faint lighting provided only a little help. I moved to the edge of a pool of water and sat down to meditate. At first I followed Plato's guidance, concentrating on my shadow being cast on the front wall of the cave, along with the shadows of my fellow pilgrims from Wisdom University. As my eyes adjusted to ambient light, I beheld the infamous shadows as dangerous illusions that would eventually be my downfall. Soon, though, the shadows invited me to move toward them. Was I being seduced by the shadows?

My first move was to step toward the limestone walls off to my left. Cool to the touch, the rock invited friendly resonance. The pool of water in front of me acted as a mirror, and then drew me into its depths. Ancestors rising out of the pool were older, much older than Plato, and they beckoned me. If I was not deceiving myself, they invited me to stay in the cave, not flee.

After a time of meditating by staring into the watery depths, I focused my attention on the shadows on the front wall which were now just behind me as I turned toward the pool and the entrance. Dancing and moving, the shadows reached out with passionate arms. I felt comforted, and a question jumped into awareness. Were the shadows an allurement of illusion as Plato taught or full of hidden truth as the ancestral guidance from the pool of water suggested?

Then, my eyes rested on an aperture at the back wall of the cave where the shadows danced. The forbidden shadows, the seat of human problems, according to Plato, pranced across a crack in the wall. I hesitated. Buddha agreed with perceiving the shadows as illusions blocking enlightenment and as seeds of *samsara*, or suffering.

These two towering figures—Plato and Buddha!

Could they both be wrong? Or at least off base?

Slowly, I inched my way into the shadows and the crevice on the front wall. Moving even closer, I experienced the opening as a vagina, seat of Earth's intimacy. These innards of Earth drew me in, and I ran my palms over the cool surface of the 250-million-year-old rock.

Then, an astonishing filament of light appeared in the vagina. How could that be in this dark cave?

I followed the light upward until a tiny aperture in the ceiling revealed the blue sky of the morning flowing down and into this feminine receptacle. My heart opened and expanded. A numinous *élan vital* flowed through me. An eros moved like a snake up my spine and shot out the top of my head.

So this was what lay behind the dancing shadows. Not illusions of our own creating but rather the numinous connecting of the sky with the fertile depths of the cave. Something about this joining of light and rock brought together a healing—one where the Divine Feminine in the Cave mingled with the Sacred Possibility of the Masculine Sky.

At that precise moment something tectonic shifted in my way of knowing.

After a long while, I felt my way along the wall in the semi-darkness back to my meditation spot by the pool. New reality swirled in my head and heart. The stars were not only outside in the sky. They rose up out of the waters and the femininity of the cave. Again I asked until it became a questioning mantra: Could Plato have been only half-right? In his haste to bring balance through transcendence had he opened a door to an imbalance we have never quite corrected? Have we all been following this half- truth into oblivion?

Is it possible that embedded in the monumental achievement of Plato in introducing the rational paradigm lies the very dark shadow he sought to escape, the seeds of our possible destruction as a species? Could it be that the most destructive shadow or illusion is not those cast on the cave wall but rather in the impulse to escape the cave?

All I knew at that moment was this: my main attraction was to the fertility of Earth where Sky found its way into a sublime experience of tantric union and included me in the ecstasy.

This pivotal truth jumped out at me only when I moved into the shadows. If I had followed Plato's imperative to flee the cave, I would have reinforced the dramatic scripts of the dominant cultures of blue and orange. Unexpectedly, the shadows so threatening to Plato became the very source of my expanded awareness, so necessary for the evolution of myself and our culture.

Keep in mind that I am not speaking metaphorically when I refer to receiving a message from the cave. I refer to EFH2 where there is an actual meaning exchange between human and cave. The cave is alive and has its feelings and thoughts, not expressed in human language but in the Mother Tongue. This spectacular primordial utterance expands the story of wisdom, instead of imprisoning me as indicated by Plato's allegory.

Sit with me for a moment in the cave, legs crossed, staring into the dark. We do not know if our eyes are closed or open because of the pitch black, as dark as the darkest sweat lodge. Meld into the stillness. Minds, quiet. Incubate, and receive the pure utterance that arises out of the womb of Grandmother Earth. Relax into that place where a sliver of light from the roof of the cave finds its way into the dark and damp femininity.

*There the Sacred becomes mid-wife to birth us into an elegant
union of Earth and Sky.*

A Grieving Plato

How could Plato's philosophical approach so full of possibility lead
us so far astray? As I indicated earlier, Plato was a wrestler with
two gold medals won at the Greek Olympics (Moody, 2010). With
his athletic background Plato brought us both the metaphor and
the practice of intimate wrestling in conversation about what really
matters in life and death.

But then, Plato's story takes a dramatic turn. Besides his
ongoing wrestling with his sexual identity, his basic approach to
reality was greatly influenced by the death of his mentor, Socrates.
Mostly, he never moved beyond that grief. He was furious with
the poets and playwrights of Athens and blamed them for writing
exaggerations about Socrates that significantly contributed to Socrates' death (Moody, 2010). In *The Republic*, Plato actually calls
all poets liars and expels them from the Republic (2005, BK. 10). I
understand both his grief and his anger, and my heart reaches out
to him as I contemplate his loss. Yet, after my cave experience, I
could not avoid any longer challenging the direction his philosophy
took after Socrates' death.

In my view Plato's grief and anger moved him to ban figures
of speech from his search for truth. The young wrestler had been
a poet and a singer of songs. Under the influence of the shamanic
Parmenides, Plato had balanced sensitivity, intuition, and a love of
the woods with emergent reason. But apparently his broken heart
hardened him and covered over his intuitions and artistic feelings
with an impersonal rationalism.

Raymond Moody raises the question of whether Socrates and
Plato were lovers? Intimates as it were? If so, it might explain how
Plato shifted his philosophical approach in the midst of his grief. It
is one thing to lose your lover and another, your mentor. But to lose
both? Devastating!

He was never the same, nor was his philosophy. His insistence
on literal truth and antagonism for symbolic truth opened the door

for both fundamentalism and reductive scientism to flourish in our current culture. We shall see how his being knocked off balance eventually tilted Western Civilization in a distorted direction.

A final comment about Plato: he who banned symbolic figures of speech from his search for truth is best remembered for his famous allegory of the cave, with its bounty of extended metaphors and poetic images.

The Future of Industrial Culture and Its Religions

Before we guide our canoe up the river to the next standing orange wave, I want to comment briefly on the future of Platonic philosophy, the Abrahamic religions, Buddhism, and Hinduism. All have been crucial players in the sprouting of our industrial/informational culture.

What shall remain of these wisdom traditions as we navigate through these standing waves in the Era of Natural Birth? Institutional religions have become largely useless to address the current planetary crisis. On the other hand, the mystic traditions embedded within the various religions are a rich resource for our descending and ascending journey.

But wait.

Even these mystic traditions themselves are often estranged from the Soul of Nature. Teachers and leaders within the mystic remnants must themselves re-orient their traditions to the Sacred within the flow of the Primordial. They, like all of us, must re-learn the Mother Tongue. A new epistemology will have to be birthed within these traditional mystics. A third way of knowing will have to emerge if these traditions are to be viable. Here are three ways of knowing (epistemologies):

- The first way of knowing is the direct access of the heart within Nature, the shamanic.
- The second way of knowing is with the mind, including philosophical logic and science.
- The third way of knowing includes the first two, as we learn not only to speak the Mother Tongue but also to speak each language of the standing waves as we descend

and ascend. Central to the third way is the communal medium through which meaning transfers occur.

This emerging third/way epistemology points to the need for a discussion of a radical new ontology, a task beyond the scope of this book. However, I offer hints in the direction I think the discussion needs to proceed. Plato, Abraham, Buddha, Muhammad, and traditional Christianity all emphasize an often imbalanced transcendence in the form of a distaste for the sensual and material. The goal of all these approaches is to take us out of the cave toward Reason (Plato), or God (Abraham), or Nirvana (Buddha). The scales of balance have tipped heavily toward the ascending current.

A chasm separates God/Reason/Nirvana from the matters of Earth in these traditions, an ontological canyon. The Being of the Beyond (Sky, God, Reason) can be spanned by Nature-based practices familiar with primal syntax. Then, and only then, can a substantial nondual practice occur equal to the task of our era. Immanence needs to balance transcendence, moored by a language both deeper and higher than usual vernacular. Most of the traditions do engage immanence, but not in a direct access of untamed Nature.

Pause.

Maybe, I have been too harsh with Brother Plato and his subsequent students, even presumptuous. Let's explore the breadth and depth of this orange standing wave to discover if that is true.

CHAPTER SEVENTEEN

Aristotle, Einstein, and The Great Relative

Trust me, if for just a moment.

We are paddling for our life in this giant standing wave, the orange eco-field. This monstrous wave dominates the U.S.A., Europe, and Japan. India, Russia, and China are set to be inundated. Turkey and Brazil, too. We desperately need assistance as we flounder to understand the nature of waves as I employ them.

Field Guide Notes Concerning Standing Waves

As we paddle for our lives from wave to wave, it is worth noting that these standing waves merge into each other. Concerned with the human element in the wave, Beck notes that individuals of the above-mentioned nations are almost always a blend of wave functions. For example: in the industrial nations, 25% of humans reside in red/blue, 50% in orange, and 25% in the next wave green (Beck, 2006). It is also important to observe that each standing wave has its light and dark, its function and dysfunction, and its hindrance and possibility for our current planetary transition.

Human and More-Than-Human Elements in the Waves

A common confusion in reading Graves and Beck arises when the reader does not notice that *Spiral Dynamics* addresses exclusively human values and cultural intelligence. When powerful forces such as external conditions like climate crises are addressed, they are not treated explicitly as aspects of a larger intelligence.

In EFH2, it bears repeating, I state that the vMEMES are merely a small bubble in the wave. Most of the standing wave is more-than-human. At the other extreme, Farina attends almost entirely to more-than-human in eco-field waves and does not take into account the human factor (Farina, 2010). In EFH2 I seek to account for both human and more-than-human factors in the waves of development. The human vMEME remains an aspect of the eco-field wave, even if that meme is estranged from the remainder of the eco-field wave.

An eco-field, it will be recalled, is that region of influence within a locale seeking both balance and evolution no matter how disturbed is one or more aspects of that eco-field. For example, British Petroleum and the U.S. government are dysfunctional aspects of the orange vMEME as related to the Gulf of Mexico. Yet, they—indeed, we—are part and parcel of the interlocking eco-fields that constitute the Gulf of Mexico, no matter how destructive or constructive we are. An eco-field is not just a beautiful mountain meadow on a warm summer day, it also may contain a freeway system, a nuclear plant, an oil refinery, a hurricane, a tornado, a tsunami, or a drought.

As we proceed, a question emerges: since we humans create vMEMES and culture itself and since the cultural memes of Western Civilization have produced the current crisis, *are we as humans, toxic waste to be eliminated? Have we become extraneous pollution floating in the waves?*

With these field notes in hand, we return to paddling in order to address these questions by probing Aristotle's downloads as his water splashes into our vessel.

Aristotle's Break with the Academy and the Mother Tongue

Athens, 366 BCE

A handsome adolescent of seventeen years from the hinterlands of Greece applies to Plato's Academy and quickly becomes a favorite of his mentor, the founder of the Academy. Plato is so enamored with Aristotle's intelligence that he refers to him as the *brain* (Moody, 2010). At first, Aristotle revels in the sacred grove of olive trees in which the Academy is located.

The grove itself is steeped in the teeming expressions of landscape, having been a sacred point of power for local shamans since the Bronze Age. In fact, Plato had selected the site in the sacred grove for his learning center precisely because it was an enticing eco-field, an action that indicates he was not entirely bereft of Parmenides's shamanic influence. The word academy (*akademia*) itself derives from a Greek root word that refers to trees (Cherniss, 1945; Moody, 2010). No doubt Aristotle's early education includes the Mother Tongue, though the rationality of orange quickly obscures possible shamanic fluency, as we shall see.

After twenty years of study with Plato, Aristotle moves across the city of Athens to establish his own school, more centered in his maturing view of reality. Aristotle calls his school, *The Lyceum*, a term that denotes higher learning (Carnes, 1984). As his school develops, Aristotle becomes aware that something he learned at Plato's academy in the olive grove is missing. Something he cannot quite name.

Then, it dawns on him.

Aristotle's Return to the Cave

In his move across the city, Aristotle eventually yearns—in my view—to return to the primordial, the first cause of things. He seems to note the error of overemphasizing the transcendence of Absolute Rationality in Plato's work and aspires to integrate a particular thing (the cave eco-field) with the Universal *form* (the Sky in the cave allegory).

He writes in Books I and VI, *Metaphysics*:
First of all things was chaos made, and then
broad-breasted earth...and love, 'mid all the gods
pre-eminent which implies that among existing things
there must be from the first cause which will move
things and *bring them together.*
(McKenon, trans., 2001:4, 25-30)

Notice my italics, *bring them together.* Is he referring to the light outside the cave and the fertile uterus within? The eternal and the sacred sensual? Brought together?

Sadly, no.

The impulse of integration in Aristotle is there, but then his pilgrimage of learning takes a unique turn. Imagine him returning to the cave Plato fled in the name of enlightenment. Aristotle senses something is incomplete in his mentor's teaching. He sits in the same cave I visited and looks around. He views the shadows on the wall.

Are the rocks and water droplets aliens to enlightenment? Should he flee?

He thinks not. But what action will Aristotle take? Then, it occurs to him: he must use the skill of reason taught by Plato and observe the aspects of the cave, and, indeed, all the material world. And not only observe, but also *classify and define.* In that way he not only can learn more about the natural order, he also can introduce more control of nature for the human species. He writes:

It is clear how we must seek and define the 'what'
In the case of natural objects,
And also that it belongs to the student
Of nature
To study even soul
In a certain sense.
    (Metaphysics, McKeon, 2001:102a, 5)

Here we see the creative urge to bring together the two worlds, and in this impulse Aristotle opens the door to modern-day biology, even science itself (Moody, 2010). His way of relating to the cave is to develop deductive reasoning. Inductive reasoning (the scientific method) would flower centuries later, but all scientists who follow stand on Aristotle's broad shoulders (Kuhn, 1996). He employs these powerful tools of reason to observe, name, and classify the elements of the material world.

Pause for a moment and take in this tool of naming, a naming that will become a modern obsession, a compulsion of categorizing that squeezes the life out of the thing named. *All seemed to go well until we humans forgot that the thing named is not the thing-in-it-self.* Herein are the seeds of the forgetting of the Mother Tongue.

Need it be so?

Unlike Plato, Aristotle seeks to embrace particular things in the cave and elsewhere. He looks within *things* and sees the essence of the Universal. He descends to the lower regions of the river, perceives the soul of *things* and recognizes that essence in the cave is the same as essence in the sky. In this sense he anticipates a holographic Universe.

He leads us in a very encouraging direction, and there is more.

In his search in the cave Aristotle envisions an actualizing force he calls *entelecheia*, an early version of evolution whereby potentiality becomes an actuality (*Metaphysics*, McKeon, trans., 2001, 1048a, 30–35). In a flash of insight Aristotle has a vision:

The acorn becomes the oak, and a life force pushes and pulls this unfolding. There is in the acorn implicit oakness.

He anticipates the developmental research I cited earlier in scientists like Graves, Beck, Kegan, Gilligan, Houston, and Fowler, all of whom researched the various elements of standing waves. We will always be in Aristotle's debt for his return to the cave. Let us honor his accomplishments for a long moment by breathing it into our souls.

A few years ago I discovered a sculpture of Aristotle on the northwest corner of the Chartres Cathedral in France. There, I reflected on his deep wisdom and on his courage to return to the shadows of the caves. He opened the door for the flowering of the Chartrian masters and, later, for developmental scientists. The Chartrian masters recognized their debt to Aristotle, as do I. In a real sense he is the parent of biology, geology, and physics. That is the good news for Aristotle, and there is also not so good news.

Devastating, actually.

What you name, you tend to put in a box and think you comprehend. The seductive power of categorizing and specializing has run amok.

Is this misunderstanding of understanding the actual illusion?

Aristotle's building of rational systems, brilliant though they were, moved the human story farther and farther away from the mysterious and fertile uterus of the cave and the luminous connection with the sky through the tiny hole in the cave ceiling.

Aristotle turned the lights on in the cave, literally. "Let there be light," he said, "So I can observe, classify, and seek rational conclusions." In his zeal to name, classify, and deduce, he covered over shamanic enchantment. He began the long process of objectifying what humans study. He led the way in objectifying all creatures which in the shamanic era had been living entities full of power, life, and vibrance. Out of his brilliance was birthed a massive push to *deduce* and *reduce* to a rational framework. The deduction and reduction eventually squeezed the breath of life out of the Western mind. We lost our soul, as Jung would note centuries later (Jung, 2009). We became enmeshed in left-brain thinking and lost the gifts of right-brain creativity and intuition, the wonder of global thinking and artistry.

This reductionist approach pulsates at the heart of the orange eco-field. Humans who had once been fluent in the Mother Tongue traded mystery for certainty, a certainty that led to arrogance and dominance of 20th-century science. We who had dug our toes in the grass and felt the dappled light streaming through the olive grove on our backs now sat at a desk in front of a computer, until one day we could no longer recall the intuitions of mystery. The light of reason shone so brightly that the shaft of light emanating from the tiny hole in the ceiling of the cave could not be seen in its exquisite coitus with Mother Earth.

I read the above paragraph to Raymond Moody—recognized by many as one of our foremost Greek scholars—and he said little. The next day, however, he told me he had been up all night pondering my massive shift in epistemology. To this day the two of us have lively discussions about my framing of Plato's *original mistake, passed down through Aristotle to us.*

Where has this objectification and impersonal classification of Nature led us?

The Control of Nature

Skip through the centuries to Francis Bacon, the 17th-century philosopher and scientist. He extended what Aristotle began by proposing it was man's God-given right to "subdue, control, and exploit the natural world and every living creature. Bacon...established reason as the basis of true religion" (quoted in Lawlor, 1991, p. 19). Or in Bacon's primary source words: "Science... comprehending all things" (Bacon, 1859, p. 27).

Such statements became dangerous logs floating in the orange standing wave. Scientists, dripping in orange water, exuded a confidence they could know *the-thing-in-itself*, objectively and mechanistically. Everything in the cave became objects to be studied rather than living aspects with an interior and a capacity for the transfer of meaning, information, and primordial wisdom. If a plant, oil field, or forest out there is merely a thing, then there is open season for control and exploitation. Hence, our current situation: humans can do exactly what we please with the environment.

And we can do it without conscience—without conscience because we received philosophical and eventually scientific permission from the Greek Fathers, the Abrahamic religions, and 20th-century science.

Questions Float to the Surface

Within this stifling system of reductive rationality, beginning questions floated to the surface within the eco-field. As early as 1781, the great German philosopher, Immanuel Kant, who lived a century after Bacon, sensed something was terribly wrong. The confidence, even arrogance, of this reductive rationality did not touch his deepest essence. The process left him cold. Kant set forth a ringing criticism of pure reason in his seminal work, *The Critique of Pure Reason* (*Die Kritik Der Reinen Vernunft*), one of the most important works in all philosophy. Kant sought a new epistemology, an alternative to Aristotle's analytic way of knowing. You simply cannot know the thing-in-itself, *das ding an sich*, railed Kant (Guyer & Wood, trans., 1998).

You cannot be so certain.

Certainty is the parent of arrogance.

Looking inside himself, Kant pointed to the moral intuition of *I ought* as the most sure footing of knowledge. He was not speaking the Mother Tongue by any stretch of the imagination, but he was hearing the murmurs of Her voice. He descended the river until he could hear something deeper than reason. After Kant, a floodgate of questions roared down the river. But, once again, I get ahead of my story. I shall return to the questioning of Western rationality as the dominant force in our culture shortly.

Let us move now to the potential of orange rationality; I must not overlook the immense gifts of this orange wave. In many ways the flowering apex of orange rationality is Albert Einstein. In a powerful paradox of Nature herself the rationality of Western Civilization produced this man who would strike out at the very roots of the certainty of rationalism.

Had reductive science at last bent back on itself,

back, back, back

toward the Mother Tongue?

Einstein's Thought Experiments and Second Thoughts

At an early age Einstein engaged in pure thought experiments like riding a light beam or wondering why the sound in an approaching train was relative to where he was sitting (Einstein, 1940). He identified himself as a theoretical physicist and thus put himself in a direct line with Aristotle, Bacon, and modern science, but with a large difference. Einstein connected his experiments in pure reason with a deep intuitive sense, more basic than religion or current science, primordial in character.

His thought experiments would lead him—and eventually cutting edge science—to mystery and uncertainty.

Consider a conclusion he reached late in life:

> "The finest emotion of which we are capable is the *mystic emotion. Herein lies the germ of all art and science.* Anyone to whom this feeling is alien, who is no longer capable of wonderment and lives in a state of fear, is a dead man."
> (Einstein, 1954, p. 23)

Dead indeed!

His utterance pulsates with the Mother Tongue, especially when he notes that the germ of all art and science is not reason but a primal emotion, a wonderment, an enchantment. Basking in wonderment and living in awe lies at the heart of the inexpressible.

Look at the Theory of Relativity through goggles tinted with *mystic emotion* as we snorkel in the orange wave. Soon we gawk, slack-jawed at the wonder of relativity. Recall that the theory of relativity is birthed by a robust fire beside an alpine lake where Einstein and his friends swam after an eighteen-mile hike to Lake Thun in Switzerland, snowy peaks all around.

If you listen, you can almost hear the crackle of the fire they built after drying off from swimming in the icy lake. They camped for days above the city of Berne in retreat from urban work in the Swiss capitol. It was as if a prodigious magnet drew these young people together. When their discussions were "in full swing little else mattered" (Clark, 1995, p. 43).

In the language of EFH2, you could say the fire, lake, and alpine forest conspired to channel the Theory of Relativity through Einstein and his friends. They were part of an eco-field, an orange standing wave, at its best, offering a startling transmission that cracked open the arrogance of modern science by enlarging the story. Their new wine broke open the old wine skins.

The scientific world in which Einstein was reared maintained it had solved all of the major problems of the Universe. A leading physics professor had advised Einstein not to enter the field because the physics of the day believed that the Universe was a closed system and that science essentially knew everything that needed to be known. There were so few problems to be solved that the faculty member doubted Einstein would be able to find an original contribution for his doctoral dissertation (Isaacson, 2007).

So much for the arrogance of pure reason.

It is estimated that only about five people on the face of Earth understood relativity when it first burst forth through the eco-field in 1905, channeled through Einstein, and published in the scientific journal, *Annalen der Physik*. There were not many people who spoke both the language of science and the mysteries of the field. Einstein's former adviser was not one of the five. Those pilgrims of science who did speak these two baffling languages called 1905 the *Annus Mirabilis, the year of wonder.*

The Year of Wonder.

The year when scientific humans rediscovered wonder.

The year when the wall of scientific certitude cracked.

That said, the science of our dominant culture still speaks the reductive language, and we are *dead persons walking, living in a state of fear*, stated Einstein, until we regain the primal fluency of wonder and awe. When he moved to Princeton, Einstein rowed daily on a near-by lake to maintain his connection to the *mysterium tremendum.*

As a connector with mystery, Einstein represents the best of the orange standing wave. Bring him aboard our little canoe. We want to take him with us on our journey up the river. We will need him to help us sort out the chaos on our upward journey seeking coherence in disorder, if not certainty. Indeed, Einstein's axiom— you can't solve a problem with the level of thinking that produced it—is at the heart of our inquiry (Einstein, 1979). In some ways you could call Einstein a scientific shaman of the 20th century, though he might, like my mentor Bear Heart, desist in advertising himself by that name.

Yes, I love this man.

However, even though we want him aboard our communal vessel, we cannot overlook his shadow side. Our bushy-haired field guide opened the door, indeed encouraged, the creation of the A-bomb. Niels Bohr and Robert Oppenheimer, at the forefront of developing the bomb, were substantially influenced by Einstein in both science and politics. These seminal scientists all knew what they were doing. They hoped the A-bomb would end all wars; however, they also knew "the bomb would make it possible to end civilization," maybe even the human species (Bird & Sherwin, 2007, p. 274).

Shortly, after the bomb became a reality, Einstein realized that he had been a principle player in leading Western Civilization to the brink of destruction. He was horrified at what he and his colleagues had wrought. In November of 1954, just a few months before his death, Einstein lamented the use of his influence to forward the creation of the A-Bomb with his famous notation: "I made one great mistake in my life… when I signed the letter to President Roosevelt recommending that the atom bomb be made…" (Isaacson, 2007, p. 629).

As Einstein accompanies us in our vessel for our journey upward, we are forced to ask questions, not only of him, but of ourselves:

- Do we have enough courage to question the epistemology which stretches backward in time from Einstein to Bacon to DesCartes to Aristotle and Plato? An epistemological map that led us to the brink?

- Can we look with awareness at a fundamental flaw not only in Greek thought but in the Abrahamic religions?

- At the same time can we appreciate the contributions of this golden heritage within this standing wave and remain balanced so as not to tip over our canoe?

Einstein as The Great Relative

We move on.

1931, the Arizona desert

Einstein visits the Grand Canyon on a train trip across the United States. Along the way he stops to view this cavernous sculpture of river and wind, arguably the most awe-inspiring view on the planet. Predictably, he is deeply moved. He looks around as if to find someone who understands his primal feeling, the wonder he will write about some twenty years later.

Out of the corner of his eyes he detects movement, subtle at first but then more obvious. A little child moves close to him, an offspring of the Hopi nation, those people who above all else intuitively grasp the inherent wisdom of this landscape and, perhaps, of this awkward gentleman. Soon the child's family joins her to stand quietly by this sophisticated, European scientist with coarse eyebrows and twinkling eyes.

They notice something, a quality, an energy, in him. They do not know him but proceed with the guidance of the inner whispering of the Grandmother tongue. The shy girl reaches up and takes his little finger in her hand, and together they stand for a long while gazing, drinking in the scripture of Nature in an amazing array of purples, violets, red, blues, yellows, and turquoises dancing across sheer rock cliffs to snakelike whitewater below in the grandeur of the canyon. Before the sun has set over the lip of the canyon, the Hopi have adopted Einstein into their tribe.

They give him a tribal name.

The Great Relative.

A name pregnant with meaning.

They honor him, and more, much more. An elder, a shamanic figure, reaches out and gifts The Great Relative with a sacred pipe. Wrinkled faces, with hair cut straight across the forehead, beam, and then with brown hands the tribal elders gently place a bonnet of eagle feathers on his unruly hair. Suddenly, Einstein's ancient, bedouin blood quickens as his cellular memory recalls the desert winds of the wilderness of Ur, Abraham's home. Now, Einstein adjusts himself, still not speaking. He shifts his left hand to hold the sacred pipe over his heart while at the same time reaching down to grasp tenderly the tiny hand of the Hopi child.

Historians of the orange standing wave have not been kind to this treasured moment. With many modern-day academicians a cynicism and pessimism of reductive thought reign. His biographers are obviously uncomfortable with photos taken of the scientific icon's adoption into the Hopi tribe; indeed, many historians pass the ceremony off casually as a tourist moment, unimportant in the larger scheme of things (Sayen, 1985).

They miss the point.

I have spent considerable time with the pictures taken of those precious moments (Museum of New Mexico Photo Archives, 78.007). I am quite familiar with the Hopi ceremony of adoption and the Native American practice of gifting sacred pipes. For the most part, such a ceremony is not engaged in lightly, Hollywood and orange historians not withstanding.

Here we encounter the best and worst of our industrial culture. The Hopi recognize the Great Relative in Einstein, the purveyor of relativity. The historians, in typical orange fashion, reduce this sacred moment to a tourist attraction. Yet, Einstein himself disagrees with this minimizing, or so it seems with his thought some years later:

> A human being is part of the whole called by us
>> *universe*, a part limited in time and space.
>
> We experience ourselves, our thoughts and feelings
>> as something separate from the rest.
>> A kind of optical delusion of consciousness.
>
> Our task must be to free ourselves from the prison by
>> widening our circle of compassion to embrace all
>> living creatures,
>
> And the whole of nature in its beauty.[1]

Einstein's soul shines forth with the possibility inherent in this standing wave. He opens our eyes to Parmenides' gift from the

---

[1] www.thinkexist.com

goddess, Alethia, once again. Is this what she had in mind when she gifted Parmenides, the ancient philosopher/shaman, with the power of reason? Is this what Aristotle intuited as the essence of things but somehow lost? Is this the whole of nature in its holographic beauty? Is this what lies behind the shadows in Plato's cave? Is this beauty what we have been escaping for millennia in the name of liberation from the cave?

> We reach underneath the splash of this orange standing wave,
> past the A-bomb,
> past the reductive thinking of scientists and historians,
> past our imbalanced transcendence,
> and, with the Hopi child touch the little finger of The
> > Great Relative.

In that touching we propel toward the next wave.

CHAPTER EIGHTEEN

Toward the Green Wave

Our sturdy vessel of nature-based community carries us across the crest of the orange wave into a trough between waves. From the bottom of the trough, we look up and see the next wave, the green eco-field. We also can look over our shoulders at Aristotle and Einstein in the wave we just left. In looking backward we see not only disenchantment with reductive science but also other debris in that wave. Bobbing in the wave are orange capitalism, climate warming from profligate lifestyles, and the rape of forests and seas, not to mention Hula-Hoops, brown sugar water, and cigarettes.

At the bottom of the trough, we need to pause and offer thanks for humans who had enough courage to question the orange wave and open the way for us to journey upward and out of the devastation while also taking with us the marriage of sense and soul in Einstein and his like. Our story now takes us to an even deeper questioning of the wave we just left.

Existentialism's Courage to Question Reason

The seeds of discontent with Plato and Aristotle rose in the 17th century with Immanual Kant, as I mentioned earlier. Then, came Blaise Pascal who *blazed* a trail to tunnel underneath reason. As a sophomore in college, I was jolted by the words of my professor, Howard Slaate (1986), when he pointed me to Pascal's insights:

"...it takes more than reason for reason to be reasonable" (p. 61). Like Kant, Pascal railed against the tight system of Platonic reason:

"The heart has reasons that reason cannot know" (p. 64).

But Pascal's voice of discontent was one in the wilderness until Soren Kierkegaard (2008) surfed into the trough of the wave with his paradoxical existentialism, followed by the ontological existentialism of Heidegger (1949) and the personalistic existentialism of Berdyaev (1939). These dissenting voices reached profound proportions in the panentheistic existentialism of Paul Tillich (1963).

Now, we hear a chorus of voices, if not yet speaking for the Mother, then tuning into Her whispers to look for choice and intent. They insisted there is more to life and the Universe than the orderly, reasonable, impersonal and mechanistic.

"Wake up! Look!" They shout.

"There is a dimension of existence, both within the self and Nature Herself, that is best described as chaotic, irrational, unpredictable, downright nonsensical, uncertain, but also intensely relational," they rail over and over through various art forms. Nietzsche looked into Plato's objection to figurative truth in contrast to literal truth, and asked this question, "As we explore the difference between literal and figurative truth, are we exploring literally or figuratively?" (Moody, 2010) Logic, Nietzsche contended, bends until it breaks back on itself.

These existentialists yearned for access to a distant domain of mystery which lies beyond the reach of reasonable analysis. In the face of their life conditions, these revolutionaries demanded personal choice, integrity, and a leap of faith, one that stretched out beyond the confines of Platonic purity, order, and scientific reduction. In the confines of our reductive reason and industrial domination there is a "sickness unto death," an epidemic of despair and an estrangement from essence (Kierkegaard, 2008, p. 1). A virus, they further diagnose, eats away at the innards of Western Civilization.

For the most part they were not aware that their profound estrangement and accompanying despair were the result of the loss of the primal in Nature. They did not return us to the cave, but they could hear murmurs from the cave. They were distant children of the Primordial.

In 1981 I wrestled with my own existential despair as I realized I had lost my deepest voice in the long and sometimes barren training of becoming a psychotherapist. I wrote in my journal just before I began shamanic studies:

"Our human estrangement from Nature leads us to a profound estrangement from our human nature. Without Nature I cannot know my true nature. Without her I am lost in my own despair." The rational component of psychotherapy assisted but eventually crashed me into a solid ceiling and, in the rebound, a cement floor. I was trapped in my own narcissism, a condition of the orange and green vMEME.

Lost Voices in the Trough of the Wave

Return to Carol Gilligan and recall that she discovered in her research that females tend to lose their soul voices, their deep human essence, at about the age of nine (Gilligan, 1982). She further found in later research that young males lost their deeper voices before the age of five (Schnall, 2007). Hal and Sidra Stone (1989) stated brilliantly in their clinical research on voice dialogue that a variety of inner voices created by the dominant (orange) culture drown out the still small voice of the soul's unique intelligence. Robert Kegan noted a developmental path of the self that included learning to listen to the inner voices, and this listening, according to his research, requires a growing objectivity coupled with a deep subjective sensitivity (Kegan, 1982).

My training with the ancient tribal circle sent me on a search to retrieve my soul, my lost voice, a voice not generally available to usual psychotherapy. Carl Jung writes about a similar journey in his paradigm shattering work, *The Red Book* (2009):

Therefore the spirit of the depths
forced me to speak to my soul,
to call upon her as a living and
self-existing being.
　　I had to become aware that
I had lost my soul
　　　　(p. 232).

Like Jung, I intuitively knew my journey was a descent into the depths rather than climbing Jacob's ladder or fleeing the cave for the transcendence of Reason. Over a ten year period of tribal training, my essence began to shine through from time-to-time. Somewhat hesitantly, I wrote about the integration of this shamanic training with the field of psychotherapy.

In 1992, I received a telephone call from Theodore Roszak; he was researching a book and had read an article I had written for *Voices: The Art and Science of Psychotherapy*, entitled "*Nature-based Psychotherapy and Shamanic Training*" (Taegel, 1992). He also had just finished reading a book of mine, *The Many Colored Buffalo*, a treatise about the return to the council of voices (Taegel, 1990). As a historian of culture and the inventor of the sociological term *counterculture*, Roszak was convinced that my clinical research and the co-creation of the Earthtribe was part of a rumbling of the deeper voices within Earth Herself. His encouraging call awakened me to a widespread whispering of the Great Mother channeling herself in many different venues.

Later that year Roszak gave a title to his book, *The Voice of the Earth* (Roszak, 1992). He expanded, in ways that I had not thought of yet, the psychological voices of Gilligan, Kegan, and Stone and Stone. In the 1960s he had coined the term *the making of a counterculture*. He used that term to describe a massive movement, one that would become the green vMEME within an ecofield. Yet, he sensed something more in the early 1990s. The very psyche of Earth Herself was speaking to and through tiny gatherings of people around the globe. In that same year, 1992, Al Gore first published his growing concern about Earth's environment (Gore, 1992).

At that same time I began teaching in earnest about the planetary, environmental crisis. I sensed a deep disturbance in a global system I would later call the eco-fields. Working with denial about our ecological disaster became a natural extension of the Mother Earth spirituality I learned from the elders. Mother Earth had first spoken to me, as She did to many of you, through Rachel Carson in her monumental book, *The Silent Spring* (Carson, 1962). The Mother's voice through Carson jolted me:

"Man has lost the capacity to foresee and to forestall. He will end by destroying the earth" (p. iv.).

Carson's prophetic writing stung me at age twenty-two, but it would take three more decades for me to fully work through my own denial. The devastation of the eco-fields was just too overwhelming to confront. Just as families keep secrets about child- and spouse-abuse, so our culture continues to keep its secrets concerning environmental abuse. Even though we see the broken bones, the cuts, and the bruises, we make up convenient stories to avoid the reality. Nevertheless, the silence is being broken. Voices heard.

Early green and prophetic voices first pointed our attention to the abuse of racial minorities, then to women, then to sexual minorities, and, at last, to the more-than-human dimension of Earth, the eco-fields themselves. In that regard Roszak noticed Earth's voice murmuring through my work, and soon I heard brothers and sisters around the planet awakening, including trees, soils, rocks, grasses, birds, and mammals. By the turn of the century Paul Ray's research revealed more than 25% of the population in Europe, the U.S.A., and Japan were finding their cultural creative voices with special attention to the environment (Ray & Ray, 2000).

Cultural Creatives were being sensitized to eco-field abuse, and sensitivity would become our central trait in this new, green standing wave. Bring those values aboard to take with us upriver as we surf to the top of this standing wave.

General Systems Theory and Science

Einstein, as the Great Relative, along with the science that followed his breakthroughs, led indirectly to a new inquiry called general systems theory, linchpin of the green vMEME. In 1933, the brilliant biologist and observer of human behavior, Ludwig von Bertalanffy, postulated a general systems point of view, beginning with the human body as a "physico-chemical system" (Bertalanffy, 1933, p. 13).

Although still captivated by his reductive background, von Bertalanffy was—likely beyond his usual awareness and culturally influenced thinking—advocating a larger web of life, patterns that reveal a reality broader and deeper than the truth of an individual part.

Pinch yourself to wake up to the radical nature of this scientific proposal of systemic reality, one we take for granted in the age of cybernetics and the world-wide web. Three years after von Bertalanffy advanced his proposal, in 1936, Konrad Ruse built the first freely programmable computer, and green systems science was off and running.[1] Eventually the flow of the river would push us to ride this wave through the 1960s toward the flowering of the green wave in the era of the Internet.

It all started in the post-modern era with von Bertalanffy who noticed that the human body had a tendency toward healing itself, and in the servicing of that noticing, he coined the terms "teleological patterns and dysteleological patterns" (Bertalanffy, 1950). He argued that the human body was a systemic whole that tended toward health and, indeed, was pulled in that direction by a force he called *telos*.

Such a notion is warmed over shamanism and heated-up Aristotle who, you will remember, called the evolutionary force entelecheia, a power that pulls the essence of a thing toward being fully realized (Aristotle, McKeon, ed., 2001). An acorn is drawn by this force toward oakness. If an entity is not moving toward its

---

[1] htmlpress.net/the-history-of-web-design/

potential, then, von Bertalanffy said, it was not sick but *dysteleological, not moving to its end.*

At about the same time, the influential paleontologist and priest, Teilhard de Chardin—stimulated by his discovery of Peking Man—advanced the notion that the cosmos itself has a systemic impulse or surge of love moving toward its fulfillment, a notion that seemed clear to him as he pondered his scientific findings (de Chardin, 1959). Coupled with computer science, general systems theory offered a new understanding of human pathology as being dysteleological or inhibiting the surge toward health or wholeness. The healthy person was seen as allowing the *telos* or *enteleccheia* to flow freely through the system.

In this standing wave we take aboard a very important paradigm. If we hinder the surge of Spirit moving through the standing waves of the eco-fields, then we will be symptomatic and finally drowned in the turbulence of the standing waves. Our task, according to the best of the green standing wave, is to identify the surge, that force moving through the fields that is trying to happen. Once identified, if only partially, then we can align with the cosmic force, doing what we can to surf with its power through the waves.

Pause with me to offer gratitude for these scientific expressions of shamanism: the surge toward wholeness within the fields. This standing wave is so important for our time that I will explore my subjective movement through this green wave in the next chapter.

CHAPTER NINETEEN

From Psyche to System to Sensitivity

As a budding psychotherapist, I was introduced to the green stand-ing wave with the hypothesis that the action of transformation lies not primarily in the human psyche but in larger systems. Contrary to most psychological and even spiritual paradigms, I was taught that individual change without systemic attention would soon disappear into chaos, rigid patterns, or, likely, an oscillation between the two.

Carl Whitaker, one of the pioneers of family therapy, mentored me in treating individuals as actually a conglomerate of systems, set in the web of life (Kniskern & Neil, 1982). In Whitaker's model a per-son's internal structure is a reflection of an introjected family system, which itself reflects the external system of a given culture.

Like the existential philosophers who influenced him, Whitaker questioned the reductionism of Freud. He particularly transcended Freud's preoccupation with sexual repression and the unconscious as primarily a repository of unacceptable wishes. The unconscious, Whitaker taught me, was not a caldron of ene-my-hoarding pathology but a vast potential for healing and trans-formation extending far beyond the person and usual reason.

In 1973, I worked briefly as a co-therapist with Whitaker as we engaged highly disturbed family systems, usually with a patient identified by the system as schizophrenic. In one demonstration at a medical school in Texas, he took me aside and explained that we could change the whole system, including the patient, by entering the depth of the unconscious system with the courage to face our own disturbances.

I did not have a clue as to what he meant.

I was accustomed to thinking of the unconscious as a domain entered through dreams or free association. How else could you enter it?

I would soon see.

On a typically warm and humid Houston day, we interviewed a family with an audience of twenty therapists-in-training, viewing by closed circuit television. Soon after we entered the treatment room—as I recall forty years later—Dr. Whitaker went to sleep. I looked at the family; they looked at me.

I was horrified.

The family itself and the professionals at the medical school joined me in judgement and indignation. Presently, Whitaker woke up. When the father in the family protested and asked Whitaker why he went to sleep, my erstwhile mentor replied, "Your family is so grooved in making your son sick that you are boring and predictable in your shoveling all your own craziness toward him. Your son is predictably unpredictable. So, I decided to take a little nap."

We all blinked. Was this family therapist crazy himself—or brilliant?

Whitaker then continued to share the results of a dream/vision he had while on his hypnogogic nap. I don't recall the content of what he said, but I vividly remember the profound quality of his awareness and the palpability of his compassion.

The family was entranced, especially the father, whose anger was transformed into respect in the face of Whitaker's authenticity. The truth Whitaker communicated was confronting, but his words came from a whimsical and compassionate place. What was this intervention? I pondered: Whitaker's dream/vision of the family constellation was not an access to his own counter-transference and repressed sexuality (Freud) or a dip into the collective and symbolic unconscious (Jung). It was something else all together.

In retrospect here is how I hold his intervention: *Whitaker was swimming in the waters of the repressed system of this particular family as part of a very local eco-field. Only, to paraphrase Jung, he was not drowning in the waters of the system as was the family.* He had complete confidence in the underlying intelligence of the system to heal itself when the therapist pointed to what was not being said or done in the field. Somehow he knew how to surf in the same waters in which the family was gasping for air.

Young as I was, I was entranced and quickly planned how to take my own naps. Whitaker sensed this in me and offered firm instructions, "Don't follow my path. You're too young to nap. Follow your own currents."

Through Whitaker and others my psychotherapeutic training introduced me to the green eco-field, one that accesses reality first-and-foremost systemically. Whitaker entered not only his own personal unconscious (orange) but, most importantly, a systemic field (green) that included the unconscious domain of the family system, as well as the eco-system of the medical school and the professional organization sponsoring him. The target of therapy was the system, not the individual. Even so, Whitaker did not venture outside the confines of his office to include the-more-than-human in the eco-field. Such a daring move came through a friend of his, Milton H. Erickson.

The Therapy of the Mountain

Whitaker introduced me to the work of Erickson, whom he called "the best therapist of the 20th century." Erickson, he told me, was a "modern day medicine man" (Whitaker, professional communication, 1973). An unorthodox psychiatrist, Erickson practiced informally out of his home in Phoenix, Arizona, and he often gave assignments to clients that ushered them outdoors (Erickson, 1979). He frequently asked clients to journey to near-by Camelback Mountain, which was a radical intervention indeed for the sometimes stodgy profession of psychiatry.

Erickson knew that the mountain was used by the Hohokam culture as a sacred site for vision quests, and he enlisted the mountain as a co-therapist. Erickson often used two trails for his clients on Camelback Mountain which were about two miles one-way in length and ascended 1,200 feet. The hiking path consisted of gravel, boulders, and some handrail-assisted sections. The trek required hikers to spend from one and a half to three hours of hiking time, depending on the physical shape of the hikers and the distance they chose.

In one case I recall, Erickson gave a married couple the vague assignment of hiking the mountain trails. When they returned to his office, he asked them who took the lead? Who lagged behind? What did they see? How did they assist each other? How did the ascent differ from the descent? (The descent was almost always more difficult.) Did the mountain itself say anything about their relationship? Since Erickson had two cases of polio over his lifetime and was limited to a wheelchair, he also benefited from the nature-based stories of his clients as they brought the outdoors to him.

My point here is not to explore Erickson's therapy techniques—brilliant and fascinating though they were—but to note how Erickson extended the domain of therapy out of the office (and the orange paradigm of the couch) into direct access of what I now call the eco-field.

Coupled with my shamanic training this approach to psychotherapy took me far outside the box of traditional therapeutic endeavors. Whitaker expanded my work into the systemic field of the family, and then Erickson guided me to treatment beyond air-conditioned space and showed me a vast consciousness in the more-than-human in Nature-near-by. Erickson also taught me reciprocity in the healing process through noticing his clients brought the wonders of nature to him. Such are the powerful information transfers from the green standing wave. The integration of Erickson's influence with my shamanic training laid the foundations for EFH2 where, in the quantum world, there is a reciprocity between the so-called objective scientist and the collapse of the wave-particle continuum.

Shamanic or Nature-based Psychotherapy

I fused Erickson's guidance and inspiration with the shamanic wisdom of Bear Heart and the tribal circle in the early 1980s. By 1990, the download splashes from the green eco-field provided me with enough information, if not wisdom, to propose a bold integration of psychotherapy and shamanism. I wrote in book form:

> As the transformative process picks up steam, therapists and clients reach another boundary. When clients cross this boundary, they see that the process is not just *psychotherapy but a transforming process*. It is evolution itself and reaches through all life, through death, and beyond. (Taegel, 1990, p. 126)

And, then I crossed a Rubicon in my thinking by suggesting a new term for my work:

> Crucial to the process is the bifocal emphasis of psychotherapist and shaman who combine to form a powerful *ecology therapy*. The synergy of these two currents of energy provides powerful impetus to the seeker (Taegel, p. 126).

So far as I know, that phrase—*ecology therapy*—was the first attempt in my profession to integrate ecological systems and psychotherapy. In 1992 Clarissa Pinkola Estes wrote *Women Who Run With The Wolves*, a work that was on the *New York Times* best seller list for 145 weeks and that pulled the wild into psychological discussion. Two years later Howard Clinebell (1994) expanded the proposal into a book called *Ecotherapy*, a model rich in green downloads but which stopped short of drawing on shamanic training. At the turn of the millennium, I wrote *Natural Mystics: Journey Toward Your True Identity*, in which I introduced a form of psychotherapy called *ecodrama* (Taegel, 2000). Bill Plotkin followed in 2003 with *Soulcraft: Crossing Into the Mysteries of Nature and Psyche*, a brilliant advance in the integration of psychology and the eco-field.

Landscape as Foreground

Slowly, the power of landscape dawned on me. Early on, I thought the ceremonies were the conduit, and they were to a certain extent. But first and foremost the field of energy in a specific locale infused healing when a balance between humans and more-than-humans occurred. Increasingly, I saw the wilder dimensions of the eco-fields as my co-therapist. My task as a therapist was to open the doors between the immediate surroundings and the humans in my care.

My aspiration—and eventually my intention—became the balancing of estranged humans with their eco-fields. Through hundreds of clinical hours I was convinced; intimacy with the more-than-humans heals humans and perhaps the eco-field itself.

About that time, I was asked to guest edit *Voices: The Art and Science of Psychotherapy* in an issue entitled, "Psychotherapist and Shaman" (Taegel, 1992). In the introduction (p. 2) to that issue, I wrote:

> A central hypothesis to my work and this issue of *Voices* suggests strongly that a *sacred place* is needed to facilitate creativity, healing, and balance, a place where the vortexes of natural energy swirl and draw the individual into dimensions of reality different from the ordinary, a place that offers pathways between, and, in short, a *place* beyond the psychotherapy office that allows the ego to stretch between realities so that new awarenesses birth themselves.

Increasingly, place, surrounding landscape, and quantum fields shaped my approach to reality.

Sensitivity: The Highest Value of the Green Eco-field

And, indeed, the role of landscape and surroundings became the focus of my unfolding map of psychotherapy. The treatment became sensitivity to the-more-than-human. Awareness, awakened through sensual and sensitive connection to the eco-field, opened doors for relief from modern anxiety, depression, and addiction. Creative interventions arose naturally and spawned expanded awareness based on beginning a learning community utilizing a new psycho-spiritual textbook written in the Mother Tongue.

The cure for mental illness? Intimacy in the Eco-field.

The Shadow Side of the Green Eco-field

So far so good in the green standing wave, but now the green wave splashes us with cold water and debris. In the years of having a center of gravity in green, a I-must-be-right self grabbed my inner microphone time and again. Even in writing this book, I re-read and sense an occasional tone of self-righteousness, bordering on arrogance. At times, there is a strong us-against-them dimension in my story. The green movement is laced with this rampant holier-than-thou attitude and led me to make pronouncements about a variety of subjects, including climate warming where I was quick to point out people who lived in denial of our planetary vulnerability. This attitude of I-have-the-answer is viral in the green wave. Were it not for my spouse, Judith, I might have remained ensconced therein. She opened the door for the next waves and quantum leaps by building bridges toward other wisdom systems like mystical Islam, Rumi, and Creation Spirituality.

Besides a tendency toward political correctness and self-righteousness there is in the green wave what I call *the horizontal trap* (Chapter Three). As we tumble in our vessel into the next trough there exists a whirlpool, a treacherous sucking motion. If we are not careful, we will see our ascent completely thwarted by these swirling waters.

A beautiful practice of this wave is to listen to all points of view. The trap lies in the tendency to think all points-of-view carry equal weight. For example, there is a qualitative or vertical difference between Hitler's rants and Gandhi's sermons. Yet the green standing wave has trouble noting the distinction because it has twisted itself into the pretzel of a radical democracy. Here we encounter in this green wave a strange mixture of self-righteousness while, at the same time, claiming equality of all points-of-view.

Go back to the fire at Deer Dancer Ranch. By the time of the fire, I had learned to engage a leadership based on competency, not necessarily green consensus. As we approached the fire, we listened to police and fire professionals in our tribe who had first-responder training. We did not stop, listen to every perspective, reach consensus before we acted. We had spent enough time in the horizontal prison to know when consensus does not work.

When our communal vessel escapes the horizontal trap, a whirlpool of the green standing wave, we then prepare ourselves for a quantum leap to the 2nd Tier.

CHAPTER TWENTY

Field Notes on the Quantum Leap

Like salmon journeying up the river of their birthplace, we ride the ascending current and reach a steep grade requiring much of us—a large waterfall higher than any faced thus far. How can we reach the next level? Perhaps, we can jump like our relatives, the salmon, or take the canoe of our communal vessel out of the water and portage to the next level. In any case, Clare W. Graves (1971) was right: a quantum leap to the 2nd Tier of evolution is required.

Punctuated Equilibrium

Speaking to this issue of the quantum leap is a theory of evolution: punctuated equilibrium. As stated in geological circles, the theory proposes that the fossil record unfolded in fits and starts rather than in a steady process of slow change (Heylighen, 1997). One source states that punctuated equilibrium is "the theory that organisms just appear out-of-nowhere on Earth." That definition may be or may not be overstated, but Graves (1971) was certainly surprised when individuals who saw reality in a very different way showed up in his research, as if they appeared on Earth out of nowhere.

Widespread research has continued, and the difference in the first six eco-fields (standing waves) and the next two in our ascent is startling enough that it seems the people whose center of gravity rests on the 2nd Tier (yellow and turquoise) do come from a different reality, if not a different star system (Beck, 2002; Fowler, 1981; Gilligan, 1982; Houston, 1987; Lovinger, 1977; McIntosh, 2007). Let us explore a bit on this upper level to see what it is like by peering into the unfolding world of quantum fields.

The Great Relative As Reluctant Field Guide

Earlier (Chapter 18), I referred to Einstein's adoption into the Hopi Nation and their gifting of a sacred pipe to this sometimes 2nd Tier scientist/field guide. Return to the photo of that moment. See him with a headdress of eagle feathers, a pipe in one hand, and a small Hopi child in the other. Hear his tribally gifted name uttered by elders, *The Great Relative*. In this pregnant instant, Einstein is a walker in two worlds: the shamanic and the newer science.

Einstein's two theories of relativity appeared as if from a star nation—punctuated equilibrium *par excellence*. Historians estimate that only a handful of scientists on the planet at the time understood his theories when they emerged in the human conversation at the turn of the 20th century (Issacson, 2007). Princeton wanted to give Einstein an honorary doctorate for his discoveries, but they had a requirement that even honorary doctoral candidates needed to pass an oral exam. The problem in their process was this: no one knew enough about relativity to examine Einstein. He was one of the first humans to quantum jump up the waterfall and then to speak in the Mother Tongue of relativity.

But Einstein himself did not understand the implications of this download from the eco-field. Parmenides received the gift of deductive thinking from the goddess Alethia on a shamanic journey. Einstein too received a gift from the unseen domain of the eco-field in the form of relativity. Though Einstein held the gift in his hands, it burned him like a hot potato. Earlier (Chapter 18) I noted that Einstein and several of his friends hiked miles into the high mountains outside Bern, Switzerland. Calling themselves the Olympia Academy, they plunged deep into the glacial lake, emerged from the swim, and built a roaring fire. Sitting in a circle they discussed the growing edge of human wisdom and eventually sprouted the basics of relativity.

It bears repeating that the mountain, the lake, and the fire imparted this newer science to the world through Einstein and the Olympia Academy. It is well known that it was a group project with his soon-to-be spouse, Elsa, being the chief mathematician. Also, we cannot overlook the influence of the eco-field as a giver of relativity through The Great Relative. Let us bestow credit on Einstein and at the same time recognize that he had not a clue as to the ramifications of relativity for revealing a new reality of the Mother Tongue, destined to become a syntax of the 2nd Tier.

What Einstein saw when he stepped through the door of relativity shocked him. So much so that he spent a good part of his adult life backtracking. But the toothpaste was out of the tube. The quantum reality Einstein uncovered was ornate, and yet can be described simply like this:

Reality is not as it appears to the rational mind.

In this micro-world of quantum fields, we enter a theater of exploration so outside our usual rational mind—and certainly the common sense of the first six standing waves—that it jolts us into disbelief. In short, the quantum fields reveal the end of human certainty. Life above the waterfall is lived without certainty.

No wonder Einstein (1979) shook his head, stating that the quantum world looked like God playing dice with the Universe. What did Einstein see once he leapt up the waterfall to the 2nd Tier that baffled him and filled him with unease? What was now set loose in the eco-field as anathema to the rational mind of Plato and Aristotle?

Particle Accelerators Reveal The Universe's Building Block

Once Einstein opened the door, young scientists rushed into the new domain searching for the building blocks of the Universe. They dared go where Einstein hesitated. They splashed in the waters above the waterfall. At first, they hypothesized the foundation of the Universe would be a microscopic ball bearing on which all the Universe rolled along like a machine in steady state of perfect equilibrium.

They were spectacularly wrong.

Let us see what they discovered instead and the direction they traveled.

1930. Cambridge, England

Two post-relativity scientists, Cockcroft and Walton used a crude transformer of 200 kilovolts to accelerate protons down an evacuated tube eight feet long as a way to view the micro-eco-field of sub-atomic particles. What they found was not a *thing* but an *event*, or more accurately, an oscillation where it appeared that particles disappeared into thin air at a certain speed. More experiments were needed. If what they were seeing was accurate, the Universe could not be accurately described as a *tiny noun or even as a collection of things* as science to that point had thought. A whole new picture unfolded for them.

They were seeing a Universe that was a web of verbs.

Yet, they asked, Could a Universe of verbs be really real?

It would take 2nd Tier thinking to explore such a possibility.

Two years later, 1932, enter Earnest Lawrence, a science *nerd* from South Dakota, who earned his Ph.D. from Yale in physics. He expanded the Cambridge experiments and subsequently drew a design of a crude accelerator on a scrap of paper, soon noting that such an accelerator would become too long and unwieldy for his laboratory. Plus, he needed a power supply much greater than usual electricity to acquire the speed he needed in order to gain more information about the quantum world.

Brilliantly, he decided to set a circular accelerating chamber between the poles of an electromagnet. The EM field held the charged proton particles in a spiral path that looked suspiciously like a labyrinth seen on the floor at the Cathedral in Chartres, or maybe the Nazca Lines in Peru or even the crop circles in England depicting a torus. The first circular accelerator Lawrence built was small enough to lift with one hand and cost $25 in material from the local hardware store to construct. His invention progressed rapidly.

By 1939 Lawrence had built a cyclotron atom-smasher which hurled particles near the speed of light, for which he received the Nobel prize in science. Here is how it worked. The magnets produced a circular magnetic field propelling the particles on a circuit. As the particles moved faster, the radius of their circular path became larger and larger until they hit the target at the outermost circle of the labyrinth.

Today, the largest of these accelerators, called the Large Hadron Collider (LHC), is near Geneva, Switzerland. It lies 574′ below the surface with a circumference of 17 miles. (Now, that is a large labyrinth.) Here is a glimpse of what these particle accelerators reveal to us in the quantum fields.

Glimpses of the Two Worlds

A new picture of reality emerged in the quantum fields. At near the speed of light the accelerated particles disappeared into the domain of waves. More accurately, the young scientists gazed upon a wave/particle continuum, revealing a layer of the world where you behold a wave form of potential particles which have the probability of collapsing into a system of particles in material form.

In short, they discovered two worlds interacting with each other.

Whew! No wonder Einstein was reluctant to believe what he saw, even when he insisted on being present at key experiments. As an aside in the story, let us not be too hard on Einstein. As reality unfolds before us on the 2nd Tier, most of us shrink from startling truth above the waterfall, whether in the newer sciences or otherwise. Mostly, we prefer to return to our own patterns of thinking and behaving, familiar as they are.

At this point in our journey we realize that the higher we go on the river, the more it begins to look like the lower regions. Somehow, with 21st-century science we bend back on ourselves and behold a new shamanic reality. Let's continue that theme for a moment.

Currently, I am exploring only one small dimension of the 2nd Tier in the form of quantum fields. It is more than most of us can digest easily, and I have not even raised the tantalizing questions that a younger physicist, Nassim Haramein, has brought into the discussion. When Haramein follows the tiny dots from atoms to particles, to quarks, to the wave/particle continuum, he proposes an infinity of dots all of which contain diminutive black holes. Infinite density becomes a black hole, one through which the shaman can travel.

But let us return to this remarkable 2nd Tier story.

The Field Guide As Tracker of Shape Shifting

In a classic experiment performed by Max Born with electron waves, the question of the role and influence of the human experimenter arose. Born explored where the experimenter was likely to find an electron wave collapsing into a specific electron particle or system of particles. More precisely, the question emerged: where in the flow of electron waves is a collapse into the material world likely to happen? And what influence does the experimenter have on the experiment?

After numerous experiments, which I will not detail here, a provisional answer emerged for these detective-like scientists. They tracked shapes of waves, and the steep wave shapes indicated where the collapse of the wave into particle was likely to happen. The gentle, evenly flowing waves did not hold the potential for moving from one world to another. On the other hand, steep amplitude in the waves possessed probability of collapse of wave into particle.

Pause for a moment in the story and gaze down the river to the shamanic era, far below the waterfall. Do we not see the shape-shifter shaman in the 2nd Tier scientist? Do we not see the ancient ones in steep and disturbed waves waiting to collapse into other worlds? Is it not possible that these ancient wise people already knew on an intuitive level what we are now discovering in explicit scientific language? Is the arc of human wisdom now bending back toward what we already know? Considering these questions, let us continue.

The story becomes even stranger to our rational ears.

A Collapse Of Waves Leads To The Material World

Let us perform a thought experiment to assist us in understanding this very important syntax of the Mother Tongue, this lingo where shaman and scientist meet in shuttling between worlds. Imagine you are in a helicopter hovering above a freeway in a typical city searching for a place in the flow of traffic where a crash is likely to occur. As the cars flow along the freeway, you see the cars getting closer and closer together, until they appear almost as discrete packets.

Then, you notice a strange creature standing at the edge of the freeway—say, a white buffalo. No wonder the cars slow down like blood coagulating as they stare intently at the out-of-place creature. In such a bottleneck, the probability of a crash is much more likely to occur than out in the country where the flow of traffic is even.

Picture thirty miles back on the freeway along open countryside where there is much space between cars. The flow of autos is close to equilibrium and balance. The amplitude is weak. On the other hand where the cars are closer together at the bottleneck, they appear as a package. Tightly packed cars increase the possibility of a crash or a collapse into a pile.

Quantum physicists call such an occurrence a *wave packet*. The packet of wave forms contains a high probability of collapsing into an electron particle at a particular time and specific place. Or, if you take Haramein's view, a possible movement into a black hole.

The Death of Pure Objectivity On The 2nd Tier

I hope I did not lose you on the leap up this waterfall because we now come to one of the most important revelations of the Mother Tongue of Nature at this new level. These early quantum scientists soon noticed that the steep wave form remained in its current structure until a measurement of the system was made. Once the experimenter observed and made a measurement; then, *shazam*, the wave form, steep as it was, collapsed into a particle, emerging into the world as a new coherence.

Listen! The axis of the history of human inquiry creaks as it turns on this quantum observation. At that moment in the quantum experiment, the hope of pure reason, pure objectivity died. First, we lost absolute certainty. Now, 20th-century science lost objectivity itself.

And the influence of measurement was only the beginning.

The Power of Interpretation
Or Story In The Co-Creation of Reality

Another crew of physicists emerged in the early 21st century: Henry Stapp, Amit Goswami, Mae-Wan Ho, Nassim Haramein, and Brian Greene, to name a few. They paddle our boat above the waterfall by pushing forward experiments. In their research they noticed another factor beyond the observational measurement contributing to the collapse of the wave into a discrete particle or system of particles. At first they could not name this new influence in the experiments, but slowly they realized how they interpreted the data influenced the outcome.

Put another way, they became aware that the conscious intention they brought to their work participated in the experiment itself. As physicist Goswami elegantly puts it:

> ...suppose we define consciousness as the agency that affects quantum objects to make their behavior sensible. (1995, p. 7)

Return to the thought experiment on the freeway. Consider for a moment that you are a Sacred Leader in the Era of Natural Birth. You hover over the freeway in a helicopter. The cars slow down to gander at the strange apparition of the white buffalo. You as the Sacred Leader are a news announcer, and you broadcast your conscious interpretation of the white buffalo as a harbinger of a new coherence in the midst of chaos. Your broadcast immediately enters most of the cars. Hearing your momentous interpretation, the cars slow down to a snail's pace until the flow collapses into a full blown traffic jam.

Thus, you as a so-called objective observer now have entered into the co-creation of the traffic jam not only through observation but by bringing your consciousness as the shaper of reality. Although this traffic analogy breaks down soon enough, roughly speaking this observation-plus-conscious interpretation speaks to what happens at ground zero in quantum field reality.

The Ceaseless Basketball Game

This window into what lies beneath the surface of reality reveals, then, tiny packets of vibrating energy, eco-fields where there is a ceaseless exchange of information, meaning, and even wisdom. These exchanges of traded information and energy are something like ongoing passing back and forth in a basketball game.

The legendary basketball player of the 1960's, Bill Russell (1979), once described the games between the Celtics and the Lakers as being more like a dance than a battle. He spoke of the two teams giving up their identities to the larger experience of flowing like waves back and forth from one end of the court to the other in forms of excellence, moving to higher and higher levels of performance, exchanging subtle information through nudges and feints, and spiraling toward higher and higher levels of performance as if they were one organism. At such times Russell said he prayed for excellence for himself and his opponents in the name of co-creation.

And, now, on the 2nd Tier it appears they, and we, transcend individual competition so prominent in the first six waves, and become one in holomovement. Let's continue to explore the heights above the waterfall, the 2nd Tier. What you have read so far is just the beginning of speaking the sometimes primal and intimate language of the newer sciences.

V

Life Above the Waterfall

CHAPTER TWENTY-ONE

Field Guides on the 2nd Tier

Stranger in a Strange Land by Robert A. Heinlein (1961) has been called the most widely read science fiction novel ever published. Synchronistically, it was written during the same time period that Clare W. Graves performed his major research, which concluded with Graves' discovery of humans reaching for the 2nd Tier. The phrase, *strangers in a strange land*, aptly describes the humans Graves discovered in the waves above the quantum jump to the 2nd Tier of the evolutionary story.

In another strange twist of the system of eco-fields, a Russian born physicist/chemist immigrated to the United States in the same year, 1961, that Heinlein published his book. His name? Ilya Prigogine, the *sine qua non* of our travel on the high waterfall of the 2nd Tier. When Prigogine arrived in Austin at The University of Texas, he was a little known scientist. Just sixteen years later, 1977, Prigogine would receive the Nobel Prize for his work with chaos and coherence in fields, thus setting the stage for him to become a primary field guide in the world that Einstein could never accept, this strange land of the 2nd Tier.

And that award was just the beginning. By the time of his death in 2003, Prigogine had redefined the very heart of physics, The 2nd Law of Thermodynamics. He has been called by some *the Einstein of the 21st century*, a title claimed by many but deserved by few. In the context of this book, I advance that Prigogine provides us with a beginning framework, a cosmic map, for exploring the upper reaches of the strange land above the waterfall, the terrain where the quantum leap lands us. His experiments give us new language to describe the waves around us. His maps constitute a near fit to our new territory. (No map really corresponds to the territory exactly.)

But I get ahead of my story here. Let us now quickly review what we have covered in the context of the Field Guide model as a way to set the stage for Prigogine's remarkable discoveries as one expression of the Mother Tongue of the 2nd Tier.

Four Essentials in Field Guide Leadership

Thus far we have explored four different aspects—field notes I call them—crucial to being field guides with the intention of guiding our vessels through the turbulent white water of a planet in birth pangs.

- We need a clear grasp of the eight standing waves delineated throughout this book. We need a much broader understanding of these waves of eco-field development than just the memetic model. Beck's (2002) memetic model examines principally the human value aspects of the standing waves and thus exacerbates the human-centric difficulty that has resulted in current global devastation. Field guides need to see themselves as one-among-many species. Human centered research and activity often intensifies our global problems.

- The two currents in the standing waves of eco-fields are *ascending* and *descending*. As field guides we need to guide the vessel down the river first and foremost, as has been the case throughout the book. Only then can we ascend to the point of the quantum leap, using shamanic power as the fuel.

- Key for field guides is the ability to *tune into the fields*. This tuning into the fields begins with a thorough examination of the inner councils of selves, the energetic forms dwelling within our inner landscapes. Earlier (2010), I advocated that retrieving the *wild heart* is essential so that the inner council can tune into the loins/fields of Earth Mother. Then, your inner council is positioned to be part of a wild wisdom community, which itself becomes a principal tuning fork into the various eco-fields.

♦ These Nature-based communities become the vessel which can best navigate all eight of the standing waves. Without this kind of community (Chapter Thirteen), surviving and thriving in the current era will be problematic at best.

♦ As this inner and outer work unfolds, we are gifted with a primal form of intimacy, a docking with the Mother Ship, or better, the Mother Tree.

Field Guides Embody the Primordial Agreement

Once we retrieve the wild heart, we have a conduit to the depths of Earth's Wisdom, a Mother Tongue referred to in this book's title. Another Field Guide for the upper reaches of the river is Teilhard de Chardin, a significant influence in Prigogine's work. Teilhard (1959), prominent scientist who was key in discovering the Peking Man in China, surveyed a lifetime of paleontological research and wrote concerning the Primordial Agreement:

> In its present state, the world would be unintelligible and the presence in it of reflection would be incomprehensible, unless we supposed there to be a *secret complicity* between the infinite and the infinitesimal to warm, nourish and sustain to the very end—by dint of chance, contingencies and the exercise of free choice— the consciousness that has emerged between the two. (p. 276)

Note important points Teilhard is making in this remarkable conclusion to his life's work.

- Humans (and I maintain all of the seen world) have the capacity to reflect with awareness on themselves and the Universe-at-large.
- This form of self-reflecting awareness results from a secret agreement or complicity of the Infinite with the infinitesimal.
- A unique form of consciousness has emerged in the movement between the worlds of the seen and the Unseen.
- This consciousness warms, nourishes, and will sustain us to the very end. Within the field there is a force pulling us toward Omega or telos.

Human's New Dialogue with Nature

Now, the table is set for us to consider Prigogine as a primary field guide on the 2nd Tier of our river journey. Seven years after he received the Nobel Prize, Prigogine (1984) wrote *Order Out of Chaos*. The subtitle of his book is *Man's Dialogue with Nature*, a phrase he employs as a new definition of science. Through this daring reframing of science Prigogine vaults us up the waterfall to the 2nd Tier. He continues to write:

> Science is a risky game, but it seems to have discovered questions to which nature provides consistent answers. (p. 5)

> Nature speaks with a thousand voices, and we have only begun to listen. (p. 77)

Exactly! Our listening is limited to our ability to speak the Mother Tongue, and Prigogine schools us in the newer version of this tongue with his precise language, born of research. Like the wisdom of the ancient shaman, Prigogine's science is a direct access into the wilds of Nature, the source and mentor for both perspectives. I push Prigogine's point even further. Not only science but also art pulsates with our new dialogue with Nature. Keep in mind humans and more-than-humans are partners, both aspects of Nature's eco-fields. Human-centered science and art lose their meaning on the upreaches of the river where reciprocity is demanded by the eco-field.

In short, there is no meaningful dialogue outside Nature in this era, on any subject. Period. The end.

Or, as the first-century poet, Juvenal puts it,

Never does Nature say one thing and
wisdom another.

What, according to Field Guide Prigogine, is Nature expressing in his translation of the Mother Tongue?

A Primary Feature of the Universe is Fluctuation

When I first was introduced to systems science in the late 1960s through the work of Ludwig van Bertalanffy (1950), the then new science emphasized the tendency of the system to drift toward equilibrium and homoeostasis. At first that map of reality comforted me as individuals and families sought my help in therapy. Using that systems directive, I kept working with the families to achieve consistent equilibrium, a calm with minimal change, a steady state, and a refuge in the storm.

Yes. A worthy goal.

It usually did not happen.

Families live in a universe of constant fluctuation, oscillation, and motion. As I engaged families seeking therapy over the next three decades after embarking on systems science, I slowly noticed that the primary characteristic of the families was fluctuation. About the time a basic equilibrium would emerge in our sessions, a new shaking would occur during the course of the time between appointments.

I felt discouraged until I discovered Prigogine's (1984) research. He makes clear that all systems contain sub-systems which are continually in fluctuation. Even if the whole appears to be in equilibrium, sub-systems are always in fluctuation, floating in what Prigogine calls a sea of chaos (p. xxix). Systems have constant friction and tension, and, while they appear to be in equilibrium, they actually are seething with fluctuations which can descend into chaos at any given moment as they drift away from previous adjustment forms no longer sustaining their life. You might wonder why such a raucous scene gives me comfort, but it does. Let us proceed to see why.

Given the fluctuating conditions in any eco-field, a primary capacity of the field guide for the 2nd Tier is the ability not only to live with chaos but to thrive in the white water, surf the waves, and delight in the joy of the ceaseless motion.

Often fluctuations become so powerful that the ensuing shaking shatters the preexisting organization of whatever current form is in place. With that reality in hand, I saw families in a different light. My job was not to preserve the current organizational form of the family but to move with the fluctuations and chaos, align with the creative urges in the family system, and be patient until a new form emerged. I propose that this situation I describe in the family therapy process is true for all eco-fields throughout the Universe. All eco-fields have built-in a self-healing urge, and even the fluctuations become part of the healing fever.

Note to field guides: structures dissipate and new structures more in tune with on-the-ground-reality-of-the-field emerge out of the wreckage of the old structures and create a different form with new information in the system.

But let us slow down the action here and see how these dissipating structures eventually form into something new.

Phase Transition and Bifurcation Points

As the organization (individual person, family, nation, corporation, university, forest, Earth, Cosmos) drifts far from equilibrium, then change becomes more and more a possibility, eventually an inevitability. The quantum waves become more steep. Amplitude increases. In my metaphor cars get closer together in traffic. Common sense based on industrial culture suggests this drift far from equilibrium is cause for despair and discouragement, and, at first, despair does prevail. This despair reveals itself in post-modern art, films, and literature: points well taken by cultural artists. However, the despair is necessary only if you continue following reductive rational paradigms that see the smaller picture of a chaos ever increasing, as did mainstream science of the 20th century.

Field guide note: don't follow the smaller version of rational human-centered thinking. Good news: when you give up being the center of the eco-field, then you do not carry the burden of change. Phase transitions are already in the making, and your task is to identify, align, and participate. Then, you open the door to being part of an attractor force within the field.

Imagine for a moment that you are learning to ski downhill. Your field instructor tells you to lean out over your boots and fly into the fluctuations of speed, snow, trees, rocks and ever-changing weather. You try to follow this instruction, but it is counter control-centered-rational, especially when you hit your first major bump and your skis and legs shake. Your usual rational mind tells you to lean back toward the equilibrium of the ground, the illusion of safety.

If you follow your culturally oriented rational mind in this case, you will fall. Yes, you may fall anyhow, but the fall is all but guaranteed if you lean back in desperation.

Paradoxically, the push toward safety actually results in little change because systems in balance and functioning well see themselves as not needing change. The urge to sit down when you hit the bumps tells you to stop the motion, a move counter to your intention to learn to ski downhill. If you want absolute safety, just sit down. See how much fun that is. The larger logic embraces tension and chaos, and eventually creates the possibility of coherence. Go ahead. Lean out over the boots into the chaos. Therein lies the emerging new form of downhill skiing.

Slowly, ever so slowly, I began to see my discomfort with what fluctuation was creating. I was a drag on the emerging coherent energy in the families with whom I worked. Although they resisted change in their culturally dominated personalities, they did not—in their better moments—want me to align with their resistance and safety strategies. In their evolutionary selves, they wanted more from me as a field guide in their eco-field. Although they could not express it in this manner, they wanted me to help them build a new island of coherence in the midst of the waves of chaos of addictions, martial strife, co-dependence, anxiety, grief reactions, and serious mental illness.

True, they came to me pushed by their pain and suffering. In that state their vulnerability called for safety, but of a deeper sort than avoiding the chaos. In their better moments they yearned for the safety of new forms of the family, more in line with the movements of Nature and their deeper souls. In their usual rational minds they wanted to lean back on their skis toward the sit-down-safety of previous family patterns, but in their souls they yearned to ski down the mountain in the direction of the joy of new patterns of behavior.

As the eco-field attempts to steady itself in fixating on control and falling backward, a false sense of harmony seduces the system into fixating on outdated patterns. Then, inevitably, as new energy enters the eco-field, the form or vessel that floats on the sea of chaos will drift more and more away from an earlier form that worked so well in previous moments. In drifting far from equilibrium, the shaking and tension increases. Big bumps appear as you lean over your skis. You contract your mind and muscles and, again, lean backwards toward false safety. But bang yourself up enough in falling on your backside and soon you will experiment with leaning over the skis despite what the patterns of your rational mind tell you.

During these paradoxical moments powerful change is just around the corner. Prigogine puts it this way in his experiments with chemistry:

It is remarkable that near-bifurcations systems present large fluctuations. Such systems seem to "hesitate"... [But then] A small fluctuation may start an entirely new evolution that will drastically change the whole behavior of the macroscopic system. (1984 p. 14)

As I embraced the fluctuations in the family eco-field of my therapy practice, then change became possible and then probable. Prigogine calls these singular moments, *bifurcation points*. A bifurcation describes a point in the eco-field of branching or forking into a qualitatively new type of behavior. Taking the fork toward leaning over the skis, you fly down the hill to the musical strands of *Ode to Joy*. Just before the bifurcation moment, there is a *shudder* in the field, as if the Grandmother of the field is catching her breath.

In that breath between lies the intimacy of the eco-field.

Mae-Wan Ho (2008), physicist and cell biologist, describes this crucial moment of change like this:

In a non-equilibrium system the transition is always to a regime of dynamic order where the whole system is in *coherent* motion. (p. 126)

Ho introduces the very important notion of coherence, our next order of discussion in seeking a Mother Tongue for the 2nd Tier

CHAPTER TWENTY-TWO

Islands of Coherence

Once you relinquish maintaining the equilibrium of the old form and once you accustom yourself to the rollicking waves of fluctuation, then an amazing moment, a bifurcation, happens.

To explore the emerging coherence, let us try an experiment which I first saw in junior high and which also is used in advanced physics, as we shall see. Picture in your mind a glass filled with a solution of salt (4 tablespoons), bluing (4 tablespoons), water (4 tablespoons), and ammonia (4 tablespoons). The solution is diffuse with particles and larger molecules darting about in seemingly random, chaotic directions, a sea of chaos as it were.[1]

Now, pour the mixture over a small piece of porous limestone rock or a length of cotton string. This piece of rock might represent the previous structural form that has drifted far from equilibrium. Over the next six hours or so, molecules in the solution will be attracted to the piece of rock (or clay, or charcoal, or string, or some other attractor).

If you select a charcoal briquette as an attractor, you likely will find that it needs attention. You may need to coat your vessel with Vaseline®, or make sure the solution is more than half way up the side of the briquette. Whether you use charcoal or a porous

---

[1] chemistry.about.com/cs/growingcrystals

piece of limestone or cotton string as your attractor, you may need to sprinkle more salt over the attractor artifact on the first or second day, depending on humidity, temperature, and air flow.

Then, on the third day of the process of growing crystals, you may need to add more of the solution to keep the crystals growing. But, be careful about dripping the new solution on the growing crystals, or the new crystals will be damaged.

Because evaporation is an energetic force in the crystal growing, the experiment needs to have free air circulation, yet no hard drafts. Warm, moist eco-fields will grow larger and faster than cool, moist eco-fields. Avoid direct sunlight because direct sunlight evaporates the liquid solution faster than the growing structure can attract molecules. One practice might be a gentle fanning of the vessel several times during the first six hours. Then, add a small fan set on a low speed setting. Or, better, place under a tree with a gentle breeze.

Now, we are positioned to engage crystal growing to explore the important eco-field occurrence of coherence, a central feature of life above the waterfall.

Respecting Outmoded Forms

Back to the ski analogy. Sometimes, it is valuable to lean backwards and sit down for safety, the inclination of the previous mode of behavior. Occasionally, the rational mind's message works best, if not for learning how to ski downhill, then for immediate safety. Sit down and take your fall if a tree is immediately in front of you. The emergent form of leaning out over the skis will have to wait, given the clear and present danger of the tree in your path. Respect and include aspects of the previous form. It may provide a seed for the emergent island of coherence, the piece of porous rock in the solution.

In our current global situation, we are called not so much to criticize the previous forms as to appreciate and discern where they have led us. Then, we can see how they are sometimes useful, but limited in terms of the new situation. That discernment frees us to sit down when we need to, while at the same time realizing our new intention is to move downhill or in the direction the grand attractor of gravity pulls us.

Living with Chaos: 2.0

Continue with the growth of crystals experiment as a lens to look at life on the 2nd Tier. The solution in the glass needs our utmost care. The molecules or particles darting around in various directions are indeed chaotic or random when it comes to our intention to grow crystals, but we do not need to rush too quickly into coherence and the new forms taking shape in the crystals.

First, we need to have the correct measurements of each of the solutions, including salt, bluing, water and ammonia. Then, we need to allow them to circulate in the glass in chaos as they mix themselves together with their rollicking fluctuations. The linear thinking of the orange eco-field assists us at this point.

In short, we need to learn to be at ease with the chaos in the solution sea, even encourage the chaos of the mixing as a prelude to the next phase of coherence. Chaos is a necessary condition of emergent coherence. In the first six standing waves chaos is frequently seen as the enemy, but on the 2nd Tier we make friends with chaos.

The Power of the Seed Attractor

All current forms eventually become outmoded and drift far from their equilibrium. No structural form, no matter how cherished, is forever. All forms drift far from balance into chaos, then emerges coherence. Such a process is the truth of the 2nd Law of Thermodynamics as redefined by Prigogine. In time the fluctuations in the field will increase and shatter the old form. More drifting. Eventually (emphasize eventually), an attractor force in the field will emerge.

Hopeful? Yes, but not always.

The Dark Attractors

The attractor force may or may not be pleasant or even immediately useful. Sometimes, the new coherence is worse than the old. The Germany of the 1930s shattered its economic and governmental form in a fluctuating field in spite of having one of the most advanced rational and educated populations in history. A sea of chaos ensued in the shattering waves of a massive depression, and then an attractor force emerged in the form of Hitler. He co-created a powerful new form that offered many solutions such as the Volkswagen auto, but then its demonic character revealed itself. Crucial in coherence is the basic character of the seed attractor. The German people opted for the easy coherence of the far right in the moment of bifurcation.

In our current Era of Natural Birth, we need to pay the closest attention to the attractor forces rising out of the field to discern whether they fit the larger intention for the good of Earth.

The Choice or Bifurcation Point: Divine or Demonic Attractors

As Prigogine vividly describes the process:

> Which direction the change takes depends on the nature of the attractor in the midst of chaos that lifts the chaos to the new order.

> If the attractor is demonic the old cycle repeats itself, which seems to be the case historically for our species. But if the attractor in the chaos were benevolent or divine the new order would have to be of that same nature.

In the ski analogy everything depends on which aspect of the inner council attracts you to lean over the skis. If, for example, the seed attractor force is channeled through the inner pusher, then you likely will lean over the boots too quickly. That attraction then becomes potentially fatal if a cliff shows up in front of you before you are prepared for that obstacle.

In the crystal growing experiment, the direction of the experiment depends on which attractor seed you place in the solution. If you place a charcoal briquette as is often suggested in the experimental lab, you may use a briquette which has been soaked in a petroleum product. Such a seed attractor will perform its attracting job in the beginning but may doom your experiment to failure because the oil mutes the growth potential of the other molecules.

If you use a piece of porous limestone or a strand of cotton string as a seed for the crystal growing, the likelihood of a beautiful crystal increases exponentially.

Primordial Attraction Creates New Forms of Community

Consider now a simple definition of crystals. Crystals are structures that are formed from a repeated patterning of sub-atomic particles, which are attracted to atoms, which are attracted to form molecules. Then, the molecules are attracted to the seed. As the molecules congregate on the attractor, they form a crystal. This powerful process is sometimes called *nucleation*.

Let us slow down the action of nucleation and see what happens because it speaks directly to our life above the waterfalls.

First, the elemental forms such as salt have to dissolve into the solution. The old form of salt drifts into the fluctuation of the solution.

Second, the particles in the chaotic solution contact each other and through the attractor force make a connection. They then form a small group, a subunit larger than the individual particle. This subunit becomes an attractor bringing more individual particles to itself. Then, the subunits are attracted to each other as they dart about in the sea of the solution moving toward the seed attractor. The particles continue to attach to the now growing crystal, causing it to enlarge, form a shape, and maintain an identity.

Third, this forming of the crystal will continue until there is an equilibrium between the particles still floating in the solution and those shaped into the new form we call a crystal.

Now, we behold an interlinking system of particles, a new tribe. Conveniently, we call this new community of particles living near equilibrium, a crystal. In our dominant culture we tend to think of it as a fixed thing, but in quantum reality the crystal is a new and thriving community and will exist for only a brief moment in the space-time continuum.

As 2nd Tier field guides, stretch for a moment into this primordial truth. Around our beautiful planet individual humans are being attracted to each other as we give up the illusion we are in this sea of chaos alone. We are forming into subunits, often centering in a seed attractor through teachers such as Jane Goodall, Jean Houston, Carolyn Myss, Elisabet Sahtouris, HeatherAsh Amara, Linda Tucker, Nassim Haramein, or Stan Grof, each with their own schools.

These seed communities lead us to the next step in the creation of a beautiful new form. Our subunits of growth communities are transcending themselves to form global learning circles, such as the Earthtribe, Wisdom University and beyond. In this next step we fulfill our calling in forming islands of coherence.

The Awareness of the Field Guide: New Communal Vessels

The field guide's aware attention paid to the co-creation of the attractor force in the field contributes crucially to the emergent form. In the crystal growing experiment many variables arise. You may need to add Vaseline®, depending on your awareness and ethical considerations concerning the use of petroleum products. If you do, then you need to be aware of the influence of petroleum on your experiment and the planet. You may need to move the experiment if there is direct sunlight. You may need to give the growing area more air, or less. You may need to add solution, but not too much. Notice that all of these human participations in the process require aware sensitivity, even congruence with the organic emergence of the crystal.

To be a field guide you need to have a reciprocal relationship with the emerging crystal community. In fact you are an aspect of the emerging crystal.

Expanding personal and communal awareness is always the additive in the process that connects particles with attractors within the eco-field. Here it is useful to return to Prigogine's definition of chaos:

Chaos is the behavior of systems in which close trajectories separate exponentially in time. (1996, p. 201)

I ponder my decades as a psychotherapist. Families and individuals come to see me with their systemic eco-field on a trajectory of separation or estrangement; and, if I am aware, I can witness this fragmentation that causes the symptoms. Let me amplify why I am hopeful in the fluctuation and chaos. Whether it is on the macroscopic scale of the cosmos or the microscopic scale of the family or the even smaller scale of the dissolving of salt in our crystal growing experiment, I find hope in Prigogine's (1984) clear voice:

The fluctuation of nonequilibrium is the source of (new) order. *Nonequilibrium brings order out of chaos.* (p. 287)

We grow in direct proportion to the amount of chaos we can sustain and dissipate (1984, p. 170)

These statements carry great power. I repeat them out-loud as I write. *The very state of fluctuation most of us avoid is the state that elicits the new order.* However, knowing about fluctuation and chaos is not enough to align with the emerging island of coherence bubbling up within the cauldron of the eco-field.

In aligning with the emergent form, I add the essential element of awareness—human and more-than-human—as the liquid that dissolves the old forms (salt, bluing, family patterns, etc.) and positions the eco-field to "grow" an island of coherence in the choppy standing waves of our journey. The implicit becomes explicit within the eco-field through an awareness *that transfers information, meaning, and, finally, untamed wisdom.* In the process of emerging coherence, it is important to note that not all of the molecules involved respond to the attractor force enough to be part of the growing crystals. These molecules participate in the dynamic process by remaining in the solution. They are essential and not to be judged by the coherence in the new form of the crystal.

I will return to this point momentarily. First, I want to explore instances of coherence building in the natural world.

CHAPTER TWENTY THREE

Coherence in Eco-fields

In her ground breaking work, prominent geneticist Mae-Wan Ho explores the physics of organisms and, relying considerably on Prigogine, forges an exploration of the emergence of coherence in the eco-field. In her original work she researches how biology links to physics through the science of coherence and of coupled processes (2008, Preface). Utilizing Ho as a field guide, consider with me important instances of coherence in the eco-fields. In coherence we witness an emerging human identity—who we are—as we swim in the eco-fields above the waterfall.

Human Identity: As Photon Fields

Neuse, Germany

For thirty years biophysicist Fritz Popp and his group of investigators have labored at the International Institute of Biophysics with a focus on light emission from living organisms.

> They have found that practically all organisms emit light at a steady rate from a few photons per day to several hundred photons per organism per second.
>
> (Ho, 2008, p. 192)

In support of Popp's work, atomic physicists around the planet are offering observations that reveal living systems as one coherent *photon field* out of which emerge different aspects of the field such as humans, grasses, and birds. Ho (2008) notes that this photon field "is maintained far from thermodynamic equilibrium, and is coherent..." (p. 195)

Everything in the Universe seems to be coherence-in-the making, arising out of an Underlying Field, which manifests systemic eco-fields.

As part of the photon field we maintain our freedom of choice while at the same time correlating with all other dimensions of the field. Thus, the phrase, "we are children of the Light," takes on an important and scientifically significant meaning.

Literally, we are rays of the Sun.

In us, the Sun takes human form.

The star systems become human flesh and dwell among us, full of grace and truth.

We humans, then, are a pattern of photon communities, and we couple our photon communities with other photon communities, all of which interact with a fluctuating eco-field in varying amounts of coherence.

Human Identity as Potential Coherence

Now, we are prepared to explore a definition of coherence.

So far in our rollicking journey through the eight standing waves, we have seen that these waves are merely eight prominent waves among trillions of waves rising and falling in the river we call a Universe. The quantum world, as we have seen, is an intricately interconnected, interdependent sacred web where every entity— from elementary particle to galaxy—evolves as a single organism, entangled with all that is.

This entangled process we call Nature. Nature, remember, is not a collection of things but rather a mind-boggling network of events. There is no such thing as a firmly fixed thing. Shortly, we shall see that the Universe has two sides, and it moves from one side to the other. I just referred to the Universe as an it, but physicist David Bohm (1995) is more accurate when he describes the Universe as *holomovement*. When we focus on the planet where we live we can see that Earth is a single organism, or, more precisely, a pattern of linked eco-fields. The deeper I look into reality the more I engage an intimate conversation at the base of known existence.

These fields are in an ongoing state of fluctuation with some aspects of the eco-fields operating at near equilibrium and other aspects living far from equilibrium. Contrary to 20th-century models of thermodynamics that proposed increasing entropy or randomness, Prigogine's brilliant model reveals that the drift far from equilibrium sets the stage for an emergent coherence, rather than unending randomness. Fluctuation and chaos are necessary ingredients in the cooking stew of coherence but not the whole story.

In my usage of the Mother Tongue, *coherence* suggests:
- a pulling together through attraction,
- an adhering through transcending difference,
- a connecting through aware coupling,
- an unfolding through emerging congruence,
- an intimacy of all aspects that creates the coherence.

Intuitively, we know if a person's speech is coherent by noticing if all the parts fit together. How we filter the exterior world through our own perception magnifies the presence or absence of coherence. So, as you and I interact through the medium of this book, a coherence arises or does not, dependent on our mutual expressions and perceptions. For me the writing of this book constitutes an effort to align myself with what I perceive to be rising islands of coherence through the fluctuations of the eco-fields in and around me. Our common understanding of coherence arises, it turns out, from the quantum or eco-field revelation of reality. In any given moment we are called on by eco-field reality to allow or disallow a coherent expression of self to arise from the fluctuations of our own inner world and mind talk.

259

Allow me to belabor this point.

Fluctuations and coherence are bound together, necessary for each other, partners in the process of unfolding reality. We, as humans, are hybrids of fluctuation and coherence, evolution in motion, dangling participles seeking a complete sentence, and, if we persist, a paragraph. As we slosh around in the waterfall of the 2nd Tier of evolution, we slowly learn how not only to be at home with coherence but also to know that the fluctuations—the change and decay all around that we see—are completely necessary to emergent coherence.

As I pause in writing and read the previous sentence, I am aware it makes only partial sense. Like you and me, the sentence is coherence in the making, not quite there. Yet, hopefully, full of congruent promise. Fluctuating nonetheless.

And what about you? You bring a council of selves to this book, brimming with thoughts and feelings. Around you a world impacts your reading, including the time of day you read. If you read these words at the end of the day, the events of the day may draw you away from creating coherence in your encounter with my words. If you talk to a friend about your reading this book, you seek to co-create an island of coherence with each sentence, born out of the fluctuations of your inner world, my thoughts, your friend, and, not to be forgotten, the eco-field around you. If you look outside for a moment, a nearby tree enters the creation of the coherence as well, particularly if you pause for a moment of intimacy with the tree. Or, perhaps, the time is not right for coherence, so the fluctuations and, to some degree chaos, continue.

In any case our identities as humans within the eco-field unfolds with emergent islands of coupling within the eco-field. Let us look inside at our cells further to explore coherence in action.

Human Identity: a Murmuration of Cells

Late Autumn

A large flock of birds, thousands of them, arise from an Oregon wetlands as I amble on an afternoon walk. All of the birds in unison hang a left, then a right, and then pull back on the stick at precisely the identical moment. As I look at them, I cannot identify what kind of birds they are much less know how they accomplish their miracles in the sky. My guess is that they are a murmuration of starlings.

They fly in swirls, spirals, and make the shape of a torus, then instantly an hourglass and other magical shapes. For most of my life I have puzzled about the highly coordinated movements of flocks of birds or, for that matter, schools of fish, always ending up with the same question: How do individual organisms share their intentions with each other "so flawlessly and instantaneously to coordinate their movements" (Ho, 2008, p. 196)?

Rupert Sheldrake, noted biochemist, offers a tantalizing hypothesis he calls *morphic* fields to address my question (Sheldrake, 1988). These fields, he proposes, provide information for the flocks of birds. His work, though not as precise or well researched as Farina's eco-fields, anticipates the integration of biology, quantum fields, and eco-fields (EFH1 and EFH2).

Morphic fields are fields in which morphic units (forms) are organized into a pattern of activity. Within the morphic field exists a morphic resonance, Sheldrake's proposal for how the field provides a feedback mechanism between itself and the morphic unit, in this case the flock of birds. The birds tune into the eco-field, drawing from the ground of information important turning signals. These signals are sent to each individual at a speed that quantum physics describes as *nonlocal*, that is beyond the linear sequence of one bird communicating with its neighbor. The birds receive the signals at precisely the same moment.

Morphogenetic fields are a subset of morphic fields and refer to organizing communication between humans and all living things, but not so-called inanimate objects within the field. In other words, the birds are programmed genetically to tune into fields (Sheldrake, 1994, p. 112). Sheldrake's work precedes the eco-field hypothesis and provides powerful clues, and Farina (2008, EFH1) carries the torch on the next leg of the journey with more focused research. Then, in EFH2 I explore, with you, the human component in the equation, and, in that manner, this book continues my boyhood fascination with the instantaneous turning of birds.

The flock soars over my head against a sapphire sky.

I ponder the mainstream of biology and its use of morphogenetic fields as describing a collection of cells by whose communication a particular organ is formed, say my heart.

Are the cells of my body like the flock of birds?

Do the various communities of cells talk to each other with a speed similar to the flocks of birds?

Do the cells of my intestines have long-range communication with my toes or my graying hair follicles?

Do I operate much like a flock of birds as a murmuration?

I wonder.

During an emergency I know that I can mobilize large pulsations of energy almost instantaneously. When danger is present, Ho (2008) suggests that "there is a system of communication that sends emergency messages simultaneously to all organs... (p. 196). Note the key phrase here: simultaneously. Faster than the speed of light? Likely, so. Like the flocks of birds, all the cells of our bodies speak to each other in a primal murmur. This long-range communication occurs every minute of every day, and the wild card is how aware we are of the process. Let's see what the implications are of this longitudinal conversation of cells.

Human Identity: Chaotic and Coherent Cells

Some cells are healthy and coherent in their communication while others seem caught in chaos. Ho's research points toward a difference "between the photon-emission characteristics of normal and malignant cells" (p. 197). More coherent cells emit less light with increasing cell density while malignant cells lose light with increasing cell density.

Is cancer the literal loss of light in our cells?

Moreover, healthy cells tend to find community through their ongoing intimacy while malignant cells reveal a tendency toward disaggregation or loss of community. The malignant cells break apart and find themselves estranged from the larger community of cells and organs.

Is cancer the result of loss of communal intimacy by whatever means?

As Ho puts it:

> The difference between cancer cells and normal cells may lie in their capacity for intercommunication, which in turn depend on their degree of coherence. (p. 197)

As humans our first and most basic use of a base network of information is the intimate matrix of cells. Our health depends on our ability to utilize awareness, choice, and practice to create community in our bodies through coherent and thus intimate, cellular conversation.

How are our cells talking? Is there tension and conflict? If so, are we intimate enough with ourselves to be aware of the tension and learn from the conflict as it arises in the field?

In summary, what we call disease may simply be the lack of community in coherent eco-fields, both in our bodies and in the larger eco-field. Or, to get to the point, it appears cancer may be related to the lack of intimacy in our cellular community as that community finds its place in the interlocking eco-fields.

Chaotic Community and Cancer Cells

Rene Dubos, microbiologist and experimental pathologist, received the Pulitzer Prize for his book, *So Human An Animal*, in which he coined the phrase, *think globally and act locally*. In a lifetime of research into human disease and its relation to the eco-field, he extracted bacteria from soil that led to the creation of major antibiotics. In his pioneering discoveries, he connected the human animal to her surroundings in such a way that larger dimensions of healing could occur.

When he studied images from global tracking units, he made a startling observation. He pored over the images of urban areas and compared them to the images of cancer cells appearing in the lens of his finely tuned microscope. He placed the photographic images of certain urban areas over the images of the cancer cells in an individual person and *discovered that they were a near match.* (Dubos, R., 1968).

Do many of us live in large, urban cancer cells? If so, do the larger cells of our cities communicate their chaos to our bodily cells? If that is so, how can islands of coherence arise? Dubos' research raises more questions:

Is cancer an outcome of our lack of community, our ignorance of the Mother Tongue, our inability for our cells to talk to each other?

How can our cells talk to each other when we live in grossly disturbed eco-fields?

Does our talking dysfunctionally create the cells of our cities which may harbor cancer?

Is the U.S. Congress a reflection of the breakdown of our cellular intimacy?

And why was there possibly no instance of cancer in North America when the Europeans arrived?[1]

Human Identity: Wisdom's Web

My mother-in-law, Eldora, will celebrate her one hundredth birthday in a few months. She is an important participant in the Earth-tribe, and, at an Earthdance, received the Nature name, *Wisdom's Web.* And with good reason: she is an embodiment of the web of wisdom. From a scientific perspective I think of wisdom's web as interlocking eco-fields.

Eldora grew up in Eastern Oregon on a 320-acre land grant she called a homestead, circa early 20th century. As a child she had little access to mainstream medicine. She nearly died of scarlet fever and a host of other diseases. In the chaos and upheaval of her body, it dawned on her one day that the animals, the trees, and other aspects of her environment possessed a remarkable capacity of healing and recovery.

She observed. She mimicked. She noticed that the animals licked and touched the points of distress in their bodies. Eldora

---

[1] www.paho.org/english/DPI/Number7_article2.htm

then touched the points of stress in her body, a form of self-massage, intuitive acupressure. She also talked to her body, sometimes tenderly and sometimes firmly. Last summer, she stubbed her foot and likely broke a bone either in her foot or in the toe. No one would know because Eldora avoids our medical system at all costs.

I observed her over a six-week period apply her healing ways. Each day she hobbled out to a tree in her back yard and placed her feet on the earth like the shamans at Dodona. She gently rubbed the dark bruises and talked tenderly to the stressed areas as she placed her bare foot directly on the surface of the Earth near the tree. The field in the form of flocks of cells flowed through the broken bones listening to the music of the spheres. Just as flocks of birds know how to turn, so her cells knew how to heal. Just as the birds soar, tuning and twisting beyond the speed of light, so her cells leapt across chasms in her broken bones, carrying minerals for rebuilding.

Eldora, Judith, and I attend a party, and I witness flocks of people hovering around Eldora, kissing her, laughing with her, hugging her, and asking her for her secrets of longevity. Some are friends and some, strangers who fast become friends. On this evening her cells broadcast to each other, to the grasses, to the trees, to the hummingbirds, and then outward through the eco-field to the cells of bodies all around her. The party comes to her as wine and food flow aplenty.

I marvel.

An intricate web, wise in its strands, weaves itself until I am slowly drawn into wisdom's fabric. Following Eldora's cue far beyond my usual shyness in social situations I too share in hugs, laughter, and naughty food in a delicious intimacy.

Human Identity: Cells and Selves

As we come to the close of this chapter and near the end of this book, I call your attention to your inner council of selves. In Chapter Nine and in a companion book, *Wild Heart* (2010), I explored with you this inner council. Is it not true for most of us that our inner world boils with busyness and fluctuations of mischief? Yet, the possibility of occasional stillness exists. With our spiritual practices we achieve moments when we sit high on a white mountain in a circle, fasting in stillness. We seek a vision, and we experience a murmuration of flocks of cells and gaggles of selves. Simple moments. Ones Alfred North Whitehead describes as *actual occasions* (1962).

During such moments our awareness shines like a laser beam on first one sub-self and then another, giving them room to talk. True, they are in tension and even in conflict with each other. Yet, if we persist in listening and facilitating their talking with each other, a coherence arises, an island within, an eco-field near equilibrium. We know it will not last. Still, the sublimity of the occasion is enough. As we stand on that island where all the cells and selves have formed themselves into a cherished unity, we can see far.

That is who we are.

Like Eldora, wildly wise.

For the moment.

The Mother Tongue oozes out of the pores of our skins as our cells sing songs that broadcast through our many selves with tender intimacy.

VI

Stories and
The Mother Tongue

CHAPTER TWENTY-FOUR

Trees, Stars, and Eco-fields

The end of our time together in this book nears. This last chapter provides a bridge to future and unknown creativity with all of us while at the same time bringing together some of my reflections on the whole of our conversation. I call it a conversation because I aspire to hear from many of you—your appreciations, your dis-agreements, and especially your elaborations. I could go on because, as you can see, I love to converse about these important matters. Nevertheless, I put a punctuation mark on our time together with this chapter, beginning the ending with a story about trees.

A Story of Intimacy with Trees

1966, Plainview, Texas, my home town

Plainview sits at about 3600′ above sea level on the steppes of North America known as the Texas Panhandle. As a county seat, the township moves at a slow pace as a low slung community shud-dering under the constant sway of mighty winds sweeping down the front range of the Rocky Mountains from Canada. Then, in a moment's notice, the winds can turn around and blow hot out of the Chihuahuan Desert in Mexico. The agricultural town is located strategically half-way between the Taos Pueblo in New Mexico on the West and the official site of the Comanche Nation near Lawton, Oklahoma on the East.

In my growing-up days, a rich mixture of tribal elders from the Pueblos, the Comanches, and the Kiowa mingled with Hispanics in the area to establish families and work wherever they could in a Texas culture known for its bias toward people of color. Anyone with brown skin was more often than not lumped together as *wetbacks* or *meskins*. Often these elders of color pushed carts with delectable tamales and soft tacos around dusty streets, or worked in the fields, or the yards of the privileged, eking out a living as best they could.

Such work occupied their day jobs, but their real love lay with informal mentoring. Hidden wisdom oozed out of their mouths as they spoke to those who would listen in a language strange to local ears. I refer here not to the mixed Spanish and indigenous phrases which enriched the streets during their day jobs but rather to the ancient utterances they used in their subtle teaching, a risky business as we shall see. The elders influenced me with their mentoring in profound ways, as they did other receptive young people, sometimes unbeknownst to the children's parents, families, or even friends.

One town leader, our local dentist, Dr. Gaynor, was an exceptional parent who took an active interest in the elders, especially Fernando Dominguez, who worked in Gaynor's yard caring for sparse trees and buffalo grass. Perhaps, Dr. Gaynor's interest in Fernando's spiritual ways arose naturally because the Gaynors were the only Jewish family in Hale County at the time and, therefore, sensitive to being a minority. Or maybe he himself yearned for a spirituality more closely connected to Nature. In any case, the elder Gaynor delighted in Fernando's mentoring of his son Mitch, a process through which the small boy was introduced to an intimacy with the trees in their front yard, likely towering sycamores and hardy Siberian elms.

One day Mitch, ten years old at the time, heard that Fernando had been arrested and petitioned his father for help. Dr. Gaynor immediately investigated and discovered that Fernando had indeed been arrested and whisked away by local officials to the State Mental Institution in Big Springs, Texas, a two-hundred bed facility that provided care for psychiatric illnesses to a fifty-eight county area the size of New England.

Our local dentist was dumbfounded.

Literally.

He could not speak.

Fernando was the most sane person he knew. How could such an atrocity happen? Immediately, Gaynor drove the 152 miles to Big Spring, often breaking the speed limit and arriving in two and half hours, according to the story told by my mother, Juanita. After a day of speaking to the psychiatrist-in-charge, and other officials, Dr. Gaynor was able to convince the administrator to release Fernando to his care. In a puzzling case of West Texas psychiatry, the officials somehow connected dental and mental hygiene.

Before Dr. Gaynor checked Fernando out, the dentist looked the psychiatrist in the eye and inquired as to why the small man with a bronze face and deep, sun drenched wrinkles was arrested in the first place.

"Oh," replied the psychiatrist-in-charge with a bored demeanor, as if the diagnosis was apparent, "He was caught talking to trees."

And that word *caught* says it all, as far as the attitude of the dominant culture is concerned, both in Plainview and elsewhere. The trees on the High Plains of Northwest Texas are few and far between. When my grandfather, Lee, arrived in the late 19th

Century, a beautiful stream fed by the Ogallala Aquifer, called Running Water Draw, ran jauntily through the town. Along its banks towered stately sycamores and rustling cottonwoods. But soon, as was the case wherever European immigrants came as purveyors of their civilization, the trees were mowed down. Lee, perhaps fueled by his mixed, likely indigenous blood, soon realized the mistake and planted Siberian elms, fast growing and fiercely hardy. The trees understood their role in the vast Southern Plains where a person could ride a horse for days and not see tree one.

They were the root of all life for the area.
They held everything in place.

Fernando ran his rough hands over the bark of a tree known locally simply as an *elm*. In the branches were two planks where neighborhood kids played. Then, there were the aforementioned, native sycamores marked by mottled bark that flaked off in large irregular masses, leaving the surface of the tree with dappled patterns of greens, whites, and grays. Fernando's favorite, as was the case with tribes all the way to Canada, was the cottonwood. From Taos to Plainview to Lawton the cottonwood appeared out of the waves of grass and wheat by streams and buffalo wallows, its leaves rustling with sacred sounds, sounds the ancient shamans of Dodona used to heal. Even today, the cottonwood is the central tree in the Sun Dance ceremony and an ancient feature of Black Elk's vision.

For speaking a lost tree language once known to all humans, Fernando was diagnosed psychotic.

As I tell this story, I can feel the bark beneath my boyish hands as my feet grab hold of the tree's sides in a shinny motion up to the first branch. How the world looks different even from that first branch! Then, I look up the trunk at patches of blue breaking through the leaves, revealing splashes of light, firing the edges of my young mind.

What was the subject of Fernando's conversation with these trees? A query to ask permission to use their bark in ceremony? Or maybe a petition to forgive all of us for our wanton cutting down of the sycamores and cottonwoods that lined the Running Water Draw traversing the town before irrigation dried up the springs? Like the Greek Christians in Dodona, we too desecrated the sacred trees. Or maybe Fernando thanked the trees for allowing us kids to climb them and even drive nails into their sides to hold up tree houses—constructed with one-by-six-inch planks nailed across limbs.

Later, as a psychotherapist I discovered that nearly everyone had a special tree in their childhood, a tree that looked after them, comforting them at a deeper level than even their human families could, speaking in primal intimacy to them even as the oceans spoke to Tilly Short in Sri Lanka about the approaching tsunami.

It was precisely Fernando's ability to talk in a syntax long forgotten by usual civilization that prompted Dr. Gaynor to give permission for Fernando to take his son Mitch camping soon after Fernando's release from the mental institution in Big Springs. Fernando took Mitch to the sacred Palo Duro Canyon, deep red rock splashes that inspired Georgia O'Keeffe. Just a scant ninety years had passed since the last wild Native Americans had roamed as they burned sage and quested in the crevices of this hauntingly beautiful canyon. There this aging shaman—fresh out of a mental institution—initiated Mitch in the skills of being intimate with the starry night, as well as the trees.

In early 2012 I flew to teach in Maui. When the pilot directed us to turn off our electronics, I glanced at an in-flight magazine. My eyes rested on a page listing the most respected physicians in New York City. One, an oncologist, had received the notation as being the best of the best in his speciality every year since 1997.

His name: Mitchell Gaynor, M.D.

Could it be the same ten-year-old that my mother Juanita mentioned in her story? I checked it out. It was the same person alright, and he had written a book on his early life, called *The Healing Essence* (1995). The book is an essay that beautifully chronicles his journey of descent to the shamanic on the Southern Plains and ascent to the latest in the newer sciences as an oncologist in Manhattan. Oncologist Mitch Gaynor began his book with a moving account of Fernando's mentoring, a source of this story.

I blinked back tears as I thought of the lonely trees that taught Fernando who, in turn, taught Mitch, who in turn learned from the stars about a healing essence, an articulate energy that accompanied him through medical school into his acclaimed practice as a cancer doctor.

Questions bob up as I finish this story:

How can we descend the spiral without losing ourselves romantically in the hunter/gatherers?

How can we face squarely the devastating *cul de sac* that Western Civilization has led us into without jettisoning the gifts of culture?

How can we have both Fernando, the indigenous shaman, and Mitch, the high tech oncologist?

No clear answers appear, but the trees, stars, and eco-fields through newer scientists like Mitch point in a creative direction.

And, as of this writing, I am emailing Mitch to explore a way to honor the Fernando of our childhood.

The Tree of Knowledge: a Mulberry Tree?

Return to Göbekli Tepe in Southeastern Anatolia about thirty miles from the Syrian border to Earth's oldest temple and the dawn of civilization. Or, that is what archeologists are now calling this archeological site. I mentioned climbing to the summit of the hill overlooking the astonishing dig to sit beneath an isolated mulberry tree. The tattered strips of prayer cloth placed on the tree by local Sufis reminded me of colorful strips of cloth hanging from branches of a juniper tree on our property back in Texas, pointing the way to a sweat lodge.

The Göbekli mulberry tree, in the same desert that yielded Abraham and Jacob, may have a direct lineage with the tree of knowledge in the Garden myth of Adam and Eve. A heady lineage, indeed. This one desert site tells a story of the human journey from hunter-gatherers to farmers. And, was it a journey of progress? To betterment? Or to a dead-end?

Jared Diamond, author of *Guns, Germs, and Steel* (1999), considers this transition to agriculture, seed of all civilization as we know it, not only to be a setback but also "the worst mistake in the history of the human race." Strong words. He goes on to write forcefully of this historical axis—which we now know happened at Göbekli Tepe—of this transition to horticulture and then agriculture. It led us, he contends, into "gross social and sexual inequality, the disease of despotism, that curse our existence." Most days I lean in Diamond's direction; some days, not.

Elif Bautman, in describing her visit to the archeological site in an article for *The New Yorker* (Dec. 19, 2011), swings back and forth between the stark reality of Göbekli's revelations of the human story taking a wrong turn and defending the civilizations made possible by that hinge in history. She returns time and again to an essential question of this book:

Was the agricultural and eventually the Industrial Revolution really a curse on our existence?

By now you know that I say, "Yes, it is a curse if we continue without the wisdom of the trees. No, if we are willing, like Fernando Dominguez, to risk a stay in civilization's mental institution for the practice of intimacy with the trees."

The mulberry tree at Göbekli speaks to me.

"I am the granddaughter of the tree of knowledge many generations removed from Eden. I carry in my cells the memories of first man and first woman who lived as respectful companions, intimate with themselves and us. They were unashamed of their nakedness, surrounded by us trees. We were pleasing to the eye and good food for them.

"Humans listened to us and noticed how we provided them with fruit. I heard Adam and Eve interpret God's mind and warning of the potential curse of a sedentary life centered on possessions. I watched with grief as I saw you humans leave behind a life of hunting and gathering wherein you worked a couple of hours a day and sought deeper life and recreation the rest of the time. I grieved your absence as you toiled behind the plow sun-up to sun-down with your new found skill at making gardens of the land.

"I saw you lose your physical height, shrinking a good six inches in stature. Why even the people who live around me today have not regained the height of your hunter-gatherer ancestors. I saw you think you were progressing as early farmers, only to have more anemia, vitamin deficiencies, younger death, worse teeth, spinal deformity, and rampant infectious diseases as you lived closer to other humans and livestock, first in villages, then cities, then nations. I saw you get completely out-of-control with your multiplying of your kind while reducing our numbers as trees to a small percentage of what Earth needs.

"When will you return to me? When will you become part of my forests? When will you give me at least as much attention as you direct to computers and malls?"

I have no ready response to the tree. Or to my thoughts I project onto the tree.

When I do not reply with answers and specificity either to the tree or to humans in my seminars, my colleagues come at me hard, accusing me of ignoring the gifts of Leonardo, Michelangelo, and Mozart, not to mention air-conditioning, rubber soled shoes, and iPads.

I have few responses, only more questions.

I know a profound sense of loss and ignorance as I seek to recover an intimacy of conversation with a single mulberry tree. I think of Jung's comment that he learned more from a single tree than from all the books he had read.

I run my hands over the mulberry tree's bark, caressing. Part of me feels hurried to leave the tree and to look at the stone megaliths, human creations. A deeper aspect within implores me to stay next to the tree. I notice serrated leaves with dots of brown. On the ground are dried up red berries, or are they black? I can't tell. I hold the berries and think of jams, wines, and breakfast.

I know that green versions of the fruit were used as an entheogen, most likely by the hunter-gatherers to evoke visions around their ceremonial fires. I long to know the secrets of the plant and to allow its medicine to course through my blood, grounding me yet sending me to heights. I imagine the taste of its sacrament to be earthy in my mouth, giving me a slight numbness. I look to the blue sky, sun above. Light streams through the leaves, a hint of Plato's limestone cave. Images of ancients shape before me, as if called forth by my touch of the green bark.

Later, I find that the bark is the sole food of the silkworm and, in that sense, this tree has given us humans all things silk. Who would know? I discover that this little tree is full of practical medicine, even a cure for ringworm. I know that trees everywhere give us medicine. I know they breathe, and without this lonely tree and its friends throughout the planet, I could not take a single breath.

And I find myself petitioning the tree, "Please, receive us back into the sacred web."

The little mulberry tree, ancestor of the tree of knowledge, is patient and quiet, intimate in its nourishment.

A Story of Stars in the Night, Stars in the Water

The return to the Sacred Web gained momentum for me as I lay on my back in the yard as a child. Or was it at age seventeen on my first wilderness quest as I looked at the night sky from the vantage point of a New Mexico lake, lightning flashing in the distance? Or have I even begun?

Sometimes, I know I have begun the return.

Sometimes, I do not.

Often, I drown in the waters of mainstream culture.

Late winter, 2010

Beside a lake on Deer Dancer Ranch, I wrap myself in a black swatch of cloth created by sailmakers near Kemah, Texas. Earthtribers use this marine canvas, a fabric called Sunbrella marine awning, to blanket sweatlodges. This particular ceremonial covering has been in use for a decade. Embedded in its fabric are prayers, sweat, steam, smoke, anguish, and untold joy from persons seeking a return to their essence, the healing essence taught by Fernando and Bear Heart, two wise persons fluent in the Mother Tongue. The absorbed aroma of sage, juniper, frankincense, copal, and rosemary combines with an early evening dew to coat my body with sweet smells.

The sun disappears behind loblolly pines, and a chill sets in as the fast grips my stomach. In my seventieth year I fast and seek visions in four different settings, over a year's span, concluding with this circle by this stream-fed lake. My intent is to expand my story, to connect with the larger tapestry, and to hit my stride for the elder years of my Earth walk.

Time folds back on itself as the night descends, colder than I expected. Have hours passed, or minutes? I nod off.

Suddenly, a voice from behind me calls my name: Will!

Throwing off the canvas, I turn to confront the intruder. My equipment consists of a sacred pipe, a conch shell, sage, and a self-powered crank flashlight. It takes thirty turns of the crank to power the beam to pierce the dark.

No one is there.

I shoulder the sweat lodge covering to hunker down and ward off the cold. Time passes.

My name is called again.

No one is there.

"This is spooky," I mutter to myself with a not very spiritual interpretation of the voice from the near-by forest.

The crisp, winter night brings forth a starry work of art. I cannot take my eyes off the glittering array. Pulling the wrap tighter in the cold, I squint and put on my glasses. The outline of the stars becomes more and more distinct. I locate the most vivid star in view, and it is brighter by half than anything I can see, save for the planets Venus and Jupiter.

And I wonder if the star has a name.

Later, when I returned from the quest, I located the star through a search engine and found it does have a name: Sirius.[1] The Dogon tribe of West Africa peered into space and received downloads from mysterious sources full of astronomical information about the star Sirius, the very one I focused on in my vision circle. Their tribal lore relates how 5,000 years ago they received information that Sirius has a companion star invisible to the human eye, that this star has a fifty year elliptical orbit around the visible Sirius, that it is extremely heavy, and that it rotates in a specific way on its axis. The Dogon have even more extensive Sirius data beyond the scope of this story.

That Sirius B existed was not news to modern humans since it had been observed as early as 1862, but what about the very specific astronomical details in the Dogon myth? In the 1930s two French anthropologists, Marcel Griaule and Germain Dieterlen, recorded many details about the second star featured in the oral traditions of the Dogon, and immediately the science of the time disputed the validity of the Dogon claims, laughing at such a yarn. Those laughing ignored the fact that the Dogon had a sophisticated astronomy 4,900 years before the Europeans even knew about the star. Evidently, the Dogon elders spoke star language, another version of the Mother Tongue.

The temperature of the Dogon tribal story of stars became tepid until 1970 when scientists, armed with larger telescopes and cameras, were able to photograph Sirius B and confirm much of the

[1] www.unmuseum.org/siriusb.htm

Dogon star data as being uncannily accurate. So accurate that Carl Sagan was moved to state at the time that the reports from the 1930 anthropologists must have been doctored with information from modern astronomers. He could not imagine that ancient people would know so much. More than Carl Sagan himself? Surely, not. But, then again, maybe so: scientists using the Hubble Space Telescope in 2011, confirmed even more extensive details of the Dogon map of the skies, fifteen years after Sagan died.

As I thought back on the night of sitting in a vision quest circle and linked it with this new star data, big questions came to me: "How could an isolated, mountain tribe with no written history, have completely accurate information concerning stars 8.6 light-years away? Information they supposedly had 5,000 years ago? Information modern astronomy could not confirm until it had invented the proper lens?"

To address my questions further, I read more of the ancient tribal stories to find that a Dogon elder, Ogotemmeli, revealed the source of their star data. According to Ogotemmeli, it seems that thousands of years ago they were visited by relatives from the Star Nations who gave them very detailed information about creation and its beginning. These ancient visitors, according to the Dogon, were quite specific in their charting of star behavior. Keep in mind, as I said before, that these visitations of elders from the stars were extensive and happened five millennia ago. And, according to Ogotemmeli, the star relatives held in great esteem the number *four*. *Four!* Wasn't that the number that came to me with transparent clarity under the stars at Göbekli? I would have to check my notes.

Relatives from the stars?

Were these same relatives reaching out to me in my vision circle? I would have to think about that.

Back in my vision circle, I wondered what time it was. A mild throb behind my eyes made me uncomfortable, a condition I attributed to my fasting and the cold. Starlight filtered through the trees all around me onto the surface of the lake, now throwing up a mild chop of waves with a midnight breeze. The starlight refracted off the water and bounced toward me, landing first on my heart, then my head, and throughout my body. Boundaries between my usual selves, the trees, and the starlight melted.

More reflections.

Everything on our planet, including you and me, is made of stardust. Our Sun is a star. All on Earth consists of particles of Sun. The story is even larger. All elements of Sun and Earth are made of dust and gas from long-dead stars, novas and supernovas who gave their lives that we might live.

I consider this above reflection. It is not precisely true. We actually are made of photon fields. A photon, offspring of Sun, is an elementary particle, a quantum of light, that once in open space takes only 8.3 minutes traveling at the speed of less than one light-year to reach the lake where I meditated. Light from the brightest star, Sirius, takes a little more than an hour to reach me. The lights mingle into a single beam.

Back in my fasting circle, the lights become part of me, joining with the photon field to permeate my body. I hear the clear water sloshing against the lake's sandy shore and sandstone rocks. The water and the rocks join my body to form a force field all around. I realize I have never before connected the dots between water and

the night sky. As I sit, I intuitively know they are deeply interconnected, entangled as it were. In this state of mind, a question comes
into my vision circle:

What is the origin of water on Earth?

That question seems simple enough, and you would think there
would be a simple answer, but apparently the question is larger than
21st-century science's answer. The current working theory explains
that water came from comets, actually snow and ice comets. Water
appeared on Earth about 3.8 billion years ago brought by a heavy
bombardment of snow and ice comets. The problem in the theory
that looms before us is that no scientist has ever seen a snow comet.
They accept the snow comets on faith.

Our solar system is chock full of water, yet no one has ever
been able to demonstrate empirically how the water formed in the
first place on the comets. However, scientists recently proposed
that the answer may live in a dusty interstellar cloud, a seedbed
of hydrogen and oxygen interaction.[2] Physicist Nassim Haramein,
on the other hand, proposes that Earth herself makes some of its
own water, though his hypothesis has scanty support at this time.
As I ponder these matters, it seems to me that the intimacy of the
eco-fields emerges out of a larger field, one I might call the *cosmo-field*. Stars and Earth merge. I make a note to extend the eco-
field hypothesis to the cosmo-field.

Back in my vision circle, the water seems to be the gift of the stars
now so near they hold me in their grasp. To shake the cold I shrug
off the canvas tarp and dance around the edge of the vision circle.
The boundary of the circle is set by a long string of prayer ties.

Let me explain the ties.

---

[2] news.sciencemag.org/sciencenow/2010/04

To prepare for a vision quest our tradition asks us to tie 405 prayer ties. To perform this meditative and prayerful task, I gather various elements in a basket: herbs, pieces of rock, leaves, and anything that touches me in a significant way. Then, I take a pinch from the basket and put it in a 3″ by 3″ cut of colorful cloth. Next, I take a length of cotton string and loop it around the cloth to make a tiny pouch and offer a prayerful meditation. At the end of the practice which usually takes months, there is a long string of 405 ties with colorful pouches of cloth, maybe thirty feet long. When unrolled, the string of prayer ties makes a circle about twelve feet in diameter, depending on how you tie the ties.

Sometimes, the question comes to me as to why 405 prayer ties. Bear Heart and the Ahe-Chay-Cha medicine circle taught me that each landscape (what I call eco-field) has many different spirits. To vision quest you need to honor each spirit of the landscape. According to Bear Heart, ancient Lakota elders discerned that there were 405 spirits in their traditional vision quest site of Bear Butte (*Mato Paha*), the most powerful land mass in their region.

Even though we have been working with this landscape of Deer Dancer Ranch for twenty years, we still do not know it well enough to number the spirits. So, we honor the ability of the ancient Lakota to know their territory and its various spirits and, thus, use their number. The number is metaphorical for us until we are more conversant in the Mother Tongue and know the number of spirits in our landscape or eco-field.

Hours—or is it minutes—pass as I dance around the vision circle. Slowly, the starlight moves across the water and lands on my heart. I find myself chanting:

Stars in the night,
Stars in the water,
Stars in my heart,
Stars in my head,
Stars in my hands,
Stars in my feet.

Then, ever so softly, I chant to the ancient Sacred Web, the matrix of eco-fields, the Star-Field, the Cosmo-Field.
I am a human being,
I am a human being,
I am a human being.

Receive me back.
Receive us back.

I listen, and an intimacy of silence, light, and darkness settles over me. There are no audible words, but I am certain, at least for the moment, that I have been heard, that I have talked with the trees, the stars, the Star Nations, and that we—Grandmother Earth and Grandfather Sky—are intimately connected.

APPENDIX I

Use of Terms

Thus far, Western psychologies, philosophies, sciences, and religions have largely focused on topics other than the most ancient themes and archetypal energy forms present in the Primordial Mind/Heart and its expressions in the Mother Tongue.

It is no wonder.

Diving into these waves requires a novel and challenging use of language. In this book we see that I am reaching for the language of the landscape, a task only for those willing to expose themselves to untamed elements, both within and without, and willing to enter into deep reflection. To launch us in our dialogue, let me be specific, if initially only suggestive, in my use of key terms.

1. **Mother Tongue Intimacy**   Many waves of wisdom have risen to the top through the human story, but in the last 150 years, reductive science and rational wisdom have dominated the human scene, to our grave detriment. The corrective and balancer arises in what I call *Mother Tongue Intimacy*. Such intimacy exudes a wisdom that includes the wild heart aspect of ourselves in our inner council of selves in such a way that we can access the template; a primal energy field crucial to the environmentally intimate conversation. Simply put: to rejoin the intimate circle of our planet's council we must speak the root language, the lost dialect at the base of all lan-

guages. Only then can we be intimate in the fullest sense. All current human languages are secondary to the more-than-human language of the eco-fields.

2. **Primordial Mind/Heart**   On the other side of the Big Bang is the Primordial Mind/Heart. How do I know? A millisecond after the Big Bang, the primal flaring forth, the Universe already had four fields in place—the gravitational, the electromagnetic, the strong nuclear, and the weak nuclear. The fields did not evolve. They were just there in operation. In the *presence of the Primordial* means touching that primal intelligence and limbic feeling with a minimum of filters currently active all around us. Such a touching opens the way to fluency in the Mother's expressions.

3. **Fields as Mother Tongue**   When we descend to the shamanic era, we discover a lost linguistic process, one where all elements of the eco-field, including humans, are able to converse. You can see this speaking of the Mother Tongue in both the Onge and Tilly Short, for theirs is the speech of humans and more-than-humans (Chapter I). But there also is an emerging syntax of the Mother Tongue through the newer sciences, especially in the science of fields, which I propose has much in common with ancient shamanic linkages to the Sacred Web.

4. **Fields**   Scientifically defined, a field is a region of non-material influence, such as the gravitational field (Feynman, 1998). Fields come to us especially in the newer sciences as expressions of the Mother reaching out to humans.

5. **Eco-field**   is a space configuration consisting of meaning carriers and living under the epistemological umbrella of a specifically-based landscape (Farina, 2007).

6. **Standing Wave**   is a description of a stage or phase of development in individuals and culture. In this book it also refers to the energy form that includes interlocking eco-fields which in turn include not only individual human development but the unfolding of the whole natural order.

7. **Inner Council of Selves** refers to our interiors as humans whereby we have a number of well-developed selves that sit around an inner table or fire circle. The inner council is usually led by an operating ego which is easily dominated by one or more of the minor selves (Taegel, 2010). In general, the Mother Tongue is not spoken today in this council because the wild element in us has been relegated to the shadows.

8. **The Inner Council as Tuning Device And Channel Selector** The flows of energy and information in the standing waves seek entry into us as individuals through the sub-selves within the council. All information has to pass through the inner council, consciously or unconsciously.

9. **Nature-based, Longitudinal Community** Spiritual communities of any sort constitute a beginning, but not a sufficient vessel for the waves of the Era of Natural Consequences. Long-term eco-spiritual communities are needed to awaken the wild heart, provide an atmosphere for listening to Nature's untamed resources, and nourish the dialogue between the wild heart and the civilized selves.

Such a broad-based community includes both humans and more-than-humans as participants in the eco-field. These nature-based communities become islands of coherence in a sea of chaos. The primary language of this kind of community is not English or any modern language but rather, I propose again and again, the Mother Tongue.

10. **Meme Codes** Richard Dawkins introduced the term as a concept for discussing evolutionary dynamics in the spread of ideas and other cultural phenomena such as Hula-Hoops and, later, Facebook. Don Beck deepened the usage to speak of template values that determine social behavior. I further expand its usage as a small aspect of the eco-field waves.

11. **White Water Waves** Throughout the book I use the metaphor of a river journey. I refer to white water history. I use that image to emphasize how perilous our journey is, but I also employ the imagery of waves in a different manner. Later, in the book I

encourage us to start our journey from a high place on the river of environmental development, including the human story. We journey down the river, and, as we paddle, we encounter eight mighty waves, symbolizing developmental phases. We float on the descending current, and, once at the bottom, we discover an ascending current.

12. **The Era of Natural Birth**   Early in the book I use the term, the *Era of Natural Consequences*, to refer to this moment in Earth's story. As the book progresses I tend to use the term, the Era of Natural Birth. Both terms are descriptive of my perception of our times; however, the latter phrase comes into my awareness more and more. In many ways, we are presiding over the death of Western Civilization and, at the same time, we are in the throes of an agonizing struggle to birth a new world with new humans who return to an intimacy with the more-than-humans.

APPENDIX II

Aims of the Book

The subjective aim of this book is to examine our interior domains as we seek to navigate the turbulent waters of the 21st century. I continue to examine our inner council of selves started in an earlier book (Taegel, 2010), and then move to see how these selves interact with our environment.

Another aim examines how standing waves in the eco-field contain important information which can be accessed primarily through a particular kind of community, one conversant in the language of Nature which lies beyond human control.

At the root of the crisis is our loss of intimacy with our surroundings, the *umwelt* (Von Uexkull, 1982). As indicated in the Gulf of Mexico oil spill, we simply do not know Earth in Her depths, literally. The Gulf tragedy issues from the joint, dare I say *stupidity*, of British Petroleum and the U.S. government in the overestimation of the effectiveness of technology as related to the depths of the Earth. The problem, however, goes deeper than governance or corporate greed. If we follow our leads, we will find that we are carried to the roots of Global Civilization itself. That takes us to another set of aims.

A further aim, then, is to probe the epistemological foundations on which Western or Industrial Civilization rests. How did we get ourselves in this mess? Beyond questioning, I acknowledge the current ineffectiveness of civilization's epistemology, while at the same time I include its best wisdom for our next world.

A parallel, more objective, effort aims at exploring a new discipline called the *Eco-field Paradigm* (Farina, 2010; Taegel, 2010). I define and integrate eco-fields with evolutionary maps of the human story, showing standing waves of development with a focus on two major currents within the spiral of the interlocking eco-fields—*the ascending and descending movement of energy propelling evolution itself.*

The descending current—the more important of the two currents in the Era of Natural Consequences—takes us deep into the Primordial Mind, the Ground of our Being (Tillich, 1963). Immersed in the loins of Earth Wisdom, we can retrieve the untamed dimension of our human possibilities, as did Tilly Short for a brief moment on the Sri Lanka coast. As we sail into the roiling waters of current eco-fields we can download facts that can become information; information that can become knowledge; knowledge that can become wild wisdom crucial for the survival of our species and thousands of other species.

Finally, and importantly, the basic aim of this book reflects my life's work: facilitating our human return to the Sacred Web, or, as we shall see, becoming aware of our place in the eco-field, as a species among species. In the shaman's wilderness, beneath the landslide of our dominant culture's devastation, hides a limbic resonance reaching out to those willing to take on the challenge of our usual operating ego's protection and control (Stone & Stone, 1989; Taegel, 1990, 2010).

Those aims are large, so allow me to address a few limits as essential to stating my hypothesis.

Limits of Inquiry

As we journey through the waves of human development in the white water of our story, the waves are replete with sediment, all

of which are computer-chip-like and contain immense information. I consider five researchers who themselves dive into the waves but focus only on a particular sediment or chip. The trace elements they research in the standing waves are:
—human values,
—human capacity to witness behavior,
—human ethics,
—human self unfolding through the spiral,
—and human spirituality.

Although there are immense complexities and myriad currents and waves in the evolutionary dynamic, I limit the discussion to the aforementioned two major currents---the ascending and, especially, the descending, or downward movement of massive energy. The complexity of biological and sociological evolution are not addressed except as a context for the elements in the above-mentioned currents. The maps of evolution engaged through the researchers transcend the reductive Darwinian and Neo-Darwinian pioneering efforts. As I explore the researchers' work, an alternative map of evolutionary consciousness emerges, one more respectful of the oral wisdom of the ancients.

Many different vessels (types of community) are appearing for navigating these two currents, but I limit the book to one vessel I have co-created over a forty-year period. The vessel of nature-based community navigates the eco-fields through the medium of the psychology of selves and shamanic work. The Earthtribe and its partner, Wisdom University, are the central examples I examine. Since this craft for traveling these waters is one I have co-created with Judith Yost and others over these four decades, it will, hopefully, shed needed light for traversing the troubled times.

I am deliberately excluding other long-term communities who seem fluent in Nature's shamanic language. I have in mind Damanhur and Findhorn, to name only two. These mature communities and their insights lie beyond the scope of this book.

Appendix III

Grammatical Themes of The Mother Tongue

As we sit in the presence of the Primordial seeking to learn this lost dialect, we slowly become aware of themes—themes which might be called basic primal grammar. This grammar states:

* that Nature is a creative and profound sheath of interconnectivity;

* that humans are part and parcel of Nature:

* that humans are Nature become aware of Herself in a self-reflective manner characteristic of but not necessarily unique to the species;

* that the major, if largely unconscious, aim of human communities is to live within an aware, reciprocal, and harmonious relationship within interlocking eco-fields;

* that such conscious engagement is not only natural, individually healthy, and culturally necessary but imperative for the human endeavor;

* that primal energy forces in Nature seek to welcome back the wayward human community into the folds of the Sacred Web.

- that this welcoming back includes epochal disturbances in the field through natural events which will destroy Industrial Civilization as we know it and open the way for a new order;
- that humans are equipped with tuning devices (now largely lost), through which can flow wild wisdom in the Mother Tongue when there is direct access to the natural order;
- and that primal trust, hope, and compassion emerge from the eco-field through shamanic ceremonies and practices in community (Eliade, 1964; Searles, 1960; Taegel, 1990; Bradley, 1997).

References

Abrams, D. (1996). *The spell of the sensuous*. New York: Random House.

Abrams, D. (2010). *Becoming animal*. New York: Pantheon Books.

Austin, S. (1996). *Parmenides: being, bounds, and logic*. New Haven: Yale University Press.

Avriel, M. (1976). *Nonlinear programing: analysis and methods*. New York: Prentice Hall.

Bacon, F. (1859). (Spedding, J., Ellis, R. & Heath, D., Eds.). *The works of francis bacon, Vol. VI*. Boston: Houghton, Mifflin. onlinebooks.library.upenn.edu/webbin/metabook?id=worksfbacon

Baldwin, J. (1905). *The genetic theory of reality*. New York: Putnam Co.

Bateson, G. (1979) *Mind and nature: A necessary unity*. New York: Dutton.

Beck, D. (2002, Fall/Winter). Spiral dynamics: The evolution of consciousness and culture. *What is Enlightenment (IV)*. openconsciousness.com

Beck, D. (2006). *Spiral dynamics integral: Learn to master the memetic codes of human behavior* (CD). Boulder, CO: Sounds True.

Beck D. & Cowan, C. (1996). *Spiral dynamics*. Malden, Mass.: Blackwell Publishers.

Becker, R. (1990). *Cross currents*. New York, NY: Tarcher/Putnam.

Berdyaev, N. (1939). *Spirit and reality.* New York: Scribner's Sons.

Bertalanffy, L. (1933). *Modern theories of development.* New York: Harper and Row.

Bertalanffy, L. (1950). An outline of general systems theory. *British Journal of Philosophy of Science, (I).*

Bierer, D. E., Carlson, T., & King, S. (1995). Shaman pharmaceuticals: Integrating indigenous knowledge, tropical medicinal plants, medicine, modern science and reciprocity into a novel drug discover approach. *Net/Science.* San Francisco, CA: Network Science Corporation.

Bird, K. & Sherwin, M. (2006). *American prometheus.* New York: Random House.

Bloom, S. (Ed. & Trans.). (1968). *The republic of plato, book VII.* New York: Basic Books.

Bohm, D. (1995). *Wholeness and the implicate order.* New York: Routledge.

Bradley, C. (1997). *Applied ecopsychology: The experience of treatment when the treatment method is nature-based psychotherapy.* (Doctoral dissertation.) The Fielding Institute. Santa Barbara, CA.

Brodie, R. (2008). *Virus of the mind: The new science of the meme.* Seattle, WA: Integral Press.

Carnes, L. (1984). *Introduction to the politics by Aristotle.* Chicago IL: University of Chicago Press.

Carson, R. (1992). *The silent spring.* New York: Houghton Mifflin.

Castaneda, C. (1972). *The journey to Ixtlan: The lessons of Don Juan.* New York: Simon and Shuster.

Cherniss, H. (1945). *The riddle of the early academy.* Berkeley, CA: University of California Press.

Clark, A. (1995). *Einstein: The life and times.* New York: Wing Books.

Clayman, C. (1989). *The American medical association: Medical encyclopedia*. New York: Random House.

Clements, J., Ettling, D., Jennette, D., & Shields, L. (1998). *Organic research: feminine spirituality meets transpersonal research*. In W. Braud & Anderson, r., *Transpersonal research methods for the social sciences: honoring human experience* (pp. 114–127) Thousand Oaks, CA: Sage Press.

Clinebell, H. (1994). *Ecotherapy: Healing ourselves, healing the earth*. New York: Hawthorne Press.

Cohen, M. (2006). *Theory of forms in history of ancient philosophy*. Seattle, WA: University of Washington Press.

Conger, J. & Pearce, C. (2002). *Shared leadership*. Thousand Oaks, CA: Sage Publishers.

Croucher, R. (2003, January 4). *Fowler's stages of faith in profile*. Retrieved on July 20, 2010 from John Mark Ministries. en.academic.ru/dic.nsf/enwiki/1950604.

Darwin, C. (Quammen, D., Ed.) (2009). *On the origin of the species: The illustrated edition*. New York: Sterling Press.

Dawkins, R. (1976). *The selfish gene*. London: Oxford University Press.

de Chardin, T. (1959). *The phenomenon of man*. New York: Harper.

Descartes, R. (Cottingham, J., Stoothoff, R. & Kenny, A., Trans.) (1988). *The philosophical writings of Descartes, Vols. I, II, III*. Cambridge, UK: Cambridge University Press.

Diamond, J. (1999). *Guns, germs and steel*. New York: W. W. Norton.

Dukas, H. & Hoffmann, B. (1979). *Albert Einstein: The human side*. Princeton, NJ: Princeton Press.

Easterling, P. & Muir, J. (1985). *Greek religion and society*. Cambridge, UK: Cambridge University Press.

Eddington, A. (1984)., as cited in Wilber, K. *Quantum questions: Mystical writings of the world's great physicists*. Boston: Shambala.

Einstein, A. (1940). On science and religion. *Nature.* Edinburg, Scotland: Scottish Academia.

Einstein, A. (1954). *Ideas and opinions.* New York: Random House.

Einstein, A. (1979). *Autobiographical notes.* Schlipp, P. (Ed. & Trans.). Chicago, IL: Open Court Press.

Eliade, M. (1964). *Shamanism: Archaic techniques of ecstasy.* Princeton, NJ: Princeton University Press.

Erickson, M. & Rossi, E. (1979). *Hypnotherapy: An exploratory casebook.* New York: Irvington Publishers.

Farina, A. (2000). *Landscape ecology in action.* Dordrecht, NL: Kluwer Academic Publishers.

Farina, A. (2007). *Principles of landscape ecology: Toward a science of landscape.* Dordrecht, The Netherlands: Springer.

Farina, A. (2010). *Ecology, cognition, and landscape: Linking natural and social systems.* Berlin: Springer-Verlag.

Federle, J. & Bassler, L. (2003). Interspecies communication in bacteria. *Journal of clinical investigation.* 112(9): 1291–1299.

Fehrenbach, T. (1974). *Comanches: The destruction of a people.* New York: Alfred Knopf.

Feynman, R. (1998). *Six easy pieces: The fundamentals of physics explained.* Harmondsworth, UK: Penguin.

Fowler, J. (1981). *Stages of faith.* San Francisco, CA: Harper & Row.

Fox, M. (1983) *Original blessing.* Santa Fe, NM: Bear and Co.

Franklin, A. B. (2002). What is habitat fragmentation? *Studies in avian biology.* 25: 20–29.

Freud, S. (1913). *The interpretation of dreams.* New York: Macmillan.

Garrison, J. (2000) *Civilization and the transformation of power.* New York: Paraview Press.

Garrison, J. & Taegel, W. (2010, October). *The wisdom factor.* Sacred Leadership Course, Wisdom University. Wimberley, TX.

Gaynor, M. (1995). *The healing essence.* New York: Kodansha.

Gilligan, C. (1982). *In a different voice.* Boston: Harvard Press.

Gilligan, C. (2002). *The birth of pleasure.* New York: Knopf.

Gore, A. (1992). *Earth in balance: Ecology and the human spirit.* New York: Penguin.

Goswami, A. (1995). *The self-aware universe.* New York: Penguin Putnam.

Graves, C. (1971). *Levels of human existence.* Santa Barbara, CA: ECLET.

Graves, C. (1974). Human nature prepares for a momentous leap. *The Futurist*, pp. 72–87.

Gray, J. (1992). *Men are from mars and women are from venus.* New York: Harper.

Greene, B. (2004). *The fabric of the cosmos.* New York: Vintage Books.

Grof, S. (1998). *The adventure of self-discovery.* Albany, NY: State University of New York Press.

Guyer, P. & Wood, A. (Eds.). (1998). *Kant's the critique of pure reason.* New York: Cambridge University Press.

Hadot, P. (2006). *The veil of Isis: An essay on the history of the idea of nature.* Cambridge, MA: Harvard University Press.

Hammond, N. G. (1986). *A history of Greece to 322 B.C.* London, England: Clarendon House.

Harner, M. (1980). *The way of the shaman: A guide to power and healing.* New York: Harper and Row.

Harvey, A., Yost, J., & Taegel, W. (2009, December). *Conscious Living.* A course intensive presented at Wisdom University. Mill Valley, CA.

Heard, G. (1963). *The five stages of man.* New York: Julian Press.

Hegel, G. (1979). *The phenomenology of spirit.* London: Oxford University Press.

Heidegger, M. & McNeil, W. (Eds.). (1998). *Plato's doctrine of truth.* New York: Cambridge University Press.

Heinlein, R. (1961). *Strangers in a strange land.* New York: Putnam.

Herbert, N. (1985). *Quantum reality.* New York: Doubleday.

Herodotus. (Godley, A., Ed.) (1920). *Herodotus, the histories, Book 2, Chapter 52, section 1.* Cambridge, MA: Harvard University Press.

Heylighen, F. (1999, July 22). Punctuated equilibrium. Retrieved December 6, 2010 from Principia Cybernetica Web pespmc1.vub.ac.be/punctueq.html.

Ho, M. (2008). *The rainbow and the worm: The physics of organisms.* Shanghai: World Scientific.

Hopi Prophesies. (2005). Retrieved September 16, 2010 from www.crystalinks.com/hopi2html.

Houston, J. (1987). *Life-Force: The psycho-historical recovery of the self.* Wheaton, IL: The Theosophical Publishing House.

Houston, J. (1988). *The search for the beloved: Journeys in mythology and sacred psychology.* New York: Putnam.

Houston, J. (2004). *Jump time: Shaping your future in a world of radical change.* New York: Putnam.

Houston, J. & Rubin, P. (2009). *Wisdom life mapping.* Seminar. Wisdom University, Oakland, CA.

Hoyle, F. (1983). *The intelligent universe.* London, England: Michael Joseph.

Hunter, J., Gutierrez, & Franklin, A. (1995). *Habitat configuration around spotted owl sites in northwestern California.* The Condor 97: 684–693.

Isaacson, W. (2007). *Einstein.* New York: Simon Schuster.

Jantsch, E. (1980). *The self-organizing universe.* Oxford: Pergamon Press.

Jung, C. (1969). *Memories, dreams, and reflections.* New York: MacMillan Press.

Jung, C. (1981). *Archetypes and the collective unconscious.* Princeton, NJ: Princeton University Press.

Jung, C. (1983). *The psychology of transference.* Princeton, N.J.: Princeton University Press.

Jung, C. (Shamdasani, S., Ed.). (2009). *The red book.* New York: W. W. Norton.

Jung, C. (Sabini, M., Ed.). (2002). *The Earth has a soul.: C. G. Jung on nature.* Berkeley, CA: North Atlantic Books.

Karpman, S. (1984). *Karpman drama triangle.* International Transactional Analysis Association: Fall Conference. New Orleans, LA.

Karpman, S. (2010). *S. Karpman.* Retrieved August 21, 2010 from www.Karpmandramatriangle.com.

Kegan, R. (1982). *The evolving self.* Cambridge, MA: Harvard University Press.

Kierkegaard, S. (2008). *Sickness unto death.* Radford, VA: Wilder Press.

Kingsley, P. (2010). *In the dark places of wisdom.* Pt Reyes, CA: Golden Sufi Center.

Kniskern, D. & Neil, J. (1982). *From psyche to system: The evolving therapy of Carl Whitaker.* New York: Guilford Press.

Koestler, A. (1990). *The ghost is in the machine.* New York: Penguin.

Kohlberg, I. (1981). *Essays on moral development.* San Francisco: Harper & Rowe.

Koffka, K. (1935). *Principles of gestalt psychology.* New York: Harcourt Brace.

Kuhn, T. (1996). *The structure of scientific revolutions.* Chicago: University of Chicago Press.

Kyokai, B. (1966). *The teaching of Buddha*. Tokyo: Kosaido Printing.

Laszlo, E. (2003). *The connectivity hypothesis*. Albany, NY: State University of New York Press.

Lawlor, R. (1991). *Voices of the first day*. Rochester, VT: Inner Traditions.

Little, E. (1989). *The Audubon society field guide to north American trees*. New York: Alfred A. Knopf.

Lovinger, J. (1977). *Ego development*. San Francisco, CA: Jossey-Bass Inc.

Mark, J. (2003, January). *Fowler's stages of faith profile*. Retrieved July 29, 2010 from en.academic.ru/dic.nsf/enwiki/1950604.

McDonald, J. (Trans.). (2010). *Taoteching*. New York: Chartwell Books.

McEvilley, T. (2002). *The shape of ancient thought*. New York: Allworth Press.

McIntosh, S. (2007). *Integral consciousness and the future of evolution*. St. Paul, MN: Paragon House.

McKeon, R. (Ed.). (2001). *The basic works of Aristotle*. New York: Modern Library.

McLuhan, M. (1967). *The medium is the message*. New York: Penguin.

McPhee, J. (1989). *The control of nature*. Canada: HarperCollins.

Mitchell, E. R. (1996). *The way of the explorer: An Apollo astronaut's journey through the material and mystical worlds*. New York: Putnam Press.

Moody, R. (2010). *Dreams and the afterlife: An odyssey to Greece*. (Seminar). Wisdom University, Mill Valley, CA.

Neihardt, J. (1959). *Black Elk speaks*. New York: Washington Square Press.

Nhat Hahn, T. (1999). *Going home: Jesus and Buddha as brothers*. New York: Riverhead Press.

Ober, C., Sinatra, S., Zucker, J. (2010). *Earthing*. Long Beach, CA: Baic Health.

Olalla, P. (2002). *Mythological atlas of Greece*. Athens, Greece: Road Editions.

Parmenides. (Blakewell, C. ed., Davidson, T., trans.) (1907). *A source book in ancient philosophy*. New York: Scribner and Sons.

Parmenides. (Coxon, A., Trans.) (1986). *The fragments of Parmenides*. Las Vegas: Parmenides Publishing.

Plato. (C. Rowe, Trans.). (2005). *Phaedrus*. London: Penguin Books.

Plotkin, B. (2003). *Soulcraft: Crossing into the mysteries of nature and psyche*. Novato, CA: New World Library.

Prigogine, I. & Stengers, I. (1984). *Order out of chaos*. New York: Bantam.

Prigogine, I. (1986). *The end of certainty*. New York: Free Press.

Puthoff, H. (1989). Gravity as a zero-point-fluctuation-determined state. *Physical Review*, 30(5), pp. 2333–2342.

Ray, P. & Ray, S. (2000). *Cultural creatives: How 50 million people are changing the world*. New York: Harmony Books.

Ray, P. & Ray, S. (2009). *Discussion in wisdom as a way of life*. (Seminar) Wisdom University, Mill Valley, CA.

Roebuck, C. (1998). *The world of ancient times*. New York: Prentice Hall Publishers.

Roszak, T. (1992). *The voice of the earth*. New York: Simon & Schuster.

Russell, B. (1979). *Second wind*. New York: Ballentine Books.

Schmidt, K. (2008, January). German research: Magazine of the deausche forschugsgemeinschaft. *Arts and Humanities (VI)*, p. 33.

Schnall, M. (2007, September 17). Conversation with Carol Gilligan at the women's power and peace conference. Retrieved July 26, 2010 from www.feminist.com/resources/artspeech/interviews/carolgilligan.html.

Searles, H. F. (1960). Unconscious processes in relation to the environmental crisis. *Psychoanalytic Review*, 39, 361–364.

Seen, P. (1985). *Einstein in America*. New York: Crown Publishers.

Sensitivity. (2011). Retrieved November 28, 2010 from Dictionary. com. dictionary.reference.com/browse/sensitivity.

Sheldrake, R. (1994). *The presence in the past: Morphic resonance and the habits of nature*. London, England: HarperCollins.

Sheldrake, R. (1995). *A new science of life*. Rochester, NY: Park Street Press.

Slaatte, H. (1986). *Contemporary philosophies of religion*. New York: University Press of America.

Smith, H. (1991). *The world's religions*. San Francisco, CA: Harper-Collins.

Spiral Dynamics (2000-2006). About spiral dynamics: Spiral dynamics and memetics. Retrieved August 15, 2010 from www.spiraldynamics.org/aboutsd_memetics.htm.

Stannard, D. (1992). *American holocaust*. New York: Oxford University Press.

Stapp, H. (2004). Theoretical model of a purported empirical violation of the prediction of quantum theory. *Physical Review* A. 72, 30–32.

Stone, H. (1985). *Embracing heaven and earth*. Marina Del Ray, CA: Devorss Company.

Stone, H. & Stone, S. (1989) *Embracing ourselves*. San Raphael, CA: New World Library.

Taegel, W. (1964). *Growth in Christ*. Atlanta, GA: Spiritual Life Publishers.

Taegel, W. (1968). *Witnessing laymen make living churches.* London, England: Word Publishers.

Taegel, W. (1990). *The many colored buffalo: Transformation through the council of voices.* Norwood, NJ: Ablex Publishing Company.

Taegel, W. (1992). Nature-based psychotherapy and shamanic training. *Voices: the art and science of psychotherapy,* Vol. 28 (4). 82.

Taegel, W. (2000). *Natural mystics.* Austin, TX: Turn Key Press.

Taegel, W. (2009, December). *Conscious living* (Notes from A. Harvey, J. Yost, & W. Taegel). Mill Valley, CA: A course intensive presented at Wisdom University.

Taegel, W. (2010). *The sacred council of your wild heart: Nature's hope in earth's crisis.* Wimberley, TX: 2nd Tier Publishing.

Tandy, D. (2001). *Prehistory and history: Ethnicity, class, and political economy.* New York: Black Rose Press.

Tarnas, R. (1991). *The passions of the western mind.* New York: Ballantine.

Tick, E. (2005). *War and the soul.* Wheaton, IL: Quest Books.

Tiller, W. (1993). What are subtle energies? *Journal of Scientific Explorarion,* 7, 293–304.

Tillich, P. (1963). *Systematic theology (Vol. 3).* Chicago, IL: The University of Chicago Press.

Tutu, D. (1962). Unpublished Address, McMurry University, Abilene, TX.

Von Uexkull, J. (1982). *The theory of meaning.* Semiotica 42 (1): 25–82.

Waters, F. (1963). *The book of Hopi.* New York: Viking Press.

Whitehead, A. (1962). *Process and reality.* New York: Vanguard Press.

Weisberg, Robert. (1992). *Creativity:beyond the myth of genius.* New York: Freeman Press.

Wilber, K. (2000). *Integral Psychology*. Boston, MA: Shambala

Wilber, K. (2003). *Kosmic consciousness*. (CD). Boulder, CO: Sounds True.

Wilber, K. (2006). *Integral spirituality*. Boston, MA: Integral Books.

Wisdom University. (2008). *About us*. www.wisdomuniversity.org/aboutus.htm.

Made in the USA
Lexington, KY
07 September 2014